Praise for *War and the Rogue Presidency*

"*War and the Rogue Presidency* is a fascinating history of the relationship between wars and the rise of the imperial presidency. If war is the mother of Big Government, it is also mother to presidents who used their expanded powers in ways exceeding the limits envisioned by America's Founders. The solution, Eland argues, is for Congress to restore its authority and restrain the 'creeping despotism' that has led to unbridled presidential power. Eland provides concrete steps Congress may—and should—take to keep presidents from going 'rogue.' Highly recommended!"
—**Jonathan J. Bean**, Professor of History, Southern Illinois University

"In *War and the Rogue Presidency* Ivan Eland chronicles the rise of the imperial presidency with great insight. But does he have a solution? It's worth pondering."
—**Mike M. Moore**, former Editor, *Bulletin of the Atomic Scientists*

"In the well-written and thought-provoking book, *War and the Rogue Presidency*, Ivan Eland convincingly demonstrates that the expanding power of the executive branch, which has resulted in the creation of the imperial presidency, is a result of our increasing involvement in foreign wars. A must read for those concerned about the decline of the checks and balances envisioned by our Founding Fathers."
—**Lawrence J. Korb**, former Assistant Secretary, U.S. Department of Defense;
   Senior Fellow, Center for American Progress; former Senior Fellow and
   Director of National Security Studies, Council on Foreign Relations

"Ivan Eland's learned and balanced book, *War and the Rogue Presidency*, identifies war as one of the chief threats to the Republic, whether we win or lose, given the effect of war on presidential power. Few subjects are worthy of greater public debate."
—**Richard Shenkman**, Founder, History News Network,
   George Washington University

"The seemingly permanent mobilization of American society since the Second World War to manage global security has produced a bloated, intrusive, and increasingly imperial and unresponsive federal government. In his book *War and the Rogue Presidency*, Ivan Eland sees clearly the danger to our freedom and outlines the Congressional and other reforms needed to find the path back."
—**Harvey M. Sapolsky**, Professor of Public Policy and Organization
   Emeritus and former Director of the Security Studies Program,
   Massachusetts Institute of Technology

"After seventy years of a monolithic, interventionist foreign policy that has ruled Washington elites, the superb book *War and the Rogue Presidency* is calling for an essential, realist American foreign policy emphasizing a robust diplomacy, military restraint, and increased congressional oversight. Author Ivan Eland has assembled an outstanding and lucid, critical examination of how the Executive must be reined in from being granted unprecedented powers to wage perpetual war globally that is subverting the Constitution, costing trillions, harming millions, trampling on civil liberties, and creating more and more enemies who endanger America. *War and the Rogue Presidency* is must reading for anyone seeking a safer, freer, and more peaceful world."
—**Rand H. Paul, M.D.**, U.S. Senator and Member of the Committee on Foreign
   Relations and Committee on Homeland Security and Government Affairs

"Adobe *War and the Rogue Presidency* is an invaluable history of the constitutional basis for Congress's war-making power that has been all but forgotten and ignored in the last two decades; and as a bonus the book also makes a compelling case linking unapproved administrative-state operations abroad with the development of the administrative state domestically—both products of congressional abdication."

>   —**C. Boyden Gray**, former U.S. Ambassador to the European Union; former Counsel to President George H. W. Bush; former Special Envoy for European Affairs and Special Envoy for Eurasian Energy at the Mission of the U.S. to the European Union; former Counsel to the Presidential Task Force on Regulatory Relief; former Chairman of Administrative Law and Regulatory Practice of the American Bar Association

"Today's domineering president and dysfunctional Congress worry Americans on the right and the left about the serious problem of the imperial—or rogue—presidency. Ivan Eland's book *War and the Rogue Presidency* explains the problem's history, highlights the combination of wars and congressional abdication that brought us to our current state, and offers an agenda to restore the Constitution's just checks and balances. There is a lot to learn from this important book."

>   —**Eugene Gholz**, Associate Professor of Political Science, University of Notre Dame; former Senior Advisor to the Deputy Assistant Secretary of Defense for Manufacturing and Industrial Base Policy, U.S. Department of Defense; author, *Buying Military Transformation: Technological Innovation and the Defense Industry,* and *U.S. Defense Politics: The Origins of Security Policy*

"Ivan Eland is one of America's top experts on U.S. presidents and their conduct of foreign policy. *War and the Rogue Presidency* is his finest book so far, and it provides a searing indictment of rapidly growing presidential abuses. Eland shows how an out-of-control imperial presidency is not only destroying America's reputation abroad, it is undermining our entire constitutional system of government and inflicting fatal wounds on the domestic liberties Americans cherish. *War and the Rogue Presidency* is essential reading for anyone who wants to help reverse that ominous trend."

>   —**Ted Galen Carpenter**, Senior Fellow for Defense and Foreign Policy Studies, Cato Institute

"Few readers, even those who start from very different political principles, will fail to be impressed with Ivan Eland's passionate, provocative and historically informed case against the 'Rogue Presidency' and his call for returning the power to declare war to the Congress. *War and the Rogue Presidency* is a timely and important book."

>   —**Hugh T. Rockoff**, Distinguished Professor of Economics, Rutgers University

"In the past half century, Americans suffered serious threats to their civil liberties and Constitutional rights during the Vietnam War (Richard Nixon and Watergate), the war in Central America (Ronald Reagan and Iran-Contra), and the post-9/11 'war on terror.' Ivan Eland's important book *War and the Rogue Presidency* not only traces the connection between war and growth of the 'imperial presidency' from the earliest days of our republic, but shows that our current national policy of seemingly permanent conflict abroad puts our rights at home very much at risk today. Just as important, he offers practical suggestions for ways that Congress might reassert its Constitutional powers in foreign policy to rein in an overweening executive branch."

—**Jonathan V. Marshall**, author, *The Lebanese Connection: Corruption, Civil War, and the International Drug Traffic* and *The Iran-Contra Connection: Secret Teams and Covert Operations in the Reagan Era*

"Ivan Eland's book *War and the Rogue Presidency* substantiates five important facts. First, wars have allowed U.S. presidents to break free of the constitutional chains that limit executive power. Second, presidents are power seeking and thus incentivized to engage in war to enhance their domestic policy prerogatives. Third, the original constitutional republic is incompatible with and being increasingly undermined by rogue, a.k.a. imperial, presidents. And, fourth, now that the chains of the Constitution have been replaced with ropes of sand, a plebiscitary despotism is emerging with the president at its head. However, Eland doesn't leave his readers hopeless. His proposals for remedying the problem of the rogue presidency may or may not succeed, for a variety of reasons. Nevertheless, in a worse-case scenario it is not unimaginable for a president to go rogue and declare war on his own domestic enemies. Today presidential powers are so vast that some future president may decide to establish the circumstances (i.e., create the crisis), and then proceed to remedy it (i.e., war). This isn't the soft despotism of bureaucratic usurpation of property rights for which we've become accustomed, but despotism with bullets flying. If this seems to be ridiculous, read *War and the Rogue Presidency* and then judge for yourself."

—**Marshall L. DeRosa**, Professor of Political Science, Florida Atlantic University

"Ivan Eland's important book *War and the Rogue Presidency* exposes the dangerous and often quasi-dictatorial power that U.S. presidents have amassed since the 20th century and how that power has resulted in a long and seemingly endless series of disastrous wars. Thankfully, Eland also provides a list of practical, concrete ways Congress and U.S. citizens can reclaim power from the executive and create something far closer to true democratic governance in this country."

—**David Vine**, Professor of Anthropology, American University; author, *Base Nation: How U.S. Military Bases Abroad Harm America and the World*

"In this fine book, Eland interweaves constitutional theory and micro-history to produce a thoughtful and insightful analysis of the war-making powers of the American President. He is relentless in his critique of both Presidents who have transgressed and Congresses which have allowed transgressions. *War and the Rogue Presidency* both extends and focuses Eland's earlier work on the fabric of power in the United States."

—**T. Hunt Tooley**, Professor of History, Austin College; author, *The Western Front: Battleground and Homefront in the First World War*

"For America's elites, no cash cow is more sacred than the military-industrial complex. Six decades after President Dwight Eisenhower warned against it, Ivan Eland shows how the refusal of Congress to meet constitutional responsibilities has led to a warfare state—with consolidation of undemocratic power in the White House. *War and the Rogue Presidency* offers a methodical indictment of congressional complicity that has ushered in perpetual war. This book challenges readers across political spectrums to face the dire realities of red-white-and-blue militarism run amuck. While spelling out how powerful forces have turned Congress into an accessory to normalize ongoing warfare, the author also provides clear ideas for how the legislative branch could end its capitulation to a brutal war machine."

—**Norman Solomon**, Founder and Executive Director, Institute for Public Accuracy; author, *War Made Easy: How Presidents and Pundits Keep Spinning Us to Death*

"Thoroughly researched and informative, the valuable book *War and the Rogue Presidency* traces the history and evolution of excessive Presidential authority, explains how this accretion of executive power is contrary to the Constitution and the vision of the founders, and argues for urgent measures to restore congressional authority and limit the ability of Presidents to drag the nation into unnecessary and unwinnable wars."

—**David Cortright**, Director of Policy Studies, Kroc Institute for International Peace Studies, University of Notre Dame; Chair of the Board, Fourth Freedom Forum

"Once more in *War and the Rogue Presidency*, Ivan Eland has given us a book that challenges orthodoxies on the left and right. A century ago, in the midst of World War I, Randolph Bourne warned that 'war is the health of the state.' Subsequent experience has made it necessary to sharpen that point: war is the health of the presidency. Eland attributes the enormous power the executive wields at home and abroad not to some purportedly inevitable forces of modernization but to executive calculation and Congressional abdication. He calls for Congress to reassert its Constitutional war powers and recalibrate the balance of power in DC. His proposals will provoke both liberals and conservatives. Few readers will be left indifferent to Eland's call to abolish the Electoral College."

—**Richard M. Gamble**, Anna Margaret Ross Alexander Chair in History and Politics, Hillsdale College; author, *The War for Righteousness: Progressive Christianity, the Great War, and the Rise of the Messianic Nation*

"I have enjoyed reading Ivan Eland's book, *War and the Rogue Presidency*. Given the mounting concern in our body politic about the extent to which the Congress has yielded its constitutional authority to a president prone to ignore the Constitution and take the expedient course without consultation with the people's representatives, it is very timely. It documents the sad series of executive usurpations of legislative authority that have transformed the American republic into a warfare state. . . . It concludes with numerous recommendations for remedial action to restore the legislative power and the civil liberties our founding fathers considered essential to preserving our liberties. *War and the Rogue Presidency* is must reading for anyone concerned about presidential overreach and the demise of the checks and balances of our constitutionally mandated separation of powers."

—**Charles W. Freeman, Jr.**, former U.S. Ambassador to Saudi Arabia; former Assistant Secretary of Defense for International Security Affairs

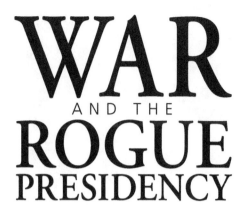

WAR
AND THE
ROGUE
PRESIDENCY

Also by the Author

Eleven Presidents
Promises vs. Results in Achieving Limited Government

Recarving Rushmore
Ranking the Presidents on Peace, Prosperity, and Liberty

The Failure of Counterinsurgency
Why Hearts and Minds Are Seldom Won

No War For Oil
U.S. Dependency and the Middle East

Partitioning for Peace
An Exit Strategy for Iraq

The Empire Has No Clothes
U.S. Foreign Policy Exposed, Second Edition

Putting "Defense" Back into U.S. Defense Policy
Rethinking U.S. Security in a Post–Cold War World

WAR

AND THE

ROGUE

PRESIDENCY

RESTORING THE REPUBLIC
AFTER CONGRESSIONAL FAILURE

IVAN ELAND

INDEPENDENT
I N S T I T U T E
OAKLAND, CALIFORNIA

Independent Institute
100 Swan Way, Oakland, CA 94621-1428
Telephone: 510-632-1366
Fax: 510-568-6040
Email: info@independent.org
Website: www.independent.org

Cover Design: Denise Tsui
Concept Cover Art: Jeremy Anicete

Library of Congress Cataloging-in-Publication Data Available

Contents

Acknowledgments

THE AUTHOR WOULD like to thank the following people for contributing to the book: David Theroux, Founder and President of the Independent Institute, provided funding for the book, as did the Charles Koch Institute. William F. Shughart II, Research Director, reviewed and commented on the manuscript. Roy M. Carlisle, Executive Editor at Independent, provided advice and expertise during all facets of book, title, and cover production. George L. Tibbitts and Melodie J. Bowler, Publication Project Manager and former Publications Director, respectively, coordinated all book production efforts. Denise Tsui designed the final version of the cover, and Jeremy Ani-cete contributed to the cover layout. Leigh McLellan did the typesetting for the book. Nicolas Jones and Maureen R. Cowhey proofread the manuscript. Eleanor Blair provided the index.

INTRODUCTION
What Is the Imperial Presidency?

THE TERM "IMPERIAL PRESIDENCY" is generally understood to mean an inflation of executive power, in both domestic and foreign policy, beyond what was envisioned by the framers of the Constitution. This book, by examining American history, demonstrates that war has been the main driver of the imperial presidency and magnifies factors that contribute to its perpetuation. The imperial presidency distorts the checks and balances of the Constitution and undermines the freedoms of American citizens. Nowadays, the imperial presidency is synonymous with "big government," because the colossus of the executive branch accounts for 99 percent of the employees of the massive federal government (currently, the federal government accounts for a whopping 17 percent of GDP). Even more pernicious is the feedback loop, whereby repeated wars cause the imperial presidency, and the imperial presidency has in turn caused a higher frequency of wars. During the period of congressionally dominant government in the nineteenth century, the United States was involved in fewer major military interventions than during the post–World War II period of the imperial presidency.

Some conservatives might say that most American wars were necessary, so the resulting imperial presidency has to be tolerated. Conservative William F. Buckley seemed to feel this way about the Cold War. Small government was great, but if America needed to put up with big government to combat Communism, so be it. Although creating and tolerating big government at home to joust with even bigger government abroad did not seem like a great tradeoff, at least Buckley grasped the relationship between big government at home and war abroad, which many conservatives still do not.

However, it is questionable whether most of America's wars, especially recent ones, were necessary for national security. In 1995, Gregory D. Hess and Athanasios Orphanides published an analysis in the *American Economic Review* showing that from the beginning of the Eisenhower administration (1953) to the end of the Reagan administration (1988), first-term presidents experiencing a weak economy during reelection years were twice as likely to initiate or escalate wars than were executives during non-reelection years or years of a healthy economy. Other scholars have also found a correlation between the executive's use of force and economic slowdowns. Still other authors have concluded that presidents use force when their approval ratings drop precipitously. Thus, domestic politics seem to play a big role in whether modern-day executives choose war or peace. Furthermore, going to war seems to be a temporary way to spike presidential popularity but can boomerang if the war drags on.[1] Particularly bad for presidents' popularity are protracted wars with high human and monetary costs that seem not to be fought for the nation's vital interests and appear not to be succeeding. Examples include the guerrilla war in the Philippines following the Spanish-American War, the Korean War, the Vietnam War, the second Iraq War, and the Afghan War.

During wars or crises, foreign or domestic, presidents tend to accumulate power because they can respond with speed and secrecy. Congress and the Supreme Court, with their problems of collective action, are usually slow to respond to such calamities. However, after the crisis is over, such institutions often reawaken and reassert themselves, at least temporarily slowing the trajectory of expanding executive power. For example, the Supreme Court declared Abraham Lincoln's use of military tribunals unconstitutional, but only after Lincoln was dead and the Civil War was over.

Pushback from other branches of government is especially strong when the initial zeal for conflict bogs down after the war doesn't go as well as planned, thus souring American public opinion against US efforts in the war. For example, as the anti-US insurgency in the Philippines dragged on after the Spanish-American War, Congress began examining misconduct by US forces and even President Theodore Roosevelt, an imperialist proponent of war for war's sake,

---

1. Studies cited in Gene Healy, *The Cult of the Presidency: America's Dangerous Devotion to Executive Power* (Washington, DC: The Cato Institute, 2008), 210.

became unenthusiastic about foreign military intervention. Because Lyndon B. Johnson and Richard Nixon were strong executives during the Vietnam War and Watergate era, the presidency got legal pushback from the other branches of government as a result of the unpopularity of those events with the public (Vietnam Syndrome), thus motivating Gerald Ford and Jimmy Carter to conduct more restrained foreign policies. After George W. Bush's invasion of Iraq turned into an unpopular quagmire, Congress and the Supreme Court pushed back on torture, warrantless surveillance of Americans, military tribunals, and indefinite detention of prisoners without trial in the "war on terror."

However, quasi-dictatorial presidents in times of crisis—such as Abraham Lincoln during the Civil War and Franklin Roosevelt during the Great Depression and World War II—are often admired by posterity.[2] It is often said that Russians like a strong leader; perhaps the same can be said for the United States during the twentieth and twenty-first centuries. But it was not always so, according to Jeremi Suri, author of *The Impossible Presidency: The Rise and Fall of America's Highest Office*:[3]

> The presidency is the most powerful office in the world. But it is set up to fail. And the power is the problem. Beginning as a small and uncertain position within a large and sprawling democracy, the presidency has grown over two centuries into a towering central command for global decisions about war, economy, and justice. The president can bomb more places, spend more money, and influence more people than any other figure in history.

Yet Suri maintains that recent presidents have failed because even though their power is great, presidents tend to overcommit, overpromise, and overreach both at home and abroad. In other words, expectations—for example, running the world—exceed even the immense presidential power amassed since the beginning of the twentieth century. For example, Suri notes that crises provoked by distant and unimportant actors have frequently preoccupied mighty American executives. He notes that American presidents now command the

---

2. Eric A. Posner and Adrian Vermeule, *The Executive Unbound: After the Madisonian Republic* (Oxford: Oxford University Press, 2010), 184–87.

3. Jeremi Suri, *The Impossible Presidency: The Rise and Fall of America's Highest Office* (New York: Basic Books, 2017), ix–x.

globe's most potent military but are often exasperated at the limitations on success using force. Although American presidents are often respected around the world, they have difficulty gaining influence in other countries. Abroad, presidents compound these constraints by overpromising to eliminate tyranny or expand democracy. Suri concludes that

> The temptation for powerful actors, especially American presidents, has been to hedge by pursuing dominance everywhere. That expansive approach has characterized our foreign policy since at least the late 1950s, and it has not served the United States or the world well.
>
> American power has underperformed because it has been overused, spread too thin by hard-working leaders who are afraid to prioritize and prefer insurance policies—at home and abroad—to selective risks.

Thus, Suri believes that we have come full circle from "creeping despotism," created by excessive royal use of the army and treasury and criticized by Enlightenment thinkers, such as Hume, Rousseau, Voltaire, Locke, and Jefferson, before and during the American Revolution.[4]

Presidential overpromising has contributed to the imperial presidency by executive expansion of power in an often-vain attempt to satisfy even higher self-created expectations. These elevated expectations of what government can do have often flowed from war.

"Creeping Despotism" Begins Early in US Foreign Policy

Although not using Alexander Hamilton's extra-constitutional creations of "inherent power" of the president as commander in chief or as "sole organ of foreign policy," even early presidents behaved as if they possessed them. George Washington, goaded by Hamilton, unilaterally issued his Neutrality Proclamation to keep the United States out of a war between Britain and US ally France, which also eroded Congress's constitutional responsibility to decide whether to declare war. Although neutrality was the right policy, arguably Congress rather than President Washington should have decided this issue.

---

4. Suri, *The Impossible Presidency*, xviii, xx–xxii, 6–7.

Without congressional authorization, Thomas Jefferson dispatched the US Navy to the Mediterranean Sea to protect US commercial ships being attacked by pirates from the Barbary states, thus putting them in a situation where they could—and did—get into a war. James Polk likewise provoked a war with Mexico to acquire its land by sending the US Army into disputed territory on the US-Mexican border without first getting congressional approval. In the early twentieth century, American presidents of both parties—William McKinley, Teddy Roosevelt, William Howard Taft, Woodrow Wilson, and Calvin Coolidge—used US troops, without congressional approval, in minor military actions in China, Latin America, and Russia. It was not until the dawn of the Cold War, however, that a president took the nation into a major war without congressional approval using inherent presidential power— Harry Truman in the Korean War. The imperial presidency had taken a huge next step.

Modern presidents use the fictitious "inherent power" to conduct actions unsanctioned by the Constitution. Presidents have appealed to inherent power to wage war without Congress's stamp of approval. This nebulous power has also been used to justify conducting congressionally unsanctioned covert operations, claiming questionable "executive privilege" as an excuse for not providing requested information to Congress, using executive agreements with foreign nations instead of legislatively sanctioned treaties, and issuing unilateral executive orders and presidential memoranda with no underpinning legislation. In effect, inherent power has allowed the president to bypass Congress completely.

Using invented inherent presidential power was only one tool used by presidents to overcome their constitutionally weak powers. Despite the checks and balances of the Constitution, the executive branch has a major countervailing advantage: It is the only one of the three branches of government that has assets in the physical world to carry out the policies of the federal government, both domestically and overseas. Government, for all intents and purposes, is ultimately the use of coercion. But the executive is the only branch to possess the means of physical force—the military and civilian federal police resources—needed to carry out policy in the real world. Congress and the Supreme Court can only hope the executive branch will enforce the results of their decision-making. Only the executive has the physical resources to act rapidly in any crisis. The president thus sets the stage on which the other actors will play. Only after any crisis is over will the other two branches try to reassert their authority. Congress could cut off funds for executive action but rarely does, because it fears being criticized for putting US forces in danger.

The number of physical resources that the executive branch can bring to a problem has always been much greater than that of the other federal branches—even at the beginning of the republic. And over time the disparity has only grown as the executive branch has grown exponentially compared to the legislative and judicial branches. For example, in the long stretches of peace during the late eighteenth, nineteenth, and early twentieth centuries, Congress retained the founders' suspicion that a standing army would threaten liberty. The US Army was kept small, was supplemented by mobilized militia to fight the few declared wars, and then was shrunk by demobilization after each war ended. Even the prestige of President George Washington would not convince Congress to incrementally augment the tiny army until Maj. Gen. Arthur St. Clair's forces were routed by Native Americans in what is now Ohio in 1791. In his farewell address, even Washington cautioned to "avoid the necessity of . . . overgrown military establishments."[5]

Only during the 1950s, after the Korean War and during the Cold War, was a permanent large peacetime standing army retained. Now the active US Army and Marine Corps consist of almost 750,000 troops, with another 580,000 troops in the National Guard and Reserves—totaling 1.3 million in just two of the US military services.

Today, the executive branch accounts for 99 percent of federal employees. In fact, since the mid-twentieth century, the executive branch has gotten so gigantic and sprawling that a large White House staff and the Executive Office of the President were created to try to manage it.

The executive also has informational advantages in foreign policy over Congress and the courts. Some of these hordes of bureaucrats collect, analyze, or disseminate intelligence or run systems that do. These include overseas diplomats, spies, and military personnel, which supply information to 17 massive intelligence agencies at home. In contrast, in domestic affairs, mem-

---

5. George Washington, Farewell Address, September 17, 1796.

bers of Congress can get a firsthand glimpse of what is happening and also have the benefit of various domestic interest groups that help them analyze it; in foreign affairs, both factors are attenuated, and Congress must rely more on the executive for information. Furthermore, elections for Congress are usually won on domestic issues, not international relations topics, giving members of Congress less incentive to care about or act on foreign policy. In contrast, foreign policy is more often important to presidential elections and a president's legacy—unfortunately, wars, unless they end in total disaster, often improve historians' rankings of a president—thus giving him powerful incentives for action. In foreign policy, the web of interest groups is thinner and weaker; the ones that do exist usually have a domestic component (for example, immigration groups and the defense industry).

Therefore, with more people, resources, information, and incentives to act, the president can regularly act first and create the playing field that constrains legislative choices. Instead of requesting legislation, the executive can use executive orders, national security directives, executive agreements with other nations, and proclamations (e.g., the Monroe Doctrine has governed US policy in Latin America since 1823) to act both quickly and unilaterally without Congress's approval.[6]

The founders drafted the constitutional checks and balances between governmental branches because they understood that an unchecked aggregation of power leads to despotism. The grim irony is that even from inception of the republic, the system of checks and balances, designed to safeguard against encroachments of power, has in fact yielded power away from Congress and to the executive.

How Did We Get into This Mess?

Why did the executive greatly expand authority, and Congress accede to this power grab in foreign affairs, which then expanded into the domestic arena? Bruce Bueno de Mesquita and Alastair Smith argue that Congress has delegated its power in foreign policy to the president simply because

6. Brandice Canes-Wrone, William G. Howell, and David E. Lewis, "Toward a Broader Understanding of Presidential Power: A Reevaluation of the Two Presidencies Thesis," *The Journal of Politics* 70, no. 1 (January 2008): 1–6

House members need to get reelected every two years and are afraid of being tarnished by failed foreign interventions. In contrast, the president has four years between elections for the public to forget any military misadventures. Also, this longer period allows presidents to use war to pursue enhanced power, accolades, riches, or electoral success—all of which James Madison believed executives were drawn to, which has not changed over time—more than the nation's security.[7]

Yet several problems exist with this simple theory. The first is that senators, whose chamber makes up half of the bicameral legislature, have even longer terms than presidents—six years. Second, the terms of members of the House, members of the Senate, and the president have not changed during the history of the country, yet not until the twentieth century—and especially the latter half of it—did the executive usurp the power in foreign policy from Congress. Any major usurpations of executive power until then did not, for the most part, "stick." Third, in the modern day, when democracy has eroded republican institutions, the main check on the powerful imperial presidency is not Congress, but public opinion serving as a restraint on the so-called "plebiscitary executive," which means that elections are as important to the president as they are to members of Congress. Fourth, on occasion Congress has been more bellicose than the executive—for example, during the Quasi-War of 1798, the War of 1812, the Spanish-American War, and World War I. Therefore, Bueno de Mesquita and Smith's line of reasoning has limited explanatory power.

Although Gene Healy, in his excellent book *The Cult of the Presidency: America's Dangerous Devotion to Executive Power*, said that no single reason exists for the expansion of presidential power in the twentieth century, he correctly concluded that congressional abdication is a key factor. He noted that Madison's idea that competing ambitions of branches of government would keep the system in balance broke down in the twentieth century, because the incentives of individual lawmakers did not cause them to sufficiently push back against executive appropriation of Congress's institutional powers. Healy

---

7. Bruce Bueno de Mesquita and Alastair Smith, *Spoils of War: Greed, Power, and the Conflicts That Made Our Greatest Presidents* (New York: Public Affairs, 2016), 11.

correctly opined that the ambition of modern-day legislators (no doubt reelection) causes them to delegate too much authority to the executive and let the president decide whether to go to war.

Members of Congress like to delegate the decision on whether to go to war to the executive, according to Healy, because they can take credit for victory and blame the president for defeat. Healy cogently compares the Congress's current role in deciding on war to the role of a university student council. The president has to show respect for Congress, just as the university administration has to show respect for the council, but everyone knows where the real power lies. (As Rome went from republic to empire, the emperor also showed respect for the Senate but wielded the real authority; the same has slowly been happening in the United States.)

Healy also argued that American empire abroad—the stationing of troops overseas on foreign bases across the globe—ensured that the president would acquire vast unilateral authority over foreign policy. The problem with this argument is that the causal arrow may be reversed. Truman was the first "imperial president" largely because of his abuse of the commander-in-chief power to take the country into a major war in Korea without congressional approval in 1950. In addition, the power of the presidency in foreign policy and national security became institutionalized in the National Security Council in the Executive Office of the President. Furthermore, unified presidential control over the military forces was established in the new Department of Defense in 1947. Also, the president could wage secret wars with a newly created Central Intelligence Agency (CIA), his own personal intelligence agency not under the military's umbrella. Yet the worldwide American empire of overseas forces and bases did not come until after the president had these powers.

In fact, the main cause of executive aggrandizement is war itself, as demonstrated in a later chapter. As Healy correctly points out, "Throughout American history, virtually every major advance in executive power has come during a war or warlike crisis." Healey also appropriately quotes Alexander Hamilton in *Federalist* No. 8: "It is of the nature of war to increase the executive at the expense of the legislative authority."[8] So maybe instead of the American overseas

---

8. Quoted in Healy, *The Cult of the Presidency*, 9–10, 162–63.

empire causing the imperial presidency, it might have been that World War II, the Korean War, and the ensuing uneasy Cold War with the Soviet Union caused it.

Even before *Federalist* No. 8 was written, James Madison, at the Constitutional Convention in 1787, lamented the ill effects of persistent wars:[9]

> In time of actual war, great discretionary powers are constantly given to the Executive Magistrate. Constant apprehension of War has the same tendency to render the head too large for the body. A standing military force, with an overgrown Executive will not long be safe companions to liberty. The means of defense angst [*sic*] foreign danger have always been the instruments of tyranny at home.

Madison's observation about the pernicious effects of the apprehension of war was borne out by the enhancement of executive power during the forty-five-year Cold War as well as the now seemingly perpetual war on terrorism. Although presidents nowadays use more well-developed federal civilian police organizations, instead of standing armies, to usurp civil liberties during wars and emergencies, since 9/11 the police have become militarized using surplus military equipment. Also, the military now has a greater potential role in law enforcement at home during crises through the creation of the Northern Command, the deployment of the National Guard and Army during emergencies, and military involvement in the war on drugs.

Unfortunately, politicians know that research shows executives who conducted war are evaluated more favorably than presidents who presided over peace and that they can take hold of more power at home when fear is stoked among the populace about a crisis or war abroad.[10] These realities create bad incentives for presidents to take excessive military actions.

Healy talks about the great responsibilities placed on the president nowadays that were not there during the Constitution's framing; the framers wanted an executive that merely carried out the congressional will in foreign policy and war and executed the laws passed at home. Healy believes that presidents seek powers commensurate with society's increased demands. Although Healy's

---

9. James MClelland and M. E. Bradford, eds., *Elliot's Debates, Vol. III: Debates in the Federal Convention of 1787* (Richmond, VA: James River Press, 1989), 208.

10. Healy, *The Cult of the Presidency*, 280–81.

aforementioned comment shows he recognizes that wars and war-like crises lead to expansion of executive power, he is less clear on the fact that increased societal expectations about the executive's roles and responsibilities originate during wars and/or significant domestic crises emanating from them. Wars, especially big or long ones, centralize federal and presidential power, and politically powerful interest groups profit from such centralization and economic regulation. The groups pressure for the precedent of federal and executive intervention during wartime to transfer into peacetime. Authors who argue that American expansion, industrialization, and globalization increased interest group demands for executive action are not wrong, but they usually fail to see that increased executive expansion to fight wars opened the door for a greater presidential role after peace was reestablished.

Historian Arthur Schlesinger, Jr. is the most famous author to see that the imperial presidency—a term he coined during the Nixon administration—resulted from American wars overseas, but then presidents attempted to translate that supremacy in foreign policy to enhanced power at home.[11] He probably overstated Nixon's role in converting the presidency of the Constitution into a plebiscitary presidency in which the populace, through elections and public opinion polling, constrains a powerful executive more than does Congress or the Supreme Court under the original Madisonian system of checks and balances. Schlesinger is largely correct in his assessment of this trajectory of the presidency, but should distribute more blame to other presidents for it instead of placing all his criticism on Nixon alone. The plebiscitary presidency is a problematic model when recent presidents have been legally limited to two terms and many have not gotten a simple majority of the popular vote[12]—and some not even a plurality of the vote.

Yet Posner and Vermeule have embraced the plebiscitary presidency. They have given up on the legalistic Madisonian systems of checks and balances to control executive aggrandizement.[13] They argue that rapid, complex economic and technological change—an updated version of Woodrow Wilson's complex society argument for more presidential power—has demanded more

---

11. Arthur Schlesinger, Jr., *The Imperial Presidency* (Boston: Houghton, 1973), x.

12. Andrew Rudalevige, *The New Imperial Presidency: Renewing Presidential Power After Watergate* (Ann Arbor, Michigan: University of Michigan Press, 2006), 271.

13. Posner and Vermeule, *The Executive Unbound.*

regulation of society at home and rapid action abroad. The cumbersome and slow collective-action problem of the relatively unspecialized legislature makes that body lose the competition to the executive branch, which commands specialized expertise in administrative agencies that have been ever more effectively brought under presidential control. According to Posner and Vermeule, the framers failed to grasp that rapid unilateral action by the executive, even with dubious or no legal authority, could create a fait accompli for Congress. In fact, in contrast to pre–Cold War presidencies, modern presidents lead and Congress follows on new initiatives at home and abroad.

Over time, Congress has delegated large chunks of its authority to the executive-led administrative state. The Supreme Court did not permit much delegation before World War II, but after the war, it became more lenient and the floodgates of congressional shirking of responsibility opened.

To substitute for honestly passing legislation that tightly governs executive agencies, Congress has delegated broad authority to them and then passed the general Administrative Procedures Act to pretend it is keeping an eye on them. The act substitutes procedural controls and judicial review for legislation mandating specific policies. In addition, when the same party controls both Congress and the executive branch, the Madisonian separation of powers is further undermined.

Furthermore, during emergencies, the president has a comparative advantage in unity, force, and secrecy compared to the Congress or judiciary. Therefore, during such crises, the other two branches delegate even more power to the executive branch. And because the administrative state is now so vast and controls so much of society, such emergencies are frequent. The cycle continues as emergencies rise and the executive branch keeps expanding in size and power at the expense of the ever-delegating legislature and judiciary. During emergencies, the Congress regularly delegates too much power to the executive.

Posner and Vermeule have accepted the progressive Wilsonian argument that the modern, complex, and rapidly changing society—when acting both at home and worldwide—needs more federal government intervention and control, exercised primarily through a powerful executive branch. In other words, the executive-centered government—in contrast to the congressional-centered government of the Constitution—was inevitable. Thus, they are resigned to constraining a potentially tyrannical imperial presidency through elections, a competitive party system, public opinion, and an American political culture that has always been leery of presidential power—that is, through a plebiscitary presidency. That the president needs to seek reelection is an especially powerful constraint on him or her. They argue that the comparatively wealthy and educated citizenry, along with the plummeting costs of information and communication, can better bind executive action than the slow and cumbersome Congress or federal courts. Even the limited check that the modern-day Congress provides on the president is done through direct appeals to public opinion rather than through legislation.

Thus, Posner and Vermeule conclude that the administrative state creates the remedy for its own maladies. The complex modern economy, which necessitated the creation of the vast administrative state, and the administrative state itself—by providing efficiency-enhancing regulation, political stability, and wealth redistribution—have increased wealth, the abundance of political information, and greater education and leisure with which to better examine presidential actions. In their minds, evidence exists of the development of such self-correcting mechanisms to the administrative state: Even as the Madisonian separation of powers has deteriorated over the course of American history, democratic processes and enhancement of civil liberties have expanded. Therefore, they conclude that modern presidents are more accountable than earlier presidents and that the potential for dictatorship in America is much lower than in the past.[14]

The problem with Posner and Vermeule's argument is that complex societies and economies do not necessarily need more government intervention and regulation. Despite gains in democracy and civil liberties, republican representative government and economic liberty have markedly declined over the course of American history. Even the executive-controlled administrative state is cumbersome and slow compared to the more rapid technologically driven changes in the market and society. The administrative state is massive, redundant, bureaucratic, and by no means fully controlled by the White House. In other words, the more complex and rapidly changing the society and economy, the less likely that the federal executive branch—with a poor

---

14. Posner and Vermeule, *The Executive Unbound*, 3–34, 61, 113, 191–92, 195, 201–02, 206.

incentive structure compared to the private sector and marketplace—will be able to regulate them efficiently or effectively. That is, the complex modern economy would likely run better without the intervention of "big brother"; as one piece of evidence, anemic post–Great Recession economic growth rates seemed to indicate that overregulation after crises, and exorbitant national debt accrued from too much government involvement in the economy, are stultifying.

By Posner and Vermeule's own admission, the federal administrative state is so vast and regulates so many areas of society that "emergencies" are much more likely to arise. If the federal government were shrunk and controlled less of the economy and society, the less specialized Congress and federal courts could again play a more effective role in regulating what bureaucracy remained—as they did from the advent of the Constitution until well into the twentieth century. Also, increasing freedom both in society and in economic markets would not only reduce the need for the vast administrative state, to which Posner and Vermeule seem resigned, but would also make America more efficient and make the Madisonian system of checks and balances viable again.

Their basic argument applies in foreign affairs as well. Posner and Vermeule vaguely allude to a more interdependent world similar to the modern, complex society at home—both demanding rapid and decisive action by the executive, with which the Congress and federal judiciary just cannot keep pace. They refer to the spurious Cold War argument that new threats, because of technology's collapse of time and space, required the expansion of executive power in foreign policy. This argument is debunked in a later chapter, which argues that the Constitution's original checks and balances system governing war was not made obsolete by the advent of nuclear weapons and long-range bombers and missiles. The original system allowed the president to rapidly respond to any attack on the United States without a congressional declaration of war. The new technology merely quickened the response time needed by the executive in that narrow category of war. Moreover, the United States has always been the leader in those technologies, including advanced nuclear and conventional weapons, which should deter—and have deterred—other countries from attacking the United States, thus making it much less, not more, likely that the president will need to muster such a rapid defensive response.

Furthermore, US wars of the twentieth century have led to a globe-spanning informal empire of alliances, military interventions into the affairs of other countries in all regions of the world, and overseas US military bases housing combat forces that can be used to patrol this expansive realm. Because the US government, although always denying it, attempts to gain global "influence" by policing the world, such a vast responsibility leads to frequent emergencies and crises. Yet these crises are usually threats to the American overseas empire, not to US national security. In times of foreign crises, the executive does have advantages of unity, force, and secrecy over the sluggish Congress and courts, with their collective-action problems. To rejuvenate these other two sides of the Madisonian checks and balances triangle, the number of emergencies in foreign policy needs to be reduced. To do so, the American Empire—which is now unaffordable with a sluggish US domestic economy dragged by a national debt of almost $22 trillion—must be shrunk substantially. US security will actually be enhanced, because less blowback terrorism will occur in retaliation for US adventurism abroad, especially in the Greater Middle East. If the American Empire is shrunk and therefore fewer wars and foreign policy crises arise, fewer US military interventions overseas would be required and thus Congress could better reassert control over foreign policy, war, and the general direction of government. Similarly, the federal courts, and especially the Supreme Court, could once again be less timid in checking extra-constitutional executive actions in foreign policy—as they were at the dawn of the republic.

Thus, although the post–World War II American Empire of globe-girdling alliances, hundreds of overseas military bases, and numerous armed interventions did not cause the imperial presidency—major world wars, a Cold War, and a "war on terror" led to both the empire and the imperial presidency—getting rid of the imperial presidency would be facilitated by drastically reducing or eliminating the empire and the many wars now fought to maintain it. To get rid of this empire, Congress would need to drastically cut the defense budget, thereby cutting the resources that fund the alliances, bases, and interventions. Congress would also need to abrogate alliance commitments and demand approval of any US forces deployed overseas, which it hasn't done in most cases during the post–World War II era. Claims for restructuring

Congress as a solution to the executive branch's overreach is discussed in a later chapter.

Posner and Vermeule argue that even as the Madisonian checks and balances have been eroded over time, democracy and civil liberties in America have increasingly thrived. Yet during the recent Cold War and continuing war on terror, we have had "red" or terrorism scares, unconstitutional domestic surveillance, torture, and violations of due process, among other erosions of civil liberties. Also, few in America worry about the lives and civil liberties of foreigners who have been killed by the many undeclared US wars on their countries during the post–World War II era of American Empire.

Finally, the Madisonian system of checks and balances, with its level of gridlock, has given the United States less government per GDP than many other industrialized nations. In contrast to the analysis of Posner and Vermeule, less government intervention in the economy may very well increase wealth, which they deem a critical factor in preventing dictatorship.

The precursor to Posner and Vermeule's analysis seems to be that of Richard Neustadt. In his book *Presidential Power: The Politics of Leadership*, Neustadt argued that the modern president's power lies in his power to persuade.[15] Sam Kernell, in his book *Going Public: New Strategies of Presidential Leadership*, took this analysis one step further and opined that presidents now spend so much time traveling and talking to the public that they have little time for governing.[16] Elaine C. Kamarck, in her book *Why Presidents Fail: And How They Can Succeed Again*, seemingly disagreed with Posner and Vermeule that the president has brought the sprawling federal bureaucracies under ever more centralized control. She cited many policy disasters that were really implementation snafus that came about because of disconnects between government bureaucracies and a White House still in campaign mode and staffed by former campaign aides, who continued to focus on political communication instead of governing.[17]

---

15. Richard Neustadt, *Presidential Power: The Politics of Leadership* (New York: Wiley, 1960).

16. Sam Kernell, *Going Public: New Strategies of Presidential Leadership* (Washington, DC: Congressional Quarterly Press, 1986).

17. Elaine C. Kamarck, *Why Presidents Fail: And How They Can Succeed Again* (Washington, DC: Brookings Institution Press, 2016), 6–15.

With advances in communication and transportation, Neustadt is right that modern presidents have gained an important advantage over Congress and the Supreme Court. In a later chapter we explore ways to strengthen those two competing branches, especially suggesting internal congressional reforms that might restore some of the national legislature's former dominance—last seen in the late 1700s, 1800s, and early 1900s.

Congress Abdicates Responsibility to the Executive

Throughout US history, the powers of the executive branch have been enhanced less by brash presidential usurpation and more by congressional abdication. Such deference is especially magnified during wartime. Such congressional delegation to the executive can be direct or by just letting the president have the playing field to himself by inaction. Over time, the Supreme Court has allowed such unconstitutional delegation of congressional power to the president. As Andrew Rudalevige, author of the *New Imperial Presidency*, convincingly concluded:[18]

> The presidency is contingently, not inherently, imperial. . . . Congress was and is the first branch of government; the constitutional structure gives Congress the whip hand. This means that when the presidency expands, it is because Congress has chosen to stay that hand.

During crises, both international and domestic, Congress has a collective-action problem. The members' individual interests may not coincide with that of the whole. The body's large size and bicameral structure, which is further fragmented by committees and subcommittees, sometimes makes it difficult to reach comprehensive solutions quickly. With the congressional "reforms" of the 1970s, the legislative body became even more decentralized as power migrated to the even more specialized subcommittees. In part, acceptance of presidential legislative agendas by Congress was the convenience of not having to sort through the many legislative proposals emanating from 535 members.[19] Because extreme decentralization was chaotic and ineffective, the

---

18. Rudalevige, *The New Imperial Presidency*, 262.
19. Rudalevige, *The New Imperial Presidency*, 265.

pendulum has since swung back to some centralization, but the Congress's collective-action problem still exists.

Yet for most of American history, as the Constitution envisioned, Congress dominated the other branches of government, including the executive. By further centralizing Congress and making the incentives of the members once again more closely coincide with that of the institution, the legislative body may be able once again to give some constitutional pushback to the imperial presidency.

After other periods of executive dominance in American history, Congress and the courts reasserted authority—for example, after Andrew Jackson's strong presidency in the 1830s, after Abraham Lincoln's near-dictatorship during the Civil War, after Woodrow Wilson's creation of the seeds of permanent big government during World War I, and after Richard Nixon's abuse of power during the Vietnam-Watergate era. Lessons might be learned from these previous reassertions of the constitutional system of checks and balances on the executive.

However, reclaiming some authority for the other branches of government now may be harder than in these other periods in American history. The federal government has ballooned to massive proportions, the vast majority of it executive branch growth. The argument that a large, complex, and modern society in a globalized world—with advances in communication, transportation, weapons, and other technologies—now requires a much bigger executive branch than in the olden days of congressional dominance has been specious yet alluring. The larger and more complex the society, the more difficulty the bloated, stodgy government, with a poor incentive structure, has in regulating society effectively and efficiently. The argument that rapidly evolving threats, most notably from nuclear weapons, should have greatly expanded executive power was also a red herring. Nuclear weapons might give the president the power to launch Armageddon, yet even they can fit within the original constitutional framework in which legitimate national self-defense can be handled by the executive; however, offensive warfare must be authorized by Congress.

The idea that George Washington's conception of the war power (only slightly more expansive than that of the Constition and Constitutional

Convention) comes from a less dangerous time in American history is a fallacy. President Washington noted in 1793:[20]

> The Constitution vests the power of declaring war in Congress. Therefore, no offensive expedition of importance can be undertaken until after they shall have deliberated upon the subject and authorized such a measure.

The modern era may be at times dangerous—Washington did not have nuclear weapons to worry about—but in his day, the newly formed, weak United States was surrounded by mostly hostile nations and empires, had a minimal military, had a huge Revolutionary War debt, and was just starting an experiment in republican government over a vast territory.[21]

Rather, in the twentieth and twenty-first centuries, the most important factor leading to bigger government and the imperial presidency has been conventional wars, especially large ones and, even more important, long wars—the forty-five-year Cold War and the never-ending war on terrorism. As Arthur Schlesinger, Jr. has pointed out, the expansion of the executive branch caused by those wars was not confined to the defense and foreign policy areas but bled into the domestic sector as well.

If the American Empire—globe-spanning alliances, military bases, armed interventions, and foreign aid—shrank because it has nothing much to do with US security and much more to do with the vanity of the US foreign policy elite, it would lessen much of the pressure to further enhance executive power. No longer trying to police the world (the United States has not been that good at it anyway) would generate fewer "crises," which tend to aggregate power in the executive branch. However, it would still remain to reduce the size of the federal government and clip the wings of the existing imperial presidency. Improvements in societal communication and transportation haven't required a more powerful executive but they have made it possible. Ever since William McKinley at the turn of the twentieth century, presidents have been able to use a national media and national transportation system to get their message directly to the people and thus put pressure on Congress

---

20. Rudalevige, *The New Imperial Presidency*, 267–68.
21. Rudalevige, *The New Imperial Presidency*, 267–68.

to enact their policy agendas (thus, Teddy Roosevelt did not invent the "bully pulpit").

Taking advantage of "new" technology—for example, railroads, telegraph, radio, and TV—to use the "bully pulpit" to speak directly to the public to promote an agenda is the most important new power that the president has acquired since the nation's founding. The usefulness of such means is magnified when what the president is selling is war. Other powers—such as the commander-in-chief power, the veto power, shared appointment and treaty power, and the power to execute and implement policies—have expanded over the course of American history but are not new. With the advent of radio and television, the media found it easier to cover one president excessively as opposed to 535 members of Congress and nine Supreme Court justices.

Over time presidential agendas became more specific and more formalized. Teddy Roosevelt's was general, William Howard Taft's was more specific, and Woodrow Wilson used the State of the Union speech for the first time since Thomas Jefferson to formally lay out his proposed program. In contrast, most presidents of the eighteenth and nineteenth centuries did not set the national agenda; Congress did. Modern presidents use their White House staffs to make most critical policies and oversee most important government operations, especially for their pet programs domestically and in foreign affairs.[22]

We will now look at the history of expanding executive power at the expense of Congress, especially during foreign policy "crises." The phenomenon begins with the first presidency of George Washington. But first, to get a baseline, an examination is needed of what the Constitution's framers at the Constitutional Convention wrote and intended executive and congressional powers to be, especially in foreign policy.

---

22. Rudalevige, *The New Imperial Presidency*, 35.

I

Constitutional Mandates
for Defense and Foreign Policy

MUCH OF CURRENT popular writing on, media coverage about, and public expectations of presidents and the presidency implicitly accept the evolved role of the office into the most powerful of the five sectors of government in America (the executive, the Senate, the House of Representatives, the Supreme Court, and the states). Nowadays, the president is not only expected to act as commander in chief of the country, but also perform other expansive functions, such as party leader, legislator in chief to get his program through Congress, and even consoler in chief when a natural or human-induced disaster reaches a certain level of loss. Yet at the dawn of the republic, the framers of the Constitution saw the president's limited roles only as defending the country from foreign attacks and executing domestic laws.

The dominant view among constitutional scholars is that post–World War II presidents have usurped vastly more power in foreign policy than the framers of the Constitution had envisioned. For example, according to Francis D. Wormuth and Edwin B. Firmage, "Articles I and II of the Constitution reveal the intent of the framers to give Congress the dominant hand in the establishment of basic policy regarding foreign relations."[1] Similarly, John Hart Ely notes that "The Constitution gives the president no general right to make foreign policy. Quite the contrary[:] virtually every substantive constitutional power touching on foreign affairs is vested in Congress."[2] Let us delve into the specifics of the founders' original concept.

---

1. Francis D. Wormuth and Edwin B. Firmage, *To Chain the Dog of War: The War Power of Congress in History and Law* (Dallas: Southern Methodist University Press, 1986), 177.

2. John Hart Ely, *On Constitutional Ground* (Princeton, NJ: Princeton University Press, 1996), 177.

The Constitution Made Congress Dominant, Even in Defense and Foreign Policy

During the colonial period and early in the American Revolution, with King George III and his powerful colonial governors in mind, colonists were concerned mainly about excesses of executive power. Thus, during the revolution, republican George Washington largely followed the Continental Congress's direction of the war.

The first American national government—the Articles of Confederation—had no executive; under new state constitutions drafted after the Declaration of Independence during the Revolution, the first state governments had strong legislatures and weak executives. Thus, later in the Revolution and just after it, concern was raised on the national level about not having a strong enough executive to effectively conduct war, to respond to insurrections like Shay's Rebellion in Massachusetts in 1786 and 1787, and to avoid being put at a disadvantage in commercial disputes with foreign nations. On the state level, concern was raised about "legislative tyranny," with unconstrained legislative bodies persecuting dissenters, canceling debt, and redistributing wealth.[3]

From 1781 to 1789, under the Articles, the Confederation had to get nine of thirteen states to agree to pass legislation, make war, approve foreign treaties, and manage the confederation—all when surrounded by British power in Canada; Spanish forces controlling Florida, New Orleans, Mexico, and Cuba; and restive Native American nations in the middle of the continent that did not want their land stolen by American settlers.[4] Under the Articles, Congress handled such foreign affairs, but with some deficiencies. The Constitutional Convention was called in 1787 to strengthen the central government—with a Revolutionary-era wariness of a strong executive (some delegates initially didn't want any executive and some wanted plural executives to dilute any person's power). However, the expectation was that any new legislative body would be the dominant branch of government and would therefore also need to be constrained.

---

3. Ken Gormley, "Introduction: An Unfinished Presidency," in Ken Gormley, ed., *The Presidents and the Constitution: A Living History* (New York: New York University Press, 2016), 4–5; and Posner and Vermeule, *The Executive Unbound*, 183.

4. Suri, *The Impossible Presidency*, 8, 35.

What resulted was a messy compromise Constitution, which was only later provided an overall vision by *The Federalist Papers* to attempt to win ratification in one state: New York. The Constitution did not provide for the total separation of powers among government branches (as commonly believed), but separated those institutions and directed them to share some key powers.

At the Constitutional Convention, the framers came very close to creating a full parliamentary system in which the majority party in Congress would always select the president. Although an independently selected president is justified in *The Federalist Papers* as a method of preventing legislative tyranny, the long-stalemated framers, hurrying to end the convention, only enshrined the independently selected executive in the Constitution when they couldn't agree on anything better.[5] And even then, in the method of presidential selection, the Electoral College, in most cases was supposed to merely nominate presidential candidates for ultimate election by the House of Representatives.

An examination of the text of the Constitution, and the debates at the Constitutional Convention surrounding the document's adoption, show that most of the limited, enumerated powers of the new federal government—including those in defense and foreign policy—were allocated to the houses of Congress, not the chief executive. For starters, as the Constitution's framers envisioned the system, the House of Representatives would in most cases elect the president, making the chief executive's job security ultimately dependent on the people's house. The framers expected that, with such a physically large country and limited public education and knowledge of candidates, prospective officeholders would be able to get an outright majority in the Electoral College only rarely; thus, they envisioned that the electors in the Electoral College would only nominate candidates for final election by the House. Even the Electoral College was a compromise between those who wanted direct election of the president by the people and those who feared an excessively powerful president, elected by the unwashed masses, and instead wanted an executive selected legislatively. In most cases, the electoral process would be a hybrid indirect system of House election with nominations provided by the Electoral College—a compromise closer to the latter camp than the former camp. The American constitutional framers were aristocrats who feared that

---

5. Posner and Vermeule, *The Executive Unbound*, 199.

the democratic masses, controlling the political system, would take away their wealth.

In fact, what independence the framers allowed the president—for example, a limited veto over congressionally passed legislation—was given to the office as a check on the expected robust power of both houses of Congress. Even the name of the office—at the time, "president" (one who merely presided over the execution of Congress's will) implied much less power than "governor" (one who governed)—indicated modesty in responsibility. The president was given the narrowly construed power of being the commander in chief of the US military and federalized militia when in battle after war had been initiated; responsibility for nominating ambassadors and other high government officials subject to confirmation by the Senate; the authority to receive foreign diplomats; the power to negotiate and submit treaties with foreign nations for Senate acceptance; the option of recommending legislation to Congress; the responsibility to execute congressionally passed laws; and the authority to pardon people convicted of crimes.[6] Most of the other powers of the new federal government, including those in defense and foreign policy, were given to Congress.

The Constitution gave the Congress the powers, among others, to provide for the general welfare; collect taxes and duties; pay debt; borrow and coin money; appropriate funds and make rules for government activities; regulate interstate commerce; establish uniform rules of naturalization; fix the standard of weights and measures; make laws on bankruptcies and counterfeiting; secure copyrights and patents; establish post offices and post roads; constitute courts below the Supreme Court; define and punish piracy and felonies on the high seas and offenses against the Law of Nations; and pass all laws necessary and proper to execute its other powers and those of the federal government.

In defense and foreign policy, in addition to approving the president's proposed treaties, ambassadors, and high defense and foreign policy officials, the Congress has the power to provide for the common defense; raise and support armies; maintain a navy; regulate land and naval forces; and organize, arm, discipline, and govern the militia and provide for calling it forth to execute federal law, put down insurrections, and oppose foreign invasions. The

---

6. US Constitution, Article II, Sections 2 & 3.

Congress also has the power to declare war and issue letters of marque and reprisal to privateers for attacks short of general war; make rules concerning capture on land and sea; and regulate commerce with foreign nations. Finally, the Congress has the power to exercise authority over locations purchased from states for forts, arsenals, magazines, naval facilities, and other federal buildings.[7] Thus, in general and even in defense and foreign policy, the Constitution gives the Congress many more powers than the chief executive.

Despite what school children learn about the "separation of powers" in the US Constitution, the document provides for separated institutions but in many cases shared powers between the branches of government to purposefully diffuse power. As for the legislative power, the president can suggest legislation, both houses of Congress must pass it, and the president can veto it, subject to a congressional override by two-thirds votes of each legislative chamber. For the more specific case of legislation to take the nation to war, the president can ask for a declaration of war, which must pass by majority vote in each house of Congress. A debate among legal scholars exists about whether the executive can veto such a declaration, but the Constitution's text doesn't make any special arrangements for this type of legislation, so the answer is probably in the affirmative.

According to an adjustment made at the Constitutional Convention, the president, as commander in chief, could respond quickly, without such a congressional declaration, but only for self-defense if the nation itself came under attack; the president's commander-in-chief role was narrowly construed as being the chief commander of forces in battle after Congress or the enemy had decided to take the nation to war. The executive can negotiate treaties with foreign nations and propose them to the Senate, but the less dexterous legislative body must advise him beforehand and during the negotiations and ratify the pacts by a two-thirds vote; the president can nominate high government officials and ambassadors, but the Senate must approve them by a majority vote. The president executes the laws but uses congressionally approved statutory language and budgeted funds to do so. To carry out the laws, the president is in operational control of executive bureaucracies, but Congress has decided what agencies exist and what they are permitted to do. Under the Constitution,

---

7. US Constitution, Article I, Sections 8 & 9.

because Congress creates executive bureaucracies and gives them their marching orders and funding, the so-called "unitary theory of the executive" exists only in the fantasyland of constitutional "separation of powers."

The president can call the Congress into special session, but he cannot dissolve the legislative body. Even the president's almost plenary power to pardon cannot be used during impeachment proceedings in Congress or for criminal purposes. The founders' intent for Congress to be the dominant branch of government is shown by the many more enumerated powers in the much longer Article I governing that body than the fewer enumerated powers for the president in the much shorter Article II governing executive powers. Furthermore, the Congress can impeach the president, but the executive cannot dissolve Congress and call for special elections.[8] In short, in most major areas where the Constitution gave the president at least some power, it also involved Congress as a check.

Some modern-day analysts have alleged that the framers left presidential powers vague—for chief executives to fill in as they went.[9] Yet the text of the Constitution indicates that although the Congress wanted the president to have some independence from Congress—for example, the chief executive's limited veto power over congressional legislation—the document is one of strictly enumerated powers. For example, the 10th Amendment reserves to the states or people constitutional powers not explicitly delegated to the federal government nor prohibited to the states.[10] With the excesses of the British central government and king in mind, the framers clearly wanted to limit the power of the federal government and especially that of the president. In the Constitution, presidential powers are explicit but purposefully limited—even in defense and foreign policy. As satirical writer H. L. Mencken said, even in the early twentieth century when the president wasn't as powerful: "No man would want to be President of the United States in strict accordance with the Constitution."[11]

Even law professors Saikrishna B. Prakash and Michael D. Ramsey, proponents of executive power, admit that "advocates of presidential primacy

---

8. Rudalevige, *The New Imperial Presidency*, 24–26.

9. Gormley, "Introduction: An Unfinished Presidency," in Gormley, ed., *The Presidents and the Constitution*, 3–4.

10. US Constitution, Tenth Amendment.

11. Quoted in Rudalevige, *The New Imperial* Presidency, 26.

have little to hang their hats on" from the Constitutional Convention. They continue: "This drafting history, with little explicit commentary on foreign affairs, should hardly encourage those who insist that, notwithstanding the lack of textual support, the President must dominate foreign affairs."[12]

Modern-day analysts who think the Constitution is vague on executive powers simply cannot believe that the framers wanted such presidential authority to be so limited. However, they have been unduly influenced by the modern conception of the presidency, which has invented, over the course of American history, many "implied" or "inherent" executive powers nowhere to be found in the Framers' Constitution. These proponents of executive power are over-interpreting the Constitution to justify the expansion of presidential power that has grown over the last 70 years into an imperial presidency and beyond. In trying to square actual practice with the text of the Constitution, proponents of executive power try to give flexibility to the Constitution that is not there. For example, constitutional scholar John Yoo asserted that if the Constitution doesn't have flexibility, "a whole lot of things we've done would be unconstitutional."[13] Rather than trying to bend the Constitution to fit bad practice, the unconstitutionality of practice should be admitted and returned to within constitutional parameters.

Let's examine how people who assert executive primacy bend the Constitution in foreign policy. First, the proponents claim that the founders were influenced by seventeenth- and eighteenth-century European political philosophers—such as William Blackstone, John Locke, and Baron de Montesquieu—to define a certain set of governmental functions as "executive" in nature. Yet these European commentators used the royal prerogative of the British monarchy as their model, which the American founders clearly and explicitly rejected. For example, in the British system, the king had the prerogative to initiate wars, whereas the American Constitution gave the power to declare war to Congress. Also, after the Glorious Revolution of 1688 and the coronation of George I, from the German Hanover House, as king of Great Britain in 1714, the British parliament became the dominant governing

---

12. Saikrishna B. Prakash and Michael D. Ramsey, "The Executive Power over Foreign Affairs," *Yale Law Journal* 3, no. 231 (2001): 287.

13. John Yoo, Comments made at the "Debate Between John Yoo and Bruce Fein on the War Power" at the Atlantic Council on February 8, 2018.

force in Britain for most of the eighteenth century. Thus, if any British model existed for the delegates of the Constitutional Convention of 1787, it was parliamentary supremacy over the king, with both legislative and executive power centered in the parliament. Even the rise of a more assertive monarch, George III, which indirectly caused the American Revolution, did not uproot the parliament-dominated underpinning of the British system, which has continued down to the present. The American colonists did not like George III's assertiveness, rejected the model of royal prerogative for their new government, and believed that the legislature was a better friend of liberty—although not without some possibility for tyranny itself.[14]

More important, proponents of robust executive power split hairs and make a questionable distinction between the language in Article I, Section 1 of the Constitution vesting congressional authority—"All legislative powers *herein granted* [my emphasis] shall be vested in a Congress"[15]—and the language of Article II, Section 1 vesting executive powers—"The executive power shall be vested in a President."[16] Alexander Hamilton originally made this "vesting clause" argument for expansive unenumerated (residual) executive power during the Pacificus-Helvidius debates with James Madison over George Washington's Neutrality Proclamation in 1793. However, modern-day proponents of executive power continue to make it, even though it is dubious.

Too much is made by these analysts of the "herein granted" wording in Article I that is absent in Article II, which they take to mean that the Congress's powers are strictly enumerated but that the president's powers are not. Yet, in fulfilling the general intent of limiting the powers of federal branches of government—later in Article II, in Sections 2 and 3—the Constitution enumerates specific powers of the chief executive (see above). Crucially, the same general pattern is found in all articles governing the powers of the three branches of national government, Articles I, II, and III: Section 1 of each article is a vesting clause that merely instructs in which branch the legislative, executive, and judicial powers, respectively, will be vested, rather than stipulating the powers assigned to each branch. Only later in each article—

---

14. Curtis A. Bradley and Martin S. Flaherty, "Executive Power Essentialism and Foreign Affairs," *Michigan Law Review* 102 (February 2004): 560, 562, 568–69, 573–74, 583–85, 593.

15. US Constitution, Article I, Section 1.

16. US Constitution, Article II, Section 1.

Article I, Section 8, Article II, Sections 2 and 3, and Article III, Section 2—are the powers for each of the three branches specifically listed. Yet the proponents of executive power attempt to read added unmentioned residual presidential powers into Article II, Section 1's vesting clause, which was meant to answer the question of where powers were being vested, not what the powers would be. Some modern-day proponents of executive power like H. Jefferson Powell admit that the text of the Constitution is not on their side and that it has been a "futile attempt, occasionally undertaken in the modern era, to make the vesting clause of Article II, Section 1, or the reception of ambassadors clause in Article II, section 3 support the weight of a broad independent executive authority." Powell instead relies on vague "structural and prudential reasoning" in his analysis of the Constitution's distribution of authority over foreign affairs.[17]

At the Constitutional Convention, James Madison asserted that "the [executive] powers should be confined and defined" because "if large we shall have the Evils of elective Monarchies."[18] The practical delegates took his advice and continued to argue about and specifically define what powers the American president would have, rather than follow European philosophers' preset conception of which powers were intrinsically executive and which were intrinsically legislative.

A doctrine in law exists called *expressio unius est exclusio alterius*—that is, when one or more things of a class are listed in a law, others not mentioned are presumed to be excluded. For example, if a law says that the official color of the United States is orange, it thus precludes the color from being black, red, blue, etc. In this case, because certain executive powers are enumerated in Article II, all others should be excluded. Moreover, Article II contains no comparable statement to the Ninth Amendment in the Bill of Rights, which states, "The enumeration in the Constitution, of certain rights [the first eight amendments to the Constitution], shall not be construed to deny or disparage others retained by the people."[19] Thus, because the intent of the Constitution was to

---

17. H. Jefferson Powell, "The Founders and the President's Authority over Foreign Affairs," *William and Mary Law Review* 40, no. 5 (May 1999): 1536.

18. Max Farrand, ed., *The Records of the Federal Convention of 1787* (New Haven, CT: Yale University Press, 1911), 70.

19. US Constitution, Ninth Amendment.

limit, by strictly enumerating, federal powers, while maximizing the rights of people and power of the states (see the previously cited Ninth and Tenth Amendments), and that no Ninth Amendment-style caveat exists in Article II governing executive functions, presidential authorities should have remained limited to only those specific powers in Article II (previously mentioned).

In other words, an expansive view of executive power in the form of unenumerated residual power does not jibe with a Constitution clearly designed to create a new federal government of strictly specified powers. In *Federalist* No. 45, James Madison succinctly stated: "The powers delegated by the proposed Constitution to the federal government are . . . few and defined" and in *Federalist* No. 14, he asserted that the central government's power "is limited to certain enumerated objects."[20] In addition, the expansive view does not comport with the framers' desire to create a republican government in which they believed the legislature would dominate. In *Federalist* No. 51, James Madison clearly stated, "In a republican government, the legislative authority necessarily predominates."[21] In *Federalist* No. 48, he reported that Congress's powers are "more extensive, and less susceptible of precise limits" than those of the executive. In contrast, he characterized presidential power as "being restrained within a narrower compass and being more simple in its nature."[22]

Also, the "herein granted" language of Article I and the more general language of Article II doesn't necessarily need to be read as meaning what Hamilton and his modern-day acolytes would like: broad executive residual authority and restricted congressional power. Under the Articles of Confederation, a Confederation Congress had preceded the Congress of the new Constitution, but no executive or judiciary in that prior national government had existed. Thus, the "herein granted" language in Article I could have had nothing to do with comparing congressional powers to executive powers under the new Constitution, but instead more plausibly to making sure the new Congress's powers were limited to those in the Constitution rather the more numerous

---

20. James Madison, *Federalist* No. 45 in Thomas A. Mason et al., eds., *The Papers of James Madison* (Charlottesville, VA: University of Virginia Press, 1985), 292; and James Madison, *Federalist* No. 14 in Mason et al., *The Papers of James Madison*, 102.

21. Madison, *Federalist* No. 51 in Mason et al., *The Papers of James Madison*, 322.

22. Madison, *Federalist* No. 48 in Mason et al., *The Papers of James Madison*, 310.

ones of the Confederation Congress. Alternatively, since the new Congress was still expected to be the dominant branch of the federal government, perhaps the "herein granted" language was designed to show the limits of federal power on the states—what would eventually be made more explicit in the Tenth Amendment.[23] Furthermore, to the extent that there are any founding statements about the Article II vesting clause, they are all statements equating general executive power only to executing the laws (according to Samuel Johnson's founding-era dictionary), thus not providing authority for residual presidential power in foreign policy that the proponents of the vesting clause would like to draw from Article II.

Finally, proponents of executive power never mention the Article III vesting clause for the judiciary. The clause is very similar to that of Article II for the executive: "The Judicial Power of the United States shall be vested" in the Supreme Court and any lower federal courts created by Congress. In other words, the clause has no words "herein granted" in it. However, the lists of cases and controversies listed as limits for judicial power were considered as exhaustive rather than as examples. This state of affairs suggests that the framers may have meant the enumerated executive powers in Article II also to be exhaustive.[24] However, many modern-day conservatives ignore the similarity of the vesting clauses in Article II and Article III, because they want expansive executive authority but limited judicial power.

The words "herein granted" in Article I also could have been put there by accident. At minimum, they were added at the Constitutional Convention by the Committee on Style, which had no power to make substantive changes to the draft Constitution.

In addition, some modern-day scholars of the Constitution bluntly assert that no one at the convention, at the state ratifying conventions, or even in *The Federalist Papers* claimed that the vesting language for the executive in Article II gave the president general power (including over foreign affairs) past the limited enumerated powers explicated later in Article II of the document—that is, the constitutional framing did not propound a theory of inherent executive

---

23. Bradley and Flaherty, "Executive Power Essentialism and Foreign Affairs," 554.
24. Bradley and Flaherty, "Executive Power Essentialism and Foreign Affairs," 553, 557.

power. Moreover, it is significant that the Virginia ratifying convention, which dealt with foreign affairs issues more than any other state convention, is not mentioned by modern-day vesting clause proponents. Hamilton invented the vesting clause only later in the Pacificus-Helvidius debate over the Washington administration's Neutrality Proclamation. In fact, at the Virginia ratifying convention, no one asserted that the Article II vesting clause gave the executive general authority over foreign affairs or even that such authority was deemed "executive" in category.[25]

James Wilson, one of the key drivers of some executive independence from the legislature at the Constitutional Convention, promised delegates that the only strictly executive power under the Constitution should be to execute congressionally passed laws and nominate personnel for the executive branch agencies.[26]

Moreover, the federalist proponents of the Constitution argued that because the document was one of strictly enumerated powers for the new federal government, a bill of rights to safeguard the people's rights vis-à-vis the government was not even needed.[27] Finally, the Ninth and Tenth Amendments also indicate the strict enumeration of the federal government's powers and all the residual being reserved for the rights of the people and power of the states. The founders, fearing that the executive tyranny of the British monarch would be transmitted to American soil, would have been unlikely to approve a boundless residual of executive power.

Proponents of the vesting clause thesis are often originalists, but the proceedings of the Constitutional Convention, the voluminous records of the state ratifying conventions, and *The Federalist Papers* provide almost no evidence to back up the vesting clause argument. Thus, proponents rely on President George Washington's slight expansion of executive power, especially in foreign policy, to provide evidence for their argument. Although the Washington

---

25. Bradley and Flaherty, "Executive Power Essentialism and Foreign Affairs," 605–06, 610.

26. David G. Adler and Michael A. Genovese, "Introduction," in Adler and Genovese, eds., *The Presidency and the Law: The Clinton Legacy* (Lawrence, KS: University of Kansas Press, 2002), xxii–xxv.

27. Healy, *The Cult of the Presidency*, 27.

administration did begin to incrementally expand executive power, the administration did not, with the exception of Hamilton, justify such expansion by citing the general vesting clause in Article II, but instead chose more specific and pragmatic rationale.[28]

In general, validation of the framers' intent for a modest role for the presidency was the experience of early American history. Executive power began increasing incrementally beginning with George Washington, especially in foreign policy, but at the end of the nineteenth century, the president still had the limited role of commanding the US military on the battlefield after the war started, enforcing congressionally passed laws, receiving foreign diplomats, pardoning convicted criminals, and sharing powers with Congress to promulgate treaties with foreign nations and to designate ambassadors and high executive branch officials.

Imaginary—that is, implied or inherent—powers for the federal government, and especially the executive branch, were first "envisioned" by Alexander Hamilton during George Washington's presidency. In the debate over whether the Constitution allowed the creation of a US national bank in 1791, a federal role in central banking could be found nowhere in the document. Yet Hamilton made the argument that Congress's constitutionally given power to coin money and regulate its value implied the power to create a federal central bank. The Constitution's "Necessary and Proper" clause authorizes Congress, "To make all Laws which shall be necessary and proper for carrying into Execution the foregoing Powers, and all other Powers vested by this Constitution in the Government of the United States, or in any Department or Officer thereof." Thus, the Constitution gave Congress, not the executive, limited power to set up a legal framework for the president or his officers to execute and enforce the laws. This constitutional provision might have allowed Congress to pass laws carrying out the coining of money and regulating its value, but it was a stretch to create a federal central bank by arguing that Congress—or any other branch of government—had "implied powers" nowhere mentioned in the Constitution.

---

28. Bradley and Flaherty, "Executive Power Essentialism and Foreign Affairs," 551–52.

Once such an imaginary power was accepted, the precedent would be used throughout American history to open the floodgates for more make-believe powers. In 1793, after President George Washington's famous Neutrality Proclamation, James Madison responded to Hamilton's *Pacificus* letters—which expounded on unstated but "inherent" executive powers in foreign policy, made necessary by the sparse enumerated powers for the executive in foreign policy and defense in the Constitution. Instead, Madison correctly asserted that the document gave Congress the power to determine content of US foreign policy and that the executive's role was limited only to implementing such legislative desires. This cogent line of reasoning resembled the president's specific constitutional role in executing congressionally passed laws domestically.

No theory of unspecified and inherent executive powers was expounded by the nation's founding generation at the Constitutional Convention and state ratifying conventions, and in 1793 Madison convincingly refuted Hamilton's invention of them out of whole cloth. That said, Hamilton's brainchild would be evoked by opportunistic politicians, especially after the large wars of the twentieth century, and thus grow the presidency. Such inherent powers, especially those mythically residing in the president's authority as commander in chief of US military forces, ultimately have led to an imperial executive branch grossly more powerful than the Constitution's framers had intended.

From the beginning of the country's history until the early 1900s, the courts recognized important responsibilities (listed above) that the Constitution had given to Congress in foreign policy. Not until the early twentieth century was the "modern presidency" born, which began when the executive branch used wars and related domestic crises to usurp congressional powers—willingly given up without much of a fight from the once-dominant legislative branch. The judiciary blessed this transfer of power by beginning to partially give in to executive action in foreign policy.

More recently, when members of Congress have tried to sue in the federal courts to overturn unilateral presidential deployment of US military forces into areas of potential hostilities, they have failed because the courts want first to see Congress try to block such executive actions before they rule on whether the legislative body's constitutional war powers have been violated. The courts view Congress as having enough incentives and tools to protect its own war powers, and if no congressional action is taken, they are reluctant to step in.[29] However, Congress may no longer have such incentives and tools to push back institutionally against aggressive presidents. Therefore, congressional reforms that restore the motivation for institutional renaissance are discussed in a later chapter.

Insights from the Constitutional Convention and State Ratifying Conventions

Although a few gray areas in the Constitution exist, they are far fewer than the proponents of executive power would claim, especially in defense and foreign policy. The text of the Constitution usually clearly delineates the powers of both Congress and the president in those areas and should be literally followed; however, it has not been. When situations come up that the text cannot address, the extensive notes that James Madison made at the Constitutional Convention in 1787, the debates in the state conventions to ratify the document, and even *The Federalist Papers*—written by Alexander Hamilton, James Madison, and John Jay to sell the proposed Constitution to the New York state ratifying convention—often can help define what the framers had intended by the text.

One such area is that of the critical war power—that is, the power to send the nation to war. The text of the Constitution says the Congress will have the power to declare war and the president will be commander in chief of the military and militias called into federal service. At the Constitutional Convention, initially no one argued that the president should have the power to begin war unilaterally. Also, a number of prominent speakers—including James Madison (author of the Virginia plan proposal), James Wilson (one of the most ardent proponents of executive power at the Convention), Roger Sherman of Connecticut, and John Rutledge of South Carolina—specifically made a case against giving the power over war and peace to the executive. Notably, Alexander Hamilton, the most zealous delegate in advocating for a powerful executive at the convention (a near monarchist), gave a speech

---

29. William M. Treanor, "Fame, the Founding, and the Power to Declare War," *Cornell Law Review* 82 (1997): 769.

arguing that the executive was "to have the direction of war when authorized or begun." He argued that the Senate should "have the sole power of declaring war."

The Convention subsequently delegated a Committee on Detail to write a draft Constitution incorporating the body's prior decisions. Unsurprisingly, the committee's draft, which detailed the executive's powers, including those in foreign affairs, came back authorizing the Congress to "make war." In the ensuing debate, Pierce Butler of South Carolina was the only delegate to clearly advocate executive power to make war. Other delegates had misgivings about giving the president the power to commence war.[30]

James Madison and Elbridge Gerry realized that in certain dire circumstances—say, an enemy invasion when the Congress was out of session—the commander in chief might need to rapidly call out troops in self-defense before Congress had the chance to reconvene and approve the war with a declaration. In those days, Congress did not meet year-round because the economy was based largely on the agricultural growing season and transportation for members of Congress by horse to the capital over hundreds of miles from the hinterlands was slow (in the modern day, the national legislature meets all year in Washington and can reconvene from recesses very quickly). Therefore, to allow the president to take immediate action in situations of self-defense, Madison and Gerry instead proposed a change that would empower the Congress to "declare war." According to Madison's notes from the Constitutional Convention, after Butler's comment above, Madison and Gerry "moved to insert 'declare,' striking out 'make' war; leaving to the Executive the power to repel sudden attacks."[31] The convention then voted to change "make" to "declare" after a clarifying comment from Rufus King of Massachusetts indicating "that 'make' war might be understood to 'conduct' it which was an Executive function."[32]

John Yoo, an executive primacist, points to Article 1, Section 10 of the Constitution—which says, "No State shall, without the consent of Congress

---

30. Treanor, "Fame, the Founding, and the Power to Declare War," 713–16; and Bradley and Flaherty, "Executive Power Essentialism and Foreign Affairs," 601.

31. James McClellan and M. E. Bradford, eds., *Elliot's Debates, Vol. III: Debates in the Federal Convention of 1787* (Richmond, VA: James River Press, 1989), 251–52.

32. Treanor, "Fame, the Founding, and the Power to Declare War," 715–16.

. . . engage in War, unless actually invaded, or in such imminent Danger as will not admit of delay"—as using the words "engage in" instead of "declare" war and making the self-defense provision explicit. His implicit point is that "declare" should mean what he believes it did in the founding era—legalizing, for purposes of international and domestic law, a state of existing hostilities already initiated by the executive.[33] Yet the Constitutional Convention's entire enterprise of rejecting existing practice and formulating a radically new system of governance was a messy process over several months. In constitutional sausage making, wording may not always be consistent. But the previously mentioned record of the Constitutional Convention's debate over the "make" or "declare" wording in the more crucial Article I, Section 8 makes it fairly clear what the framers intended by using the word "declare"—Congress is responsible for initiating war—any previous custom be damned.

According to law professor Arthur Bestor, "The phrase 'declare war' [in the Constitution] was universally understood as synonymous with what the Articles of Confederation had described as [Congress's] 'sole and exclusive right and power of determining on peace and war.'"[34] On this issue the Constitution was just following the prior Articles of Confederation, except for the change of wording by Madison and Gerry at the Constitutional Convention to provide for self-defense by the executive. This point is probably the best rebuttal to the pro-executive camp's assertion that the term "declare war" was meant only in a legalistic sense to legitimate an existing state of hostilities and not meant as the power to initiate war.

Much of the rationale for the imperial presidency arose in the latter half of the twentieth century allegedly because of the rapid-response requirements of nuclear escalation during the Cold War. Even scholars claiming to be "originalists," such as Judge Robert Bork, jumped on the bandwagon of executive war without congressional approbation by arguing that such a presidential power was needed for the modern age, because the executive could move more secretly and rapidly than Congress.

---

33. Yoo, Comments made at the "Debate Between John Yoo and Bruce Fein on the War Power."

34. Arthur Bestor, "Separation of Powers in the Domain of Foreign Affairs: The Intent of the Constitution Historically Examined," *Seton Hall Law Review* 5 (1974): 527, 555–613.

Yet because the Constitutional Convention dealt with the need for speed in such emergency self-defense situations, the president did not need to grab more power in national security—and Congress did not need to acquiesce to it—but only follow the original conception of the framers. Over the centuries, the weapons may have advanced but the ability for the president to respond if the United States was under nuclear attack, or the threat of such an attack, was already built into a Constitution then almost 200 years old.

In addition, with the advent of the Cold War, the country's traditionally advantageous geographical position—separated by two massive ocean moats from the world's centers of conflict—had not changed. In fact, replacement of hostile empires on US borders at the founding with modern-day weak and friendly neighbors, the post–World War II reduction in cross-border aggression, and possession of the globe's most potent nuclear arsenal probably has made the United States even safer from attack using conventional forces. Thus, no unilateral executive power to take the country rapidly into offensive conventional wars around the globe needed to be added, but eventually arose using the Cold War as an excuse. In a republic, conventional wars benefit from the careful consideration that representatives of the people give to war initiation and the political benefit that goes with the imprimatur of majorities of the large membership in both legislative chambers. One person is not taking the nation to war on a whim or out of self-interest, with the costs of blood and treasure flowing downward to the common citizen—much as the kings of Europe did in the late eighteenth century.

At the Constitutional Convention, the framers were so intent on the people's representatives making the decision to use armed force that they required congressional approval even for limited martial action short of all-out war. In the text of the Constitution, Congress must approve letters of marque and reprisal to authorize privateers—government-sanctioned private pirates—to use force to capture enemy ships and their contents, which were to be exchanged for money. Thus, the Constitution's two provisions governing military action—granting Congress the power to grant letters of marquee and reprisal and the power to declare war—were in the same clause in Article I, Section 8 and were thus meant to be read together. They are the only two war-commencing provisions in the Constitution; the executive is assigned no war-instigating authority in Article II of the document, which specifically enumerates the executive's limited powers.

Although most of the scholarly debate over the war power hinges on the delegates' discussion in the Constitutional Convention, the debates in the state ratifying conventions are even more crucial to discerning the founding generation's intent. After all, the Constitution, drafted in secret by the Constitutional Convention, was only a proposal until made the basic law of the land by getting at least nine of the thirteen original colonies to ratify it in open conventions. Alexander Hamilton, James Madison, and John Jay authored *The Federalist Papers* to advocate for ratification of the Constitution in the crucial state of New York. Hamilton, in *Federalist* No. 25, noted that in the late eighteenth century, most wars went undeclared and letters of marquee and reprisal were sparsely employed.[35] Yet as Hamilton noted later in *Federalist* No. 69, America's founders were creating something new in governance. By the declaration of war and letters of marque and reprisal clauses of the Constitution, the framers clearly gave the Congress the ability to initiate wars, both large and small.

Even Hamilton, an extreme outlier at the Constitutional Convention who would have preferred near-monarchical powers for the American chief executive, argued in *Federalist* No. 69 that the president's commander-in-chief power in the newly finished Constitution was well short of being kingly. The British king could declare war and raise and regulate military forces, but the American chief executive could not; the US Constitution assigned those functions to Congress. In sum, Hamilton asserted that the president's power as commander in chief "would amount to nothing more" than being the "first general and admiral of the Confederacy."[36] Thus, Hamilton even believed that executive power was restricted to "the direction of war when authorized or begun."[37] During this period, Hamilton did not contend the vesting clause argument that would give the president unenumerated powers as commander in chief or in any other manner. James Iredell, also during ratification of the Constitution, made a very similar comparison of the British

35. Treanor, "Fame, the Founding, and the Power to Declare War," 709.
36. Alexander Hamilton, *Federalist* No. 69.
37. Healy, *The Cult of the Presidency*, 24.

king to the American president, saying that the king "has also the authority to declare war. The President has not the power of declaring war *by his own authority* [author's emphasis] . . . the power of declaring war is expressly given to Congress."[38]

Modern-day pro-executive and pro-Congress analysts agree that Hamilton's and Iredell's opinions were some of the most influential on the subject during ratification. Yet if the president's role is limited to the battlefield, the executive has a role only in executing wars after they have been initiated, which is the exclusive task of Congress.

James Wilson, one of the principal architects of the independent executive branch in the Constitution, told the convention in his home state of Pennsylvania, which was charged with ratifying the document, that "This system will not hurry us into war; it is calculated to guard against it. It will not be in the power of a single man, or a single body of men, to involve us in such distress; for the important power of declaring war is vested in the legislature at large."[39] In the understanding of this key proponent of presidential power, unilateral executive war was precluded and a congressional declaration of war was the same as a national decision to enter hostilities.

Evidence from the state ratifying conventions also reinforces the desire of the founding generation to have the Constitution retain the same understanding of the war power embodied in the Articles of Confederation. As Robert Livingston noted at the New York convention: [40]

> But, say the gentlemen, our present [Articles of Confederation] Congress have not the same powers [as Congress would have under the Constitution]. I answer, They have the very same . . . [including] the power of making war.

In fact, at the state ratifying conventions, anti-Federalists, who opposed ratification of the Constitution, alleged that the document gave both the power of

---

38. Jonathan Elliot, ed., *The Debates in the Several State Conventions* (Philadelphia, PA: J. B. Lippincott, 1907), 107–08.

39. Quoted in Charles A. Lofgren, "War-Making Under the Constitution: The Original Understanding," *Yale Law Journal* 81 (1972): 685.

40. Elliot, ed., *The Debates in the Several State Conventions*, 278.

the sword and purse to Congress. In response, some Federalists acknowledged this state of affairs, but defended it, including Oliver Ellsworth: [41]

> [Does] it follow, because it is dangerous to give the power of the sword and purse to an hereditary prince, who is independent of the people, that therefore it is dangerous to give it to the Parliament—to Congress, which is your Parliament—to men appointed by yourselves, and dependent upon yourselves?

Thus, the comments of neither the Federalists nor anti-Federalists at the state ratifying conventions appear to relegate Congress's power to declare war to merely a legalistic ratification of presidentially initiated war. In fact, anti-Federalists, opponents of the new Constitution and losers of the ratification debates, feared that Congress would have both the real power to initiate war and then also have the authority to provide the money to carry it out. The Federalists countered that the new American system would have more checks on the executive than in the British system—in which the king declared (initiated) war and the parliament funded it.[42] If the founders hadn't equated "declare" with "initiate," the anti-Federalists likely would not have been worried about the Congress merely having both a power of legalistic affirmation of an existing state of war and the power to fund any conflict. Furthermore, at North Carolina's ratifying convention, James Iredell noted that the executive should have command of the military forces, because of the need for secrecy and dispatch (speed of action), but that Congress's power to declare war would check the president's power as commander in chief.[43] Congress could not do so if its power to declare war did not initiate war and instead came only after the president had begun hostilities. Thus, no statements at the state ratifying conventions seem to corroborate the pro-executive argument that the Constitution's phrase, "The Congress shall have Power to declare War," was designed merely to be declaratory under international law rather than a real decision on whether or not to take the nation to war.[44]

---

41. Elliot, ed., *The Debates in the Several State Conventions*, 195.
42. Bradley and Flaherty, "Executive Power Essentialism and Foreign Affairs," 607.
43. Bradley and Flaherty, "Executive Power Essentialism and Foreign Affairs," 622–23.
44. Bestor, "Separation of Powers in the Domain of Foreign Policy," 608.

However, pro-executive analysts, many of whom are conservatives, have noted that throughout American history, the many cases of executive-initiated war have made that practice constitutional. Yet, this vein of thought seems similar to the Left's "living Constitution" argument, which conservatives denounce when discussing other sections of the great document and their variance with actual practice. Moreover, just because executives have breached the founders' framework for the war power should not make violations of the Constitution legal. Except for the aberration of the Korean War, the use of unilateral executive war has usually occurred only for smaller military actions, and even in those cases, has accelerated dramatically only in the twentieth and twenty-first centuries. In the first military actions of the late eighteenth and early nineteenth centuries, the founders' framework was largely followed and also for almost all major wars up until the mid-twentieth century.

Not only did Hamilton agree that Congress had the war power, but also appeared to agree that Congress had an important role in shaping the nation's foreign policy. In *Federalist* No. 75, Hamilton cautioned that "The history of human conduct does not warrant that exalted opinion of human virtue which would make it wise in a nation to commit interests of so delicate and momentous a kind, as those which concern its intercourse with the rest of the world to the sole disposal of a magistrate created and circumstanced as would be a President of the United States."[45] Unfortunately, after the Constitution was ratified, Hamilton then hypocritically began pushing for ever-more executive power in foreign and military affairs, but his comments in *The Federalist Papers* indicate the general climate at the time of the nation's founding constrained him from saying so before the document became the basic law of the land.

Early in the republic's history, key framers alluded that the Constitution assumed that the lone executive, prone to seek glory, would be more tempted to war than would the many members of Congress, and thus they placed the power to initiate wars with the legislative body. In late 1789, Thomas Jefferson

---

45. Alexander Hamilton, *Federalist* No. 75.

wrote to James Madison that the Constitution provided an "effectual check to the Dog of war."[46]

In 1793, under the pen name of Helvidius, arguing against the constitutionality of President George Washington's Neutrality Proclamation, Madison summarized the founding generation's reason for giving Congress the war power in the Constitution:[47]

> War is in fact the true nurse of executive aggrandizement. In war a physical force is to be created, and it is the executive will which is to direct it. In war the public treasures are to be unlocked, and it is the executive hand which is to dispense them. In war the honors and emoluments of office are to be multiplied; and it is the executive patronage under which they are to be enjoyed. It is in war, finally, that laurels are to be gathered, and it is the executive brow they are to encircle. The strongest passions, and most dangerous weaknesses of the human breast; ambition, avarice, vanity, the honorable or venial love of fame, are all in conspiracy against the desire and duty of peace. Hence it has grown into an axiom that the executive is the department of power most distinguished by its propensity to war.

Essentially, Madison, who played a central role in crafting the war powers clause at the Constitutional Convention, believed that the executive branch— the only branch of government with actual physical assets to make things happen in the real world—would have too much power in both deciding whether or not the nation went to war and then directing the assets to execute that policy. Thus, Madison concluded that "in no part of the constitution is more wisdom to be found, than in the clause which confides the question of war or peace to the legislature, and not to the executive department." His

---

46. Letter from Thomas Jefferson to James Madison, September 6, 1789, in James Morton Smith, ed., *The Republic of Letters: The Correspondence Between Thomas Jefferson and James Madison 1776–1826, Vol. 1* (New York: W. W. Norton & Company, 1995), 631, 635.

47. James Madison, "Helvidious Number 4," in Robert Rutland et al., eds., *The Papers of James Madison, Vol. 15* (Charlottesville, VA: University of Virginia Press, 1985), 108–09.

statement indicated he thought vesting the war power with Congress was maybe the most crucial element of the document.[48]

In 1793, while as president, George Washington gave his interpretation of the war power that the Constitutional Convention had created. His important statement implies that even he found that congressional declarations of war were not merely legalistic codifications of an existing state of hostilities. "The constitution vests the power of declaring war in Congress; therefore no offensive expedition of importance can be undertaken until after they shall have deliberated upon the subject and authorized such a measure."[49] Washington's conception—based on Hugo Grotius's rendering of international law, of which many of the Constitution's framers were familiar—was similar to that of the convention when they changed Congress's war power from "make" to "declare" to allow the president to take emergency actions in self-defense. However, Washington might well have gotten some pushback from many of the other framers for narrowing offensive actions required to have prior congressional approval to only any "offensive expedition of importance."

Of course, at the time of the Helvidius-Pacificus debate over President Washington's Neutrality Proclamation, Madison was even more radical than Washington:[50]

The right to decide the question whether the duty & interest of the U.S. require war or peace under any circumstances, and whether their disposition be towards the one or the other seems to be essentially & exclusively involved in the right vested in the Legislature, of declaring war in time of peace; and in the P. & S. [president and Senate] of making peace in time of war.

---

48. James Madison, "Helvidius No. 4," *U.S. Gazette*, September 14, 1793, Reprinted in Gaillard Hunt, ed., *The Writings of James Madison 1790–1802: Comprising His Public Papers and His Private Correspondence, Including His Numerous Letters and Documents Now for the First Time Printed* (1906).

49. James Wilson and George Washington quoted in Bueno de Mesquita and Smith, *The Spoils of War*, 11–12, 63.

50. Letter from James Madison to Thomas Jefferson, June 13, 1793, in Rutland et al., eds., *The Papers of James Madison, Vol. 15*, 29.

Early in the republic's history, supporting the view that a declaration of war was not interpreted as only legally validating an existing condition, but was in fact a decision to enter hostilities, was a Supreme Court ruling (1801). Chief Justice John Marshall, from the Federalist Party opposing Madison, seemed to validate Madison's view of the war power and a statement by President Thomas Jefferson (1805) agreeing with both Madison and his archrival Marshall on the matter. According to Chief Justice Marshall: "The whole powers of war being, by the constitution of the United States, vested in congress, the acts of that body can alone be resorted to as our guides in this inquiry [of whether 'war' existed]."[51] President Jefferson stated: "Congress alone is constitutionally invested with the power of changing our condition from peace to war."[52] All three passages even imply that the president could not veto declarations of war, unlike regular legislation. That view may have been dominant at the founding, but this legislative exemption to a presidential veto is not in the final written Constitution.

The Constitution's requirement for Congress to approve letters of marque and reprisal—limited offensive actions to commission privateers to attack and capture enemy shipping—seemed to imply that Congress needed to approve even small offensive actions in advance. But even following Washington's bastardized version of the founders' intent at the Convention might be better than the current practice of unilateral executive war for all but the biggest conflagrations—for example, US invasions of the sovereign nations Grenada and Panama and the full-scale air wars in Bosnia, Kosovo, and Libya were presidential wars with no prior congressional approval.

In 1798, in a correspondence between James Madison and Thomas Jefferson:[53]

The constitution supposes, what the History of all . . . [governments] demonstrates, that the Ex[ecutive] is the branch of power most

---

51. *Talbot v. Seeman*, 5 U.S. (1 Cranch) 1, 28 (1801)

52. Annals of Congress, 9th Congress, 1st Session (December 1805), 19.

53. Letter from James Madison to Thomas Jefferson, April 2, 1798, in *The Republic of Letters*, 1031–32.

interested in war, and most prone to it. It has accordingly with studied care, vested the question of war in the Legisl[ature].

American history proved Madison right that the president generally would be more prone to war than Congress but proved him wrong that the written Constitution would be an effective barrier to such executive hyperactivity.

Regarding the general potential for executive or legislative abuse in the new constitutional order, James Madison believed that unlike in Britain, which had a monarch, in the American Constitution, "where the executive magistracy is carefully limited, both in the extent and the duration of its power," aggrandizement by Congress was much more likely than by the executive.[54] In this more general case, Madison's prediction also turned out to be very wrong, and executive expansion of power during wartime would help cause this tragic outcome writ large. Both presidential aggrandizement in war and its wider effects on enhanced presidential power are the themes of this book, as are why this has happened and how to change it.

---

54. Quoted from *Federalist* No. 48, 257.

2

America's Aggressive Expansion

Presidential Authority in the Eighteenth and Nineteenth Centuries

IN THE EIGHTEENTH and nineteenth centuries, up until William McKinley was elected in 1896, only three presidents temporarily expanded their powers greatly—Thomas Jefferson, Andrew Jackson, and Abraham Lincoln. In general, presidential power was restrained by the founders' original intent in the Constitution that Congress should be the dominant branch of the central government and by the Tenth Amendment, which gave most governmental power to the states and kept the functions, and effectively the size, of the federal government small. In addition, Congress controlled patronage positions in the small government. Finally, the president had no means of controlling the executive branch; even in the late nineteenth century, the president had only a small number of clerks and administrative staff. Thus, in this decentralized milieu, bureaucratic administration in the executive departments took place without much presidential influence, and congressional committees controlled the autonomous executive branch organizations, including their all-important budgets.[1] In foreign policy, according Harold Koh, "None of [the early] presidents ever claimed that he possessed inherent constitutional powers as chief executive or commander-in-chief that lay beyond legislative control."[2] This chapter shows that in the eighteenth and nineteenth centuries,

---

1. Kenneth R. Mayer, *With the Stroke of a Pen: Executive Orders and Presidential Power* (Princeton, NJ: Princeton University Press, 2001), 113–15.

2. Harold H. Koh, *The National Security Constitution: Sharing Power After the Iran-Contra Affair* (New Haven and London: Yale University Press, 1990), 80.

the presidency up until the Spanish-American War in 1898, with the exceptions mentioned, was an institution still limited by the framers' vision.

George Washington Was a Genuinely Republican, If Flawed, Founder

Although George Washington liked the accoutrements and circumstance of power, he was a republican and proved it when it counted. He amazed European governments by retiring from the military after winning the American Revolution (or at least helping the French to win it) and did the same after only two terms as president. Yet he exhibited republicanism even during the American Revolution.

According to Judge David J. Barron, author of the book, *Waging War: The Clash Between Presidents and Congress 1776 to ISIS*, Washington could have done what he pleased as commander of the Continental Army during the war. However, he chose to prosecute the war through the direction of Congress, even when it came to battlefield tactics. At one point in the conflict in late 1776, Congress evacuated the colonial capital Philadelphia for Baltimore to avoid a mutiny by American soldiers. During their brief absence, Congress gave Washington sole authority to conduct war. After Congress reassembled, the equilibrium between them and the embattled commander in chief was restored. Furthermore, Washington once sent a letter saying that he could not countermand a decision by Congress. And there were times when he disagreed with what Congress wanted him to do, but he obeyed anyway. (Although Washington was commander in chief of the Continental Army during the war, a century or so before, commanders in chief had served under King Charles I but were explicitly ordered to take direction from the British parliament—a history that Washington knew, as did delegates to the later Constitutional Convention.[3])

Washington's behavior during the war—deferring to Congress's direction of the war and turning his sword into Congress at the end of it—set the precedent for the Constitutional Convention in 1787 giving most of the na-

---

3. David J. Barron, *Waging War: The Clash Between Presidents and Congress 1776 to ISIS* (New York: Simon and Schuster, 2016), 3, 10–12, 17, 24.

tional security powers to Congress, not the president. On one important issue, Washington had to reluctantly yield to Congress—that of a standing army.[4] Republican thought believed standing armies were a threat to liberty, and in the later years of the American Revolution, Congress feared the Continental Army's aggressive insistence on receiving promised pensions. As a result, the legislative body had ordered Washington to decommission all regiments of that army, except about 800 troops to guard weapons and ammunition at forts. Although it seems unfathomable today, for decades after the revolution, even during periods of threatened war and actual conflict, the fear of a standing army continued in the republic. After the revolution was over, despite Washington's immense prestige and advocacy of a small standing army, Congress would not recruit more than the single regiment created in 1784. Militia would need to round out any force.[5]

As a republican president, Washington was deferential to Congress in most cases but began incrementally to augment executive power, especially in the security realm. He was determined to make the president's voice heard in foreign policy.

George Washington Slowly Begins to Erode Congress's Constitutional Powers in National Security

George Washington rejected the huge sprawling ministerial executive branches of European kings and chose to keep the presidency small. And although, as a professional military officer, he was skeptical about the capabilities of militias during wartime, he also realized the threat to the republic from a large standing army. Therefore, he advocated a small standing army (not in the Constitution), a modest navy, and state militias that could be federally called up in times of emergency. Compared to the modern-day imperial presidency, George Washington had limited executive powers—he would define goals for legislation and enforce laws when passed, while leaving the details of the statutes and the funding of them to Congress. Despite his respect for Congress, even he tried to make the most of his powers, expanding them past

4. Thomas Fleming, *The Strategy of Victory: How General George Washington Won the American Revolution* (New York: Da Capo Press, 2017), 256.

5. Fleming, *The Strategy of Victory*, 263.

what the debates creating and ratifying the Constitution indicate the framers had intended.

According to law professors Curtis A. Bradley and Martin S. Flaherty, Washington's incremental expansion of executive power "offers a cautionary lesson against too easily drawing inferences about the understanding of the Founders from post-ratification practices."[6] Because proponents of reading general executive power into the Article II vesting clause have little to support their theory in the Constitutional Convention, the state ratifying conventions, and even *The Federalist Papers*, they tend to focus on the Washington administration's incremental expansion of executive power. Yet history shows that the administration did not often use the vesting clause rationale to justify such expansion and instead chose the more cautious route of merely stretching some of the limited number of enumerated executive powers in the Constitution's Article II, Section 2.

Washington was able to get away with this slight expansion of executive power, especially in foreign policy, because at the time he assumed the office of the presidency in 1789, he had more prestige than the new Constitution. He infused legitimacy into the document and the office of the president that would last far beyond his presidency.[7]

The debate over power between the branches of government began almost immediately after Washington took office. The Congress created three executive departments—War, Treasury, and Foreign Affairs—but a famous debate erupted over the provision that the president could fire the secretary of foreign affairs, should that become necessary, without the approval of the Senate. The Constitution required the Senate to approve the president's nominations for such government offices but was silent on their removal, except to say that they could be impeached. Although not a consensus or even a majority, some in Congress argued that the Article II vesting clause gave the executive the unenumerated power to fire executive branch officials without congressional consent; others argued against the viability of the vesting clause and for the strict enumeration of executive powers; still others thought Congress should use the "necessary and proper" clause to fill in what the Constitution had

---

6. Bradley and Flaherty, "Executive Power Essentialism and Foreign Affairs," 626, 636.
7. Suri, *The Impossible Presidency*, 19, 24, 28, 36–37.

omitted; and yet others argued against Congress correcting such constitutional "defects," because this action effectively would be amending the document without doing so formally. The members of Congress in 1789 seemed to agree that the president could fire cabinet officials, but they disagreed on whether the president's authority derived from the Constitution or Congress. Nevertheless, Washington showed that cabinet members served at his pleasure rather than being rival ministers in his government.[8] As for the vesting clause, the minority who supported it did so narrowly, arguing that the president should have the tools to execute the laws, not that the executive had a residual of unenumerated powers in foreign affairs.[9]

The basic debate about whether or not the executive could fire cabinet officials without Senate approval would last another century, leading to the impeachment of a president after the Civil War, until it was finally resolved in the late 1800s—unsurprisingly in favor of the executive not being required to get the upper chamber's approval for a dismissal. Yet reading the Constitution literally would seem to indicate that such executive officers could not be dismissed by anyone unless they died in office or were impeached, thus leading to a relatively permanent, and probably uncontrollable, bureaucracy. In this respect, the Constitution was probably flawed but has never been amended to fix this problem.

In 1789, shortly after taking office, to assert the executive's role in foreign affairs, George Washington wrote to European powers that all correspondence to the US government should be addressed to the president, not Congress. Because the Constitution authorized the president to negotiate treaties with foreign countries (subject to Senate ratification) and to receive their ambassadors and ministers, Washington's action probably was constitutional, but the hallowed document still gave most powers in foreign affairs and defense to Congress.

Henry Knox, Washington's secretary of war, had convinced him to place responsibility for Indian affairs in the Department of War, because that action would strengthen the presidency. It also showed that the new government

---

8. James T. Patterson, "The Rise of Presidential Power Before World War I," *Law and Contemporary Issues* 40, no. 2 (Spring 1976): 41.

9. Bradley and Flaherty, "Executive Power Essentialism and Foreign Affairs," 656–64.

regarded Native Americans fundamentally as a threat that might require the use of force. Nevertheless, Knox advocated for purchasing lands from the tribes that white settlers wanted and persuading Indians to settle in other areas where the federal government could "protect" them. As American history unfolded, however, this policy unfortunately morphed into grabbing Indian land in violation of treaties signed with them and forcing Native Americans onto reservations containing the worst land imaginable. Even during Washington's presidency, Native Americans uncooperative with Washington's efforts to negotiate peaceful ceding of Indian lands were suppressed using force.

The Miami Indians of Ohio, led by Little Turtle, initially routed the one-regiment regular army and militia in 1790 and then an expanded two-regiment army and militia in 1791 before Congress, still suspicious of a peacetime standing army throughout Washington's two terms as president, increased the very small regular army enough to quash the Indian uprising.[10] Washington appointed "Mad Anthony" Wayne to command the expanded, but still small, army of four regiments to carry out this mission.[11] Yet the framers at the Constitutional Convention, who gave Congress the power to "raise and support Armies," had authorized no peacetime standing army at all, because they feared that it might quash citizens' liberty.

In the early 1790s, shortly after George Washington took office, Congress itself authorized the use of confidential funds for diplomatic purposes in violation of the Statement and Accounting Clause of the Constitution. That clause states, "A regular Statement and Account of the Receipts and Expenditures of *all* [author's emphasis] public Money shall be published from time to time." Congress appropriated money to an account completely controlled by the president, but he could hide from the public how the money was spent. The president could certify that the funds had been spent without supplying vouchers or other documentary evidence, as standard accounting procedure required. This early precedent of not publishing certain expenditures using taxpayer funds has been retained and expanded to allow confidential funds in many other appropriation accounts not related to US diplomacy or war-

---

10. Fleming, *The Strategy of Victory*, 263–64, 275.

11. Thomas Fleming, *The Great Divide: The Conflict Between Washington and Jefferson That Defined America, Then and Now* (Boston, MA: Da Capo Press, 2015), 116–17.

time spending. Today, the Department of Treasury publicizes a statement of receipts and expenditures, but billions of dollars of spending are hidden from public view and are not even subject to audit by the congressional Government Accountability Office.[12]

Secretary of the Treasury Alexander Hamilton's successful quest to create federally managed taxes to finance Revolutionary War debt and a national bank to deal with that debt, although not directly related to defense or foreign affairs, eventually would have implications down to the present in national security. Although the Constitution assigned Congress the power to regulate international and interstate commerce and Secretary Hamilton saw a Bank of the United States as an essential tool in carrying out that function, the Constitution did not explicitly give Congress or the executive the power to create one. In fact, delegates at the Constitutional Convention had rebuffed James Madison's proposal that Congress be given the authority to charter banks and other corporations.

Notwithstanding, in 1791 Congress gave Hamilton his national bank, based on "implied powers" of the federal government in the Constitution—as he erroneously argued for in his influential *An Opinion on the Constitutionality of an Act to Establish a Bank*.[13] Yet the Tenth Amendment to the Constitution, ratified later that same year, seems to directly contradict Hamilton's reading into the document nonexistent powers, declaring that if a power is not specifically delegated to the federal government, it resides with the people or the states.[14] Thomas Jefferson thus opposed Hamilton's National Bank, correctly believing that the Constitution permitted only states to charter banks. However, Hamilton's fictitious "implied powers" (similar fiction involves "inherent" powers for the presidency) for the federal government would live on down through the centuries, especially acting as a precedent for not only expanding the federal role in society but also that of the executive branch.

In an example of the implicit use of the similarly fictitious "inherent powers" of the president not found in the Constitution, Washington, in April

---

12. US Constitution, Article I, Section 9; and Louis Fisher, *Presidential Spending Power* (Princeton, NJ: Princeton University Press, 1975), 202–03, 205, 207.

13. Fleming, *The Great Divide*, 102–03, 134.

14. US Constitution, Tenth Amendment.

1793, unilaterally issued without prior congressional approval, a Neutrality Proclamation. The Proclamation announced that the United States would remain impartial in the European war, then ongoing between Britain and Revolutionary France, warning Americans neither to assist belligerent ships nor to carry arms and ammunition to them. Most Americans thought it was wise for the United States to remain neutral in a war between the major powers of the day. Staying out of wars, which are always costly in lives and money, if possible is always a good idea—especially if the nation doing so is new and very weak compared to belligerents that are the superpowers of the era. However, Washington was implicitly claiming an "inherent" presidential power, not found explicitly in the Constitution, to declare that the state of peace would be maintained. In essence, he was preempting Congress's crucial constitutional power to declare war, according to James Madison.

From the debates at the Constitutional Convention, however, it was clear that the framers, thinking of the British king's unilateral power, were afraid to invest one person with the power to take the nation to war. Too many European kings had taken their countries to war for questionable reasons, with the costs—in blood and treasure—flowing downhill to their subjects. Washington offered only the lame excuse that Congress was out of session and that he didn't want to alarm the populace by calling it back into a special session. Twice he declined to call Congress back. He thus created the policy of neutrality on his own without prior congressional authorization. (At the outbreak of the Civil War in 1861, Lincoln later used this same tactic of acting unilaterally while Congress was out of session, but for war-like ends and on a much grander scale.)

After President Washington's Neutrality Proclamation, James Madison responded to Secretary of the Treasury Alexander Hamilton's Pacificus letters. Those letters had promoted inherent executive power in foreign affairs by asserting that the executive was "the organ of intercourse between the Nation and foreign Nations"—arguing that the Constitution empowered the executive to negotiate treaties and execute laws—and also by noting the difference in vesting language in Article I versus Article II of the Constitution. The vesting clause argument was debunked previously and contradicts Hamilton's earlier argument at the Constitutional Convention and in *The*

Federalist Papers that the executive would only have those powers enumerated in the Constitution.

Hamilton admitted that specific powers in foreign policy traditionally thought to be executive in nature—for example, regarding the critical powers of declaring war, granting letters of marque and reprisal, making treaties, and making appointments—were either given to Congress or shared with it, but these were "exceptions and qualifications" to the general grant of presidential executive power granted in the vesting clause of Article I, Section 1. He concluded that "with these exceptions, the executive power of the United States is completely lodged in the President."[15] His argument turned the concept of strictly enumerated constitutional powers on its head.[16]

Hamilton acknowledged that Congress had the power to declare war, which may include the power to determine whether the United States "is under obligations to m[ake] war or not." (This refuted executive power proponents' claim that Congress's power to declare war was regarded by the founders as only a legalistic affirmation in international law of an existing state of conflict initiated by the executive.) Hamilton continued:

> If the Legislature have a right to make war on the one hand—it is on the other the duty of the Executive to preserve Peace till war is declared; and in fulfilling that duty, it must necessarily possess a right of judging what is the nature of the obligations which the treaties of the Country impose on the Government [alliance treaties with France promulgated in 1778]; and when in pursuance of this right it has concluded that there is nothing in them inconsistent with a state of neutrality, it becomes both its province and its duty to enforce the laws incident to that state of the Nation. The Executive is charged with the execution of all laws. . . . It is consequently bound, by faithfully executing the laws of neutrality, when that is the state of the Nation, to avoid giving a cause of war to foreign Powers.

---

15. Alexander Hamilton, "Letters of Pacificus No. 1" (June 29, 1793) reprinted in Henry Cabot Lodge, ed., *The Works of Alexander Hamilton* (New York: G. P. Putnam's Sons, 1904), 438–39.

16. Brion McClanahan, *How Alexander Hamilton Screwed Up America* (Washington, DC: Regnery Publishing, 2017), 84.

To justify Washington's Neutrality Proclamation, Hamilton concluded, "That clause of the constitution which makes it his duty to 'take care that the laws be faithfully executed' might alone have to be relied upon."[17] So the vesting clause argument, claiming residual executive power, likely was not even Hamilton's primary argument to justify Washington's proclamation.

In response to Hamilton's dubious analysis, Madison, in his Helvidius essays, correctly maintained that the Constitution gave Congress the power to determine content of US foreign policy and that the executive's role was limited only to implementing the legislative desires. This cogent line of reasoning resembled the president's specific constitutional role in executing congressionally passed laws domestically.[18] In addition, Madison convincingly argued that it was not safe to let those who conduct wars be the judge of whether to start, continue, or halt them—that is, mixing policy formulation with implementation was dangerous.[19] Given that Washington was interpreting whether the US-French alliance allowed the United States to stay neutral in a war involving Revolutionary France, he was not just enforcing existing law; a policy of neutrality was making foreign policy in a new situation—properly Congress's responsibility. By interpreting the treaty, Washington was really usurping powers not given to him in the Constitution by eroding Congress's power to declare war. Secretary of State Jefferson also argued as much in Washington's cabinet but got nowhere.[20]

Madison believed that the Neutrality Proclamation wounded US honor by ignoring American duties to France under the US-French alliance, created in 1778, whereby the French had helped Americans win American independence from Britain. In the treaties of alliance, both countries had promised to support each other if one was attacked by another country, but the question arose whether Revolutionary France's wars were offensive or defensive. Revolutionary France had declared war on Austria, Prussia, Holland, Spain,

---

17. Alexander Hamilton, "Letters of Pacificus No.1" (June 29, 1793) reprinted in Harold C. Syrett and Jacob E. Cooke, eds., *The Papers of Alexander Hamilton, Vol. 15: June 1793 to January 1794* (New York: Columbia University Press, 1969), 40–43.

18. Suri, *The Impossible Presidency*, 40–42.

19. Rudalevige, *The New Imperial Presidency*, 28.

20. Saikrishna B. Prakash and Michael D. Ramsey, "The Executive Power over Foreign Affairs," *Yale Law Journal* 3, no. 231 (2001): 335, 338.

and Britain. Also, Secretary of the Treasury Hamilton and Secretary of War Henry Knox argued that because the forms of government in both France and the United States had changed since 1778, the United States could suspend the alliance treaties while considering whether to abrogate them. In contrast, Secretary of State Jefferson argued that treaties were between countries, not governments, and therefore still needed to be honored. Thus, it could be argued that Washington's neutrality proclamation did not just reaffirm the state of peace unless Congress declared war, as Hamilton had argued; in fact, given the alliance, US status was somewhat ambiguous. France and other countries could have interpreted Washington's proclamation as abrogating the alliance.

Also, the proclamation's edict warning Americans not to assist either belligerent, nor American ships to carry arms and ammunition to them, seemed to be an attempt to change domestic law without the consent of Congress, which the Constitution gave the legislative power. (A court at the time ruled as such.) Nevertheless, in an early congressional acquiescence to a presidential fait accompli, Congress later codified the cabinet's rules of neutrality in the Neutrality Act of 1794. Neutrality was the right policy, but Washington should have recalled Congress to set the policy rather than first unilaterally doing so himself, leaving the legislative body with a fait accompli.

In preparation for Washington's fifth annual message to Congress, to be delivered in December 1793, a debate between Hamilton and Jefferson then ensued about how to characterize the Neutrality Proclamation. Hamilton wanted to characterize it as an example of the president's unambiguous power to set US foreign policy, whereas Jefferson, trying to make the best of an already issued executive proclamation, wanted to present it as a description of the status quo—America was at peace and was unwavering in maintaining that status. In this dispute, Washington grew cautious and sided with Jefferson, saying that he had no desire to interfere with Congress's power to decide between war and peace.[21] That intention was admirable, but his proclamation, when Congress was out of session, still required Congress, if it wanted war, to override a very popular executive—therefore at least somewhat compromising Congress's constitutional role of declaring war.

---

21. Fleming, *The Great Divide*, 154, 156–57, 184.

In conclusion, by making the Neutrality Proclamation stick, George Washington had asserted executive primacy in US foreign policy, excepting Congress's role in declaring war and ratifying treaties. Also, Washington conducted day-to-day diplomacy with little congressional influence, set the agenda of US foreign policy, elucidated the country's national interests, and created realities on the ground to make his foreign policy a fait accompli.[22]

Also in 1793, the ambassador from Revolutionary France to the United States, Citizen Edmond-Charles Genet, was attempting to recruit Americans to attack Spanish-held Florida and New Orleans. Although Spain and France had been allies when trying to poke Britain by supporting the American Revolution, they had fallen out over the French Revolution. In response to Genet's activities, the anti-French, Federalist-controlled US Senate passed a bill that forbade Americans from attacking a nation with which the US government was at peace. The pro-French, Democratic-Republican-controlled House of Representatives nixed the bill. The governor of Kentucky, supporting the House, declared that he had no authority to prevent any Americans from taking New Orleans. With Congress at loggerheads, Washington decided to exercise some of the powers he believed the executive had. He signed a proclamation banning a wildcat military expedition, which was originating in Kentucky. (This action probably set a precedent for modern presidents, who often unconstitutionally legislate by executive order when Congress refuses to do so.)

To enforce his proclamation against the wildcat military expedition, Washington ordered Gen. "Mad Anthony" Wayne to intercept any armed individuals moving down the Ohio River to the Mississippi River bound for New Orleans. Although Congress should have acted to prevent this expedition, which could have ensnared the United States in a war with Spain, Washington's action was of dubious constitutionality. The reason is that no insurrection existed against the US government, and the Constitution requires states to ask for assistance when a domestic disturbance occurs, which the governor of Kentucky was not about to do.[23] Also, Washington asked the French to recall the obnoxious Ambassador Genet.

---

22. Suri, *The Impossible Presidency*, 42.
23. Fleming, *The Great Divide*, 189.

Modern-day vesting clause thesis proponents argue that only that clause—that is, a general foreign affairs power—could explain Washington's actions during the Genet crisis. However, Washington's handling of the Genet affair led to much debate within the nation, but none of it involved the vesting clause. In fact, Washington's actions could be justified under his powers to receive foreign emissaries and to enforce the laws.[24]

Yet, in 1793, Washington declined a request from the state of Georgia to defend settlers there from Native Americans. He did so because he thought only Congress could approve of such a move.

The next year, Washington—somewhat ironically, given that the American colonists had purportedly revolted against and separated from Britain because of British taxation—as commander in chief, called out state militias, the largest military force he had ever commanded, on behalf of the young federal government to put down an armed anti-tax protest in western Pennsylvania, the Whiskey Rebellion. In this case, farmers felt they were being asked to pay heavy taxes on sales of distilled spirits, made from their grain, to a federal government that was favoring wealthy business and banking interests championed by Washington's Secretary of the Treasury Hamilton. The farmers were interfering with the collection of the federal tax, but rebellion or insurrection was probably too strong a word to describe their actions because they were not trying to overthrow the government. Yet Washington saw the unrest as another Shay's Rebellion of 1787, which played a big role in prompting him to support the calling of the Constitutional Convention in the same year.

Washington asked Pennsylvania's governor to use the state's militia to intimidate the protesters, but the governor replied that local law enforcement could handle the matter. The protest dissolved before the 13,000-man multistate militia force, with Washington at its head, even got to Pennsylvania. Washington had to rely on militia because Congress, fearing executive abuse of the commander-in-chief role, kept the standing army very small. Only twenty men were arrested by Washington's force; of those, eighteen were acquitted, and Washington pardoned the remaining two.

---

24. Bradley and Flaherty, "Executive Power Essentialism and Foreign Affairs," 664.

Washington might be criticized for overreacting to the crisis, but under the Militia Act of 1792, Congress gave him the power to call out the militia in times of invasion and insurrection. Article I, Section 8 of the Constitution gives Congress the power "to provide for calling forth the militia to execute the laws of the union, suppress insurrections and repel invasions." In other parts of Article I, Section 8, however, Congress is given direct power, for example, "to declare war" or "to raise and support armies," likely making delegation of these specified responsibilities unconstitutional. In the case of the militia, the phrase "to provide for" means that the legislative body could assign to the commander in chief the responsibility for calling out state militias, as the Militia Act delegates. Washington, however, still had to abide by stringent congressionally passed laws governing where and for how long the called-out militia could be deployed.

However, calling the Whiskey Rebellion an "insurrection" was a stretch. Because the farmers were not trying to overthrow the government, the uprising was more of a tax protest. Thus, Washington's greatest transgression may have been a violation of the Constitution's provision that either a state legislature or governor had to request the federal government's help in putting down domestic violence. Washington was clearly cognizant of this constitutional requirement, because he initially asked the Pennsylvania governor to take care of the problem. When the governor, who knew much more about the local situation than did Washington, refused such dire action, Washington overreacted and cobbled together a huge multi-state force. As the outcome showed, the response was "overkill" for such a limited protest.

The real issue for Washington was making the populace submit to the new government's taxes, without which the federal government could not function. Washington's most important goal was to get the protestors to submit to federal authority, which they had already done by agreeing to resume paying the tax, even before he sent the multi-state militia there. In short, Washington probably overstated the generality of the rebellion and its threat to undermine federal authority. Washington did set a precedent for future executives to use federal and state military forces to enforce federal law over state objections—Abraham Lincoln during the Civil War and Dwight Eisenhower, John

F. Kennedy, and Lyndon B. Johnson during the civil rights movement (however, the scale of the Civil War certainly qualified it as an "insurrection").[25]

The Constitution's stipulation was that the Senate would provide "Advice and Consent" for treaties the president negotiated with foreign nations. The founders, including Washington, understood that this meant that the Senate would consult with the executive prior to and during the negotiation of treaties; however, the first president became frustrated with the Senate's process in personal meetings with that body during treaty negotiations with the Southern Indians. After this episode, Washington asked for the Senate's advice only in writing, but even those requests were inconsistent. Eventually, Washington set an unwritten norm that he would not allow the Senate to collaborate in advance on instructions for US treaty negotiators, nor would he submit draft treaties to that body during the negotiating phase, but only completed treaties for final ratification. This extra-constitutional norm has persisted down to the present.[26]

Not following the Constitution backfired on Washington when his administration negotiated the Jay Treaty with Britain in 1794. He sought the Senate's approval of Jay's appointment to negotiate the treaty but did not formally send Jay's negotiating instructions to that body. In one of the first abdications of congressional authority to the executive in American history (another was the Neutrality Proclamation), a request for Washington to provide such instructions to the Senate was voted down by that body. In June 1795, Washington presented the finished treaty to the Senate for ratification. A public furor ensued. Had Washington been more transparent with the Senate about what he was negotiating with the British, the uproar might have been much less.

In 1796, Washington refused to give the House of Representatives documents concerning the negotiating instructions for the treaty, which many people thought violated US neutrality by siding with Britain over France. The real reason for the refusal was that the treaty was embarrassing and extremely unpopular, because it heavily favored Britain to avoid war with that nation.

---

25. Suri, *The Impossible Presidency*, 38.
26. Posner and Vermeule, *The Executive Unbound*.

The agreement, signed by the pro-British, Federalist-dominated Washington administration, granted preferential trade status to British exports to the United States but not vice versa; limited US trade with the West Indies; allowed the British Navy, hovering off US shores, to seize almost any shipments bound for France as contraband; and said nothing about British impressment of American sailors at sea. The treaty did, however, reduce the number of British troops in Canada, increase trade with Britain and its colonies, and pledged British payment for any American goods seized on the oceans. Washington's refusal to provide the requested information to the House was based ostensibly on the Constitution's treaty-making power being confined to the president and the Senate.[27]

However, the House, being asked to provide funds to implement the treaty, had a right to the documents. The House should have refused to vote money for execution of the treaty until it got the documents, but this instance is one in a long line of congressional capitulations to aggrandizement of power by the executive during American history. However, the House acquiesced, and an ill-advised precedent was set that the House would not use its funding power to examine future treaties signed by the president and ratified by the Senate. Also, this episode set a bad precedent for future presidents withholding needed information from the people's branches of government, including through what would become the bogus doctrine "executive privilege." Finally, France's pique over the pro-British Jay Treaty contributed to the causes of the Quasi-War with that nation during the John Adams administration.

In any event, with the Jay Treaty episode, Washington's usurpation of some of the Senate's advice role on treaties, and the legislative body's acquiescence to it, show that even early post-Constitution practice might not always comport with the founding consensus on the divvying up of constitutional powers. The Senate did, however, condition ratification of the treaty on suspending the article limiting US trade with the West Indies—thus establishing the precedent for the Senate conditionally ratifying treaties. Both Britain and the Washington administration agreed to this modification.

---

27. Fleming, *The Great Divide*, 207–09, 221; and Suri, *The Impossible Presidency*, 43–44.

All in all, Washington, although probably asserting too much presidential power in foreign policy, largely respected Congress's powers, even when that body was investigating Alexander Hamilton. [28]

Quasi War with France

In the history of congressional-executive interaction on the war power, the undeclared Quasi-War was very important. Although French depredations against US shipping, which violated US neutral rights, were a sideshow to the war between Britain and France, the conflict is close enough to the founding that it illustrates, for the most part, how the framers intended the war power to be properly exercised. The Congress ran the show with detailed instructions about how the president was to conduct the war—even stipulating rules of engagement for forces in battle.

The French had been angered by President Washington all but renouncing the US-French alliance, established during the American Revolution in 1778, by Washington's aforementioned Neutrality Proclamation in early 1793, and by the US signing of the pro-British Jay Treaty in late 1794.

Although then-secretary of the treasury Hamilton had been pushing for the use of "inherent" presidential power four years before in defending Washington's proclamation, he initially took a much more restrained approach during the Quasi War when out of office as the informal head of the Federalist Party. Laudably, in 1797, Hamilton indirectly, through the Federalist cabinet, advised President John Adams to avoid asking Congress for a declaration of war against France and instead ask it to authorize legislation that only augmented defense measures. Such defenses included enhancing US sea power, putting cannon on cargo ships, improving coastal defenses, and raising a large "provisional" (rather than standing) army. Adams did so, did nothing to start a full-scale war, and instead opted to redouble his efforts to get France to make peace.

---

28. Stanley Elkins and Eric McKitrick, *The Age of Federalism: The Early American Republic, 1788–1800* (New York: Oxford University Press, 1993), 415–49.

However, Hamilton became less restrained as the crisis proceeded. In 1799, he proposed that Congress, in advance, authorize the president to declare that a state of war existed if negotiations with France failed. Congress declined this conditional, formally declared war, and heavily regulated the conduct of the executive even during this limited conflict. In all, it passed more than twenty laws stipulating the rules of engagement for military action. President John Adams followed Hamilton's initially prudent indirect advice, claiming no questionable executive war power and accepting this extensive congressional direction. Also, Adams acted as if he did not have the unilateral power to abrogate the alliance treaties with France, which had been created during the American Revolution in 1778.

Adams wanted to arm merchant vessels and build new warships, using the latter to protect merchant convoys instead of having the vessels just performing a coastal defense mission. However, Congress was afraid that with such a large military force, the president might put it in a situation in which war was inevitable, no matter what the legislature intended. In short, even if the commander in chief didn't have the constitutional authority to start a war, a large military gave him the means to do so in practice. Congress allowed Adams to build new warships (with lots of required specifications) but allowed him to use the Navy only for coastal defense and not for protecting convoys, which was a mission more likely to lead to war. He also was not initially given the power to arm merchant ships or to raise a provisional army. Later, after France tried to extort US peace envoys in the XYZ Affair (named for the anonymous diplomats), Congress became more interested in war than was Adams (one of the few cases of this occurrence in American history). It gave Adams a navy and a larger provisional army than he had originally requested. Congress also eventually allowed Adams to arm merchant ships and capture armed French vessels loitering off the American coast trying to intimidate American shipping. Yet Congress refused to allow the general capture of French vessels. And when Adams went slightly beyond congressional authorization and targeted French vessels in the Caribbean beyond those hostilely lurking off America's coast, the Supreme Court eventually overruled him (back then, the court was not scared to get into "national security" cases, as it is today). The court's ruling solidified the constitutional requirement that the president, even during wartime, must follow congressionally passed laws, even those enumerating tactical rules of engagement governing battle.

As commander in chief, when Hamilton became too hubristic as head of the provisional army, Adams fired him, the secretary of war, and the secretary of state and disbanded the army. Adams took such measures only after British Admiral Horatio Nelson decimated the French fleet at the Battle of the Nile in 1799, and France was no longer an invasion threat to America. Yet jettisoning the army caused a fissure in the Federalist Party that would lead to Democratic-Republican Thomas Jefferson's election in 1800. The Federalists split into the Adams peace faction and the Hamilton pro-army faction.

In general, Adams kept the nation out of a full-blown war with France and largely stayed within Congress's tight guidelines for the limited military action that was authorized.[29] He did send a peace commission to France in 1799, despite opposition from Congress and most of his cabinet, but the Constitution does give the president the power to negotiate treaties with foreign governments, even if he does not agree with the constitutional advice given by Congress. However, Congress, during the treaty ratification process, can then constitutionally pass on any outcome of his efforts. His Federalist Party was against this peace initiative, because it wanted to keep followers in an anti-French mood for the elections in 1800. Yet Adams's pursuit of peace—despite that initiative harming his chances of being reelected president—was courageous, because more people would have died if the effort had been postponed until after the election.

However, the Quasi War also showed that military action, even short of formal war, could lead to the erosion of the American political system and civil liberties at home. Taking advantage of the conflict, the Federalist Congress passed, and Adams signed, the Alien and Sedition Acts in 1798. The acts were ostensibly needed for security during the war but really were designed to stifle the Democratic-Republican Party's opposition to Federalist government policy. The Alien Acts gave the president the power to throw 30,000 French immigrants, most of them fleeing the brutality of their own revolution, out of the country. In violation of the right of free speech guaranteed in the First

---

29. Barron, *Waging War*, 42–45, 48–49, 50, 52, 54–55, 66–67.

Amendment, the Sedition Act made criticism of the government a criminal offense. Adams used the law to vigorously prosecute Democratic-Republican newspaper editors who criticized him. Also, Thomas Jefferson and James Monroe, the Democratic-Republican leaders, were afraid of being arrested by the Federalists. To respond to French cruelty to American sailors, Congress even authorized Adams to inflict equal mistreatment of Frenchmen in America.

Madison and Jefferson wrote the Virginia and Kentucky Resolutions opposing the Sedition Act. Jefferson declared that the Constitution was a pact among the states and that any federal laws passed that exceeded the powers delegated to the central government by the Constitution could be nullified by the states. That argument would cause conflict later in American history. Yet Madison noted that the Constitution was not a pact among states, because the state legislatures didn't ratify it; state conventions chosen by the people did. If a state legislature tried to nullify a federal law, it could be accused of aggrandizing powers it didn't possess.

Despite these oppressive acts, the federal government was still so small when it moved from Philadelphia to Washington in 1800, it needed only seven packing crates to carry the archives of all executive agencies.

Thomas Jefferson: The Louisiana Purchase and Other Constitutional Usurpations

Despite Thomas Jefferson's opposition to the Alien and Sedition Acts during Adams's presidency, when he became president he encouraged state governors to go after opposing newspaper editors, saying that a "few prosecutions of the most prominent offenders" might render other obstreperous editors more reticent.[30] He believed such actions were legal because the First Amendment only applied to the federal government, not the states (this changed with the adoption of the Fourteenth Amendment after the Civil War). In this way, more prosecutions of editors for free speech occurred in the hypocritical Jefferson administration than under the Sedition Act during the Adams administration. In addition, not a fan of an independent judiciary, Jefferson wrote a letter to Congress complaining about the "seditious" conduct of Federalist

---

30. Fleming, *The Great Divide*, 324.

Supreme Court Justice Samuel Chase, who had called the Jefferson administration a "mobocracy," and implied that Chase should be impeached. The House of Representatives obliged, but Chase was thankfully acquitted. These later events cast into doubt Jefferson's defense of free speech, made famous by his earlier opposition to Adams's Alien and Sedition Acts.

One characteristic of Thomas Jefferson, illustrated by these examples, which is usually buried in the adoration of the man by historians, is his often-hypocritical nature. For example, the author of "All men are created equal" in the Declaration of Independence was not only the owner of slaves, but broke a promise to free them after his death—as George Washington's will did after his wife Martha's death. An even more important instance of Jefferson's hypocrisy was violation of his strict constructionist view of the Constitution—that is, if the document does not say the federal government or the executive has the power to do something, it should not be doing it. Jefferson was one of the few powerful chief executives during the nineteenth century (the others being Andrew Jackson and Abraham Lincoln), a century in which the presidency operated largely as the restrained office that the framers of the Constitution had envisioned. While in office as president, Jefferson repeatedly violated his strict constructionist ideology. In his battle with the independent judiciary, he used executive privilege (long before the term was created by Dwight Eisenhower) to push back against Chief Justice John Marshall, his nemesis, by arguing that he could withhold a letter from the court and ignore a subpoena to testify before it. He later backed off on these claims but was never called on to do either—this timidity with the court being one reason that some scholars make the dubious claim that he left the presidency weaker than he found it. Jefferson got along much better with the then-small Congress—with which he had long-time personal relationships with its leaders—and thus dominated the legislature as no president has ever done since because of its increasing size and internal specialization into committees.[31]

Despite his strict constructionist ideology, Jefferson adopted the view of inherent executive power espoused by his nemesis, Alexander Hamilton, when purchasing the Louisiana Territory in 1803 without a constitutional

---

31. James T. Patterson, "The Rise of Presidential Power Before World War II," *Law and Contemporary Problems* 40, no. 2 (Spring 1976): 42–43.

amendment or congressional approval; when spending funds that Congress had not appropriated to replenish ammunition stocks when war seemed likely after the British seized the USS *Chesapeake* in 1807; and as commander in chief, when sending US naval forces to the Mediterranean to counter the Barbary pirates without congressional approval.

One of the most famous episodes of executive aggrandizement occurred during Jefferson's presidency: the purchase in 1803 of Louisiana from Napoleon, the leader of France. Although Jefferson did resist congressional pressure to take Florida and New Orleans by force (Congress had authorized Jefferson to raise a force of 80,000 to do so, and Jefferson's successor, James Madison, took West Florida in 1810) and continued to negotiate with cash-strapped Napoleon to buy the Louisiana Territory, Jefferson had no authority to add new territory to the country. Nowhere in the Constitution does it say that the United States could acquire new lands; a constitutional amendment was required, and Jefferson knew he needed one. Yet, Jefferson was in a hurry to buy the vast area of land from Napoleon and pushed through the land grab, constitutional requirements be damned. The land-hungry Congress acquiesced to his aggrandizement of executive power, as it did to the Neutrality Proclamation of George Washington, and as it would continue to do throughout American history.

Jefferson seemed unduly afraid that Napoleon would change his mind about selling the vast land. Even so he could have committed immediately to purchase it, let Congress ratify that treaty, and later asked Congress to propose a constitutional amendment allowing the United States to add territory, subject to ratification by the states. Congress and the states likely would have been very agreeable to the quick ratification of such an amendment. Instead, he merely let Congress ratify a treaty that doubled the size of US territory—one of the first instances in American history of a president circumventing a constitutional requirement. A constitutional amendment was never sought. Using this method of acquiring Louisiana was especially hypocritical, because Jefferson had criticized Alexander Hamilton's grandiose assertions of inherent executive power in foreign policy during the Washington administration. Thus, the way Jefferson conducted the Louisiana Purchase severely wounded the "strict constructionist" method of interpreting the Constitution, and the father of that school of thought did the damage himself. Unlike George Washington, however, Jefferson didn't just call out existing militia but persuaded Congress to authorize 80,000 militia to put down any trouble in the new territory.

In 1806, Jefferson received alarming word that his former vice president, Aaron Burr, had organized an army and was involved in a conspiracy to detach western territory, making it into a separate country, with British ships said to be sent to the mouth of the Mississippi River to reinforce him. Jefferson believed Burr was trying to deprive him of the Louisiana Territory, the biggest and maybe the only significant accomplishment of his presidency.

Initially, Jefferson was inclined to send US gunboats down the river to block the British vessels, but he didn't want to overstep congressional appropriations law that probably didn't authorize money to fund gunboats that might kill Americans. Also, laudably, Jefferson initially did not want to give Congress any excuse to expand the federal military, create a standing army, or impose martial law. Instead, Jefferson wanted to rely on local militias to address the threat.

However, unscrupulous Gen. James Wilkinson, commander of a federal military force, went to New Orleans and asked the Louisiana territorial governor to suspend habeas corpus, thus preventing those arrested from challenging their detention. The governor refused to do so. Nevertheless, Wilkinson ordered that people allegedly involved in the Burr conspiracy be rounded up, placed in military custody, sent back to Washington, and denied freedom—even if local civilian courts issued writs of habeas corpus demanding their release. Neither Congress nor the Louisiana legislature had authorized Wilkinson to place prisoners in military custody and suspend habeas corpus.[32]

The Constitution says that in case of domestic violence, states must request federal military assistance and that only Congress could suspend habeas corpus. Wilkinson did both without any such authorization. As the head of the Democratic-Republican Party, an organization at least theoretically suspicious of excessive executive power, Jefferson now faced a conundrum, because he had promised to end the creeping presidential authority from years of Federalist party rule. Yet he endorsed Wilkinson's illegal actions in the heat of the moment and trials for the suspects in Washington, violating the constitutional

---

32. Barron, *Waging War*, 59–65, 68–72.

provision that gave the accused the right to a civilian trial in the locality in which the crime occurred. Furthermore, the Congress declined to validate illegal acts retroactively by suspending habeas corpus after the fact; if Burr's conspiracy had posed that much of a threat (it did not), Jefferson should have gone to Congress in advance for such a suspension.

As he did in the impeachment of Supreme Court Justice Samuel Chase, Jefferson ignored the separation of powers in the Constitution and interfered with Aaron Burr's trial. Even though Jefferson was a lawyer, he angrily and publicly pronounced Burr guilty before the trial for treason had even begun. Fearing that Jefferson would hang Burr, John Marshall, Chief Justice of the Supreme Court, decided to preside in person over Burr's trial. In the trial, Marshall ruled that, unlike a king, President Jefferson was no more immune from a subpoena than any other citizen. Yet Jefferson declared that he would decide what papers to turn over to the court. Under threat of impeachment if he ruled in Burr's favor, Marshall did so anyway. The ruling was important, because in the future, the government could not convict opponents of putative or theoretical treason. An apoplectic Jefferson then threatened to prosecute Burr's attorney, Luther Martin, and renewed his attempt to undermine the independence of the judiciary by calling for a constitutional amendment enabling the president to remove any federal judge, if the executive got a two-thirds majority in Congress to agree.[33]

In 1807, when the captain of the British ship *Leopard* wanted to search the USS *Chesapeake*, moored at Hampton Roads, Virginia, for British sailors who might have deserted (the British had a chronic shortage of sailors to fight the French Navy in the Napoleonic wars), the captain of the *Chesapeake* declined. The *Leopard* then attacked the American ship and left three Americans dead. Jefferson feared a British invasion or at least a menacing British fleet off America's coast. However, Jefferson purposefully didn't call Congress back into session to deal with the threat because he believed much sentiment for war might exist. Yet Jefferson needed to augment US defenses quickly and therefore entered into contracts for gunpowder and materials with which to build gunboats. The problem was that Congress hadn't appropriated any money for gunboat construction, which the Constitution says is the only way federal

---

33. Fleming, *The Great Divide*, 349–56.

money can be spent. Although Jefferson was doing the opposite of trying to take the country to war unilaterally, sometimes executive efforts at making peace are also unconstitutional—as was George Washington's Neutrality Proclamation described earlier.

Jefferson believed that, in a crisis, the executive or his field commanders could unilaterally do things without Congress's approval, especially if the president thought Congress would eventually approve it. (Congress did later approve of Jefferson's unilateral defensive actions.) At that later date, Jefferson believed that Americans' spoiling for a fight after the *Leopard*'s attack would have waned.

Unfortunately, even after the war fever had lifted, Jefferson believed that embargoing all US trade with the British was the right policy.[34] The Embargo Act of 1807 was not only unpopular, but the drastic federal measures to enforce it resembled a police state and created famine in the American agricultural paradise. Not only was all overseas shipping prohibited but also all intra-coastal marine transportation as well. Thus, Thomas Jefferson, supposedly the biggest proponent of liberty in American history, enforced what one historian called the most draconian law in US history. Although Congress bowed to Jefferson's desire to shoot himself in the foot, along with the country, he usurped the Constitution by enforcing the embargo using an executive order to impose martial law—thus suspending due process and other constitutional protections. He did not believe he needed judicial warrants to arrest people and seize their property.[35] Anyone who loaded food or goods on to an American ship needed a permit, but federal inspectors had a right to prevent anyone from going to sea who they merely suspected of intending to violate the embargo, a seeming violation of the Fourth Amendment's standard that there be "probable cause" that a crime had been committed. The embargo was a failure and was terminated on Jefferson's last day in office. One main reason was that even though US exports to Britain were ended, British exports to the United States in British ships were still legal because the federal government needed the tariff revenues.

---

34. Barron, *Waging War*, 72–76, 78–79.

35. Fred Kaplan, *Lincoln and the Abolitionists: John Quincy Adams, Slavery, and the Civil War* (New York: HarperCollins, 2017), 352–53.

Jefferson was also a bit sketchy in staying within strict constructionism during the naval war with the Barbary pirates of North Africa. Although staying within the general framers' framework of the war power, he expanded the self-defense exemption for executive military action. Without congressional approval, Jefferson sent the US Navy to the Mediterranean Sea to defend American merchant ships against Barbary state pirates and privateers. Jefferson commanded the Navy to the Mediterranean Sea while the legislative body was out of session; he told naval commanders to avoid offensive action until he got a declaration of war from Congress.[36] Yet in his orders as commander in chief, to retaliate against state-sanctioned pirates, US ships should "chastise their insolence—by sinking, burning, or destroying their ships wherever you shall find them," did not seem entirely defensive in nature.[37] A convincing argument could be made that the framers of the Constitution intended that the executive exemption for self-defense, to the requirement for a congressional declaration of war, applied only when the nation itself was under attack, not its commerce overseas.

Despite (or because of) Jefferson's orders, one US naval commander got aggressive anyway and started the war. Thus, even at this early date in the republic's history, the incident shows how a president's abuse of the commander-in-chief power to put US forces potentially in harm's way can increase the potential for igniting spontaneous war, thereby usurping Congress's constitutional power to decide whether the nation goes to war.

After Jefferson, the head of a party that originated to combat excessive executive power, left office, he even anonymously endorsed the dangerous argument that in times of national danger, the president could break the law. (This was the same argument George W. Bush invoked to severely erode American civil liberties after the 9/11 attacks.)

With Britain's war with Napoleonic France again heating up, the British blockade of Europe was leading to the abuse of neutral rights of American merchant ships, and the British shortage of sailors was leading to the continued impressment of American sailors into the British Navy. Yet Jefferson rejected a treaty with the British—pledging that they would offer redress to

---

36. Matthew Crenson and Benjamin Ginsberg, *Presidential Power: Unchecked and Unbalanced* (New York: W. W. Norton & Company, 2007), 70.

37. Quoted in Patterson, "The Rise of Presidential Power," 42.

any American mistakenly kidnapped—which possibly could have averted the War of 1812.

War of 1812

American history textbooks usually attribute the causes of the war to British impressment of sailors on American ships and to their Orders in Council, which violated US neutral shipping rights by prohibiting neutral countries from trading with France, Britain's long-standing enemy. Yet the impressment of sailors had attenuated greatly by the start of the war, because the British pulled their ships back from the US coast to avoid antagonizing American maritime transport. Also, to avoid conflict with America, the British rescinded the Orders in Council. However, due to slow transportation across the ocean, word did not come until the United States had already declared war on Britain.[38] After the declaration, a British envoy approached Madison with a proposal to return both nations to peace, but President James Madison said, perhaps coyly, that he was duty bound to carry out a war until Congress rescinded the declaration, which Congress could have done but did not. However, Madison could have pressured Congress to rescind its declaration of war, using the British peace proposal as leverage, but did not.

Furthermore, impressment and the violation of neutral shipping rights had been going on since the Washington administration, because the wars between the British and French had also been going on that long. Yet if such depredations had recently become so onerous, why was the region of the United States most affected by them—seafaring New England—the most avidly against war with Britain?

The American move toward war with the British did not begin in earnest until after 1810, when the War Hawks were elected to Congress. These western members of Congress wanted to grab, using force, British Canada, which was a slave-free area that could be used to balance entrance of Florida, a prospective slave state, into the Union. In 1811, scared that Florida would pass from Spain to another foreign power, President Madison asked Congress for authority to take "temporary possession" of the area and, in secret session,

---

38. Bueno de Mesquita and Smith, *The Spoils of War*, 65–68.

the legislative body appropriated $100,000 in secret funds to do so. The public did not know about this secret law until Congress published it years later in 1818.[39]

Predictably, after the War of 1812 started, one of the first acts of the United States was to invade Canada. These western men also wanted the removal of remaining British military outposts in the West.[40] The outposts were still there in violation of the treaty ending the American Revolution, but the United States had also breached the treaty by not paying back loans owed to the British. If the outposts were removed, American settlers could push westward and steal Native American land.

Also, the War Hawks better funded the army, to capture territory in Canada and in the west, but skimped on the navy, which would have been the service used to counter British impressment and violation of neutral shipping rights—another indication of the likely foremost goal of the war. Actions often speak louder than words, but so oftentimes in American history and politics, analysts and the public believe the bogus rhetoric.

According to Hugo Grotius, the premier teacher of international law at the time, a congressional declaration of war would only be needed for offensive actions—not ones done in self-defense. George Washington's interpretation of the war power created at the Constitutional Convention, and that of James Madison, who was also familiar with such a rendering of international law, largely followed that of Grotius. Therefore, defending against British impressment of American sailors and violation of US neutral shipping rights, under this conception, perhaps would not have required such a declaration. Yet Madison did broach the subject of a declaration and Congress approved one, thus leading to the suspicion that the real purpose of the war was an offensive invasion to grab Britain's Canadian colonies, according to Bueno de Mesquita and Smith.[41]

President James Madison was much less enthusiastic about war than was Congress (another of the few instances in American history in which this was the case). For example, earlier in 1810, the Senate authorized the president,

---

39. Fisher, *Presidential Spending Power,* 214.

40. Ivan Eland, *Recarving Rushmore: Rating the Presidents on Peace, Prosperity, and Liberty* (Oakland, CA: Independent Institute, 2009), 38–45.

41. Bueno de Mesquita and Smith, *The Spoils of War,* 63–64.

at his discretion, to order the navy to actively protect US shipping against the French and British. In a move that is rarely seen—a politician limiting his power—Madison protested that this was an unconstitutional delegation of congressional war power to the executive. The House of Representatives agreed with Madison and rejected the resolution. This episode seems to indicate that early in the republic's history, despite Thomas Jefferson's earlier "defensive" actions to protect US seaborne commerce without congressional approval during the earlier Barbary Wars, the self-defense exemption from the requirement for Congress declaring war generally was regarded as existing only for an attack on US territory.

At the time, candidates for chief executive were nominated to run as their parties' standard-bearers by the congressional party caucuses. The War Hawks made it clear that if Madison did not get behind a war with Britain, he would not be re-nominated on the Republican ticket for a second term and instead one of his two pro-war rivals would be. Madison's ideology favoring liberty and avoiding war—historically, the latter had usually usurped the former—lost out to the personal desire to be reelected; he reluctantly opted for battle. Nevertheless, in lieu of requesting that Congress declare war, his message to the legislative body said war was its decision to make and merely invited the members to deliberate on the question. Still he hadn't necessarily needed to send such a message. Also, he could have vetoed any such declaration, but chose to sign it even though he had long thought war with powerful Britain would be risky and that the issues could be less costly resolved through peaceful means.

The War of 1812 was the first major declared war in American history, and Madison largely followed the framers' intent of letting Congress be in charge of it; he largely carried out their dictates. Even on the home front, with his Republican Party having been victims of the Sedition Act during the Quasi War with France in the late 1790s, Madison did not want Congress to give him powers to make criminals out of Federalist Party opponents, using war as an excuse. He ignored the urgings of former president Jefferson and Supreme Court Chief Justice Joseph Story to prosecute such dissidents.

During the war, Madison laudably avoided the kind of severe abuse of civil liberties perpetrated during the Quasi War. The War of 1812 was one of the few major wars in American history in which large-scale civil liberties violations on the home front were not perpetrated; generally, it is the exception that proves the rule. However, Madison's general, Andrew Jackson, did illegal things in New Orleans, going even further than Gen. James Wilkinson had done years before during the Burr crisis. Jackson declared martial law with no congressional authorization, failed to lift it once the British had left, and jailed a federal judge who had issued a writ of habeas corpus to free a prisoner that Jackson had taken. Jackson's martial law suspended habeas corpus, meted out military punishments on civilians, and snuffed out a free press. Although the jailed judge held General Jackson in contempt of court for his illegal actions and Madison—unlike Jefferson, who secretly approved of General Wilkinson's earlier similar actions—reprimanded Jackson in writing through the secretary of war, Madison eventually caved in to the victorious hero of the battle of New Orleans. Madison did not push his criticism of Jackson too far. After all, Jackson's win in the war's last battle—after peace had been negotiated in Europe, but was yet unknown in the United States—bailed out Madison from the otherwise foolish and inconclusive war.[42]

Astonishingly, after the US declaration of war on Britain, Madison generally had trouble getting Congress to provide the men, money, and war supplies to adequately prepare for it. Also, Madison—unlike Jefferson and more like Adams—did not try to substantially expand his power during war. Again, this presidential restraint would prove to be the exception during American history. Perhaps the reason is that Congress—not the executive—ran both the Quasi-War and the War of 1812. (The Quasi-War, however, did involve violations of civil liberties driven by Congress.)

In many conflicts in American history, the United States won the war but lost the peace. But in the War of 1812, the United States lost territory during the war but recovered it during peace negotiations. America's performance in battle left a lot to be desired; the greatest victory was Andrew Jackson's defeat of the British in early 1815, but that was after the war ended with the Treaty of Ghent signed in late 1814. Yet the United States regained territory in eastern Maine and finally got the British to evacuate their outposts on the American frontier. The latter development was important, because it opened the West for genocide and ethnic cleansing of Native Americans and the stealing of

---

42. Barron, *Waging War*, 94–97.

their land (that is, American westward expansion). Declaring war on a global superpower can be risky, and in the end, the relatively weak United States had achieved only slim benefits in return for the lives and money expended. Alternatively, if the United States had lost the war, it could have lost its recently won independence or become a vassal state of Britain. The American public was so relieved at conclusion of the war, however, that the public was willing to believe that a tie was a win, and thus Madison was plausibly able to declare victory.[43]

The First Forty Years of the Nation's History Indicate the Founders' Intent Vis-à-vis the War Power

David J. Barron best sums up the framers' intent on the constitutional power to conduct war:[44]

In the forty years after General Washington first took command of the Continental Army [1775–1815], war had seemed to come to America in all its guises: uprisings, half-wars, battles at sea, skirmishes at home, and then, war in its fullest and against no less a power than England itself. But these conflicts produced little precedent to suggest the president—by dint of his title, commander in chief—enjoyed an exclusive, uncontrollable power to determine the conduct of war. The Constitution did not by terms secure it. The delegates to the Constitutional Convention did not seem to endorse it. Congress had passed laws—most especially in restricting naval movements during the Quasi War—that were predicated on the assumption that the Constitution was not intended to enshrine it. The Supreme Court issued rulings rejecting it. Presidents conducted themselves as if they did not have it.

Justice Joseph Story, writing one of the great constitutional treatises, summed up the standard view as it stood by the century's third decade: Congress's war powers were "unlimited in every matter essential to its efficacy," including the "formation, direction, and support of the national forces." Story thought the Quasi War exemplary. It had

---

43. Bueno de Mesquita and Smith, *The Spoils of War*, 87–88.
44. Barron, *Waging War*, 99.

been "regulated by the diverse acts of Congress, and of course [had been] confined to the limits prescribed by those acts."

Similarly, David Currie concluded that early executives believed that only an attack on the United States justified unilateral war on the part of the president. Finally, a famous modern legal adviser to the State Department, Judge Abraham Sofaer, wrote, "At no point during the first forty years of activity under the Constitution, did a President . . . claim that presidents could exercise force independently of congressional control."[45]

Monroe Doctrine

In 1817, however, James Monroe, under his authority as commander in chief, unilaterally sent Gen. Andrew Jackson into Spanish-held Florida to fight the Seminole Indians. Jackson's reckless conduct nearly caused a war with Spain. Also, Monroe invented the unconstitutional executive agreement with other nations, which set a bad precedent and would be used by subsequent presidents to circumvent the stiff constitutional requirement of Senate ratification of treaties, which demanded a two-thirds majority vote.[46] Nowadays, unsurprisingly presidents sign many more executive agreements than treaties—even on major issues, such as Barack Obama's nuclear deal with Iran.

As South and Central American nations broke away from Spain and formed republics, to prevent the re-encroachment of Spain, Britain, and France into the Western Hemisphere, James Monroe and his secretary of state, John Quincy Adams, issued the Monroe Doctrine in 1823.[47] The doctrine, audacious because initially the new weak United States had little punch to back it up, was an informal unilateral presidential action that did not have the effect of law or even congressional approval. Nevertheless, the doctrine is still in effect today and has had an enormous effect on US dominance of the Western Hemisphere. The doctrine originally pledged that the United States would stay out of European wars if the European powers would not expand their attempts to intervene in the Western Hemisphere. Eventually, the first part

---

45. Quoted in Crenson and Ginsberg, *Presidential Power*, 325.
46. Patterson, "The Rise of Presidential Power," 45.
47. Kaplan, *Lincoln and the Abolitionists*, 166.

was dropped, but the second part has held. This unilateral, executive-imposed, and precedent-setting doctrine—and ones that followed in its path, such as the Truman Doctrine, the Eisenhower Doctrine, the Nixon Doctrine, the Reagan Doctrine, the Carter Doctrine, etc.—enhanced executive power in foreign policy.

James Polk—a subsequent, aggressive president—expanded the doctrine from preventing European military intervention in the Western Hemisphere to precluding even foreign diplomatic intervention. He also banned any transfer of territory in the hemisphere to European powers, even if the people living in the territory wanted it.

In the first decade of the twentieth century, Theodore Roosevelt provided a corollary to the doctrine, which stated that the United States would intervene in any Latin American country that had internal instability (for example, debt unpaid to Europeans) that could cause a European great power to intervene in the Western Hemisphere. This corollary was just an excuse to use ostensible hemispheric protection from foreign powers to meddle incessantly in the affairs of poor Latin American countries.

Andrew Jackson's Expansion of Executive Power

The great expansion of the electorate led the country to become more democratic during Andrew Jackson's candidacy and time in office. Jackson converted the presidency from an administrative office into a political one, as leader of a mass political party.[48] Forever after, presidents deemed themselves direct representatives of the people. And the reality somewhat mirrored presidential conceptions. Roughly around this time, party conventions took the place of congressional caucuses in nominating presidential candidates. And although the Electoral College still existed, it became "democratized" by most states assigning their electoral votes to the winner of the popular vote in the state instead of the system operating the way the framers had originally intended. The framers more republican intention was state legislatures selecting experts to nominate a better sample of presidential candidates than the uninformed public could muster, then to have the House of Representatives,

---

48. Patterson, "The Rise of Presidential Power," 39.

in most elections, choose among them to select the chief executive. So for most of American history, the Electoral College has operated in a perversion of the founders' vision, and thus merely has distorted the popular vote.

Prior to Andrew Jackson, most presidents, starting with George Washington, were even more conservative about vetoing congressionally passed legislation than the Constitution allowed. Despite this requirement not being in the Constitution, they vetoed legislation only if they believed it was unconstitutional. However, Andrew Jackson came into office and began vetoing bills just because he thought they were bad policy—the most famous of which was renewal of the authorization of the Second National Bank of the United States. Jackson alone vetoed twelve bills, more than double the number of the combined total of the six presidents who served before him.[49] After Jackson, presidential vetoes for policy reasons just became part of the political landscape, but this change was one of the rare expansions of executive power that was constitutional. However, in withholding a draft veto of the renewal of the bank from Congress, Jackson dubiously expanded what would later become "executive privilege" to shield internal executive branch deliberations. Also, he pushed back on the Supreme Court's questionable ruling that the bank was constitutional. Without congressional approval, he transferred federal monies from the national bank to state-chartered banks. Furthermore, Jackson was zealous in his removal of government officials, even though the Constitution is silent about how officials could be removed once the president nominated them and they were confirmed. He replaced them with his own political cronies and thus created a spoils system that would become a quagmire for presidents for most of the nineteenth century.

President Jackson deployed the military and threatened to use force, if violence occurred, when South Carolina nullified (refused to enforce) a federal tariff law. However, Congress later authorized the use of force. In the end, Congress enacted a compromise tariff and federal intervention was avoided. Nevertheless, Abraham Lincoln used Jackson's precedence to later suppress secession (states nullification of all federal laws).

However, when the state of Georgia nullified a federal treaty guaranteeing land to the Cherokee Indian tribe and the Supreme Court ruled in the Indi-

---

49. Rudalevige, *The New Imperial Presidency*, 36.

ans' favor, Jackson urged Georgia to ignore the court's ruling. Also, although Jackson was willing to send troops to South Carolina when the state nullified federal tariff law, he did not send forces to protect the Indians from whites when Georgia nullified the treaty and pushed the Indians westward. In fact, in 1830, Jackson got Congress to pass the Indian Removal Act to drive Indian nations off land that had been guaranteed to them by more than ninety treaties, and he used the army and militia to evict Native Americans from their homes.

The executive branch did not change much in size or organization during Jackson's presidency, which, despite his strong personality, was more bluster than reality.[50] As a reaction to the perceived presidential excesses of Andrew Jackson in the early 1800s, Congress reasserted its powers for the rest of the nineteenth century—except for Lincoln's dictator-like presidency during the Civil War. The model of this anti-Jackson congressional resurgence should be looked to in the present day to bolster sagging congressional power against a now imperial president.

As a reaction to Jackson's seemingly powerful presidency, a new Whig Party was formed (not to be confused with the small government Whig Party in Britain) that stood for little else except to be anti-Jackson. The increased party competition caused voter participation to soar to 80 to 90 percent. Such public mobilization and political activism strengthened the people's houses of Congress vis-à-vis the executive. In addition, party discipline increased in Congress, making a congressional majority much stronger in pushing back against the president. Powerful congressional leaders arose, and the speaker of the House was treated as more powerful than the president. By the 1840s, however, both the Whig and the Democratic parties were experiencing sectional issues—for example, slavery and the tariff.

Annexation of Texas

Americans originally had migrated to Texas, which was then part of Mexico, at the invitation of the Mexican government, which wanted a bulwark against Indian attacks in sparsely populated areas. The Americans brought their

---

50. Patterson, "The Rise of Presidential Power," 42–43.

slaves with them. The Mexican government had outlawed slavery in 1829. Whether Texas would be slave or free was a major reason for Texas fighting for independence from Mexico, which was attained in 1836. Although Texas became an independent republic, it wanted to be annexed into the United States. However, a debate on slavery was raging in the United States too and many in the North did not want to admit another slave state or states from the country of Texas.

In April 1844, US president John Tyler—negotiating with Sam Houston, president of Texas—reached a treaty of annexation. In June 1844, the Senate failed to muster a two-thirds majority to ratify the treaty. After pro-annexation James Polk won the presidency in November 1844, lame-duck President Tyler, in December 1844, asked both houses of Congress to pass his treaty by a simple majority. Just before leaving office, in early March 1845, Tyler signed the annexation bill. Although Tyler was an excellent president otherwise—he went against his own Whig Party to keep the federal government small using his veto pen—this circumvention of the Constitution's high bar of a supermajority vote in the Senate to approve treaties with foreign governments set a bad precedent. In the future, with this precedent in mind, presidents would create unconstitutional executive agreements with foreign governments that would be approved by only a simple majority of both houses. In fact, some executive agreements with foreign nations nowadays are not even put up for congressional approval at all.

The Mexican War

Although the strict constructionist view of the Constitution, which prescribed congressional direction of wars, still held at the time of the Mexican War, the conflict was the first to demonstrate how a president abusing his power as commander in chief of military forces could diminish the war power of Congress by presenting the body with a fait accompli. (Future presidents would use this model to usurp the war power from Congress.)

In one of the most dishonorable wars in American history, President James Polk, after failing in his bid to buy a chunk of Mexico's territory, provoked a war with the weaker Mexico to steal the land by force of arms. What is now the southwestern United States—including valuable ports in California, especially the sheltered port of San Francisco—was obtained in such a disreputable manner.

The border between the recently acquired Texas and Mexico was in dispute. The United States said Texas stretched south to the Rio Grande River, whereas Mexico asserted that the southern border of Texas was the Neuces River, which was north of the Rio Grande. The Mexicans had the better historical claim, which Polk implicitly recognized by unsuccessfully trying to buy the area between the two rivers from Mexico.

In 1846, Polk sent a US military force into the disputed territory between those rivers. He expected the Mexicans to defend what they believed was their territory by attacking the American army. They did and killed or captured forty American soldiers. In effect, Polk had successfully provoked the shooting in order to invade Mexico, defeat the country in war, and grab its land as spoils. In fact, by blockading the Rio Grande River—internationally, a blockade has always been considered an act of war—it could even be concluded that Polk had started the war.

After these aggressive actions, Polk then demanded that Congress declare war, which it did. In fact, he and his cabinet had already decided to ask Congress for a declaration of war when news of the Mexican attack arrived at the White House. Now they could justify it in terms of an alleged Mexican invasion of American territory.

Many justifiable complaints arose from opponents of the war, including Abraham Lincoln, who as a congressman introduced the "Spot Resolutions," demanding to know whether the spot on which US troops had been attacked was on American soil. Polk had essentially invaded Mexico, then duped Congress into declaring war by claiming that the Mexicans were the attackers, when they had merely defended their territory. In the incident, Congress merely censured Polk for his aggressive actions, a rather meaningless rhetorical action that had not been a power assigned to the legislative body in the Constitution (the first censure had been against Alexander Hamilton, the secretary of the treasury under President George Washington).

Nonetheless, Polk's assertion of his power as commander in chief to deploy troops in a manner that would likely precipitate a conflict—in this case, doing so in a provocative manner to trick the adversary into starting a war—was an abuse of that power, and the troop deployment could and should have been constitutionally overruled by Congress before the conflict started. Congress should not have waited until after the fighting started to censure the president.

After this episode, Congress still controlled the power to start wars, but Polk had demonstrated how presidents could erode that power by placing troops in provocative places or situations, baiting the adversary to attack. This instance set a bad precedent, which would lead to similar incidents later in American history.

Polk also eroded Congress's budgetary power. Before and after Polk, executive agencies and congressional committees negotiated agency budgets without presidential involvement and with congressional dominance of the process. However, Polk required that agency budgets be given to him first; he then sent a unified executive budget to Congress. This process did not survive Polk's tenure in office but did set a precedent that would be resurrected successfully by Warren Harding in 1921, leading to a permanent unified executive budget and erosion of one of Congress's foremost constitutional powers—control over federal spending. In American history, precedents are regularly instituted (often during war), abandoned, and then later resurrected. Another example is Martin Van Buren's creation of an Independent Treasury, which was a substitute repository for the federal government's cash instead of a national bank, but it was repealed after he left office; the Treasury was then institutionalized by Polk. Thus, Polk used the Mexican War to aggrandize power that a peacetime president would not have been able to accrue.[51]

Coerced Trade with Japan

In American history, the "opening" of isolated Japan is considered a good thing. However, perhaps not so much for the Japanese. In 1852, President Millard Fillmore sent Commodore Matthew Perry and his armed flotilla of ships to coerce Japan to trade with the United States. He was able to do so.[52] At the turn of the twentieth century, McKinley conducted a similar unilater-

---

51. Crenson and Ginsberg, *Presidential Power*, 86–87, 93.
52. Eland, *Recarving Rushmore*, 97–98.

ally decided military intervention to cooperate with the Europeans to coerce trade with China.

Secession, Civil War, and Reconstruction

Secession

Although President James Buchanan is now widely criticized by analysts for letting the country slide into civil war, he believed he could not legally use force to prevent the southern states from seceding without Congress's approval. Buchanan believed that although the Constitution prohibited the secession of states from the Union and the forming of a confederation or compact (Article I, Section 10), it also prevented him from taking military action unless the South used violence against federal facilities or the North. Buchanan's Attorney General Jeremiah Black told him that the Constitution was a contract the states could not break and that the Union was "perpetual." The Articles of Confederation, the prior American government before the one enshrined by the Constitution, had declared that the Union was perpetual, and although the later Constitution didn't use these same words, it alluded to them by declaring in its preamble that the goal was "to form a more perfect Union."

Article I, Section 8 of the Constitution indicates that Congress has authority, rather than state governments, over forts, arsenals, dockyards, and other federal facilities in the states. Thus, the change in the Constitutional Convention of Congress's authority from making war to declaring it implies that the president has the authority to take self-defense measures to protect federal property in the states without congressional approval if Congress is not in session. However, this provision likely applies only in the event of a foreign invasion. The same section of the document authorizes the Congress "to provide for" calling forth the militia to execute the laws of the Union, suppress insurrections, or repel invasions. Unlike the other congressional war powers, such as declaring war or raising and supporting armies, this provision seems to allow congressional delegation. In the Militia Act of 1795 and Insurrection Act of 1807, Congress authorized the president, under certain circumstances, to call up militiamen (in the former statute) or regulars (in the latter law), without getting prior congressional permission, to execute the laws, put down an insurrection, or defend against a foreign invasion. To enforce federal laws, Buchanan had put down a Mormon rebellion in Utah in 1857–1858 and abolitionist John Brown's attack on the federal arsenal at Harpers Ferry, Virginia, in 1859 to steal weapons to use in hoped-for slave rebellions.

In a written opinion, Attorney General Black concluded that the power of the commander in chief "is to be used only in the manner prescribed by the legislative department. [T]he President cannot accomplish a legal purpose by an illegal means, or break the laws themselves to prevent them from being violated." Thus, the use of the 1795 and 1807 statutes had to be kept within narrow bounds. Even though the southern states had no legal right to secede, Black concluded that such secession was not a declaration of war. Secession should be answered with the continued enforcement of federal law; in southern states, tariffs should be collected and federal facilities protected. If a federal fort was attacked, Black said that the commander in chief could use force, but only under the limits of the two laws against only those who had violated the law or attacked the fort, not in a general war against seceding states. States could not be coerced into remaining in the Union. Secession was illegal but so was using force to nip it in the bud, opined Black. Black later noted that during the long transition period between the Buchanan and Lincoln administrations, not even president-elect Lincoln questioned his legal analysis.[53]

In December 1860, during that transition period, South Carolina became the first state to secede from the Union. To enforce federal law and better defend federal facilities, Buchanan requested legislation to let duties be collected on Navy ships offshore and to allow the executive to call up regular troops and accept volunteers. All such proposed legislation failed. Buchanan can hardly be blamed for Congress's intransigence in the face of crisis.

In early January 1861, South Carolinians fired on a supply ship called "Star of the West," which was trying to resupply the vulnerable federal Fort Sumter in Charleston harbor. When the ship came under fire, it retreated without resupplying the fort. Buchanan, still trying to avoid war, did not

---

53. Quoted in Barron, *Waging War*, 119–21.

push the issue by sending other more heavily armed ships to again attempt the resupply. In April 1861 after taking office, Abraham Lincoln, much more eager to enter a war with seceding states, would not only send such ships but notify South Carolina that they were coming, thus generating a predictably hostile reaction from South Carolinian gun batteries in Charleston. Those batteries, getting word that supplies were arriving to the fort by ship, fired on the fort itself, starting what is still the most massive war in American history. Lincoln did not limit the use of force to those who attacked the fort, as former Attorney General Black's legal analysis would have required, but launched an invasion of the South and undertook unconstitutional measures to allow him to conduct the war, such as increasing the size of the army, imposing a naval blockade on southern ports, and suspending habeas corpus.

Seen through the lens of the all-powerful modern presidency—or even the near-dictatorial presidency of his successor, Abraham Lincoln—Buchanan seemed to be fiddling while Rome burned. However, Buchanan's (Black's) constitutional interpretation comported more with the framers' vision than Lincoln's almost-anything-goes approach. Unlike Buchanan, Lincoln could, and did, take advantage of Congress being out of session when he provoked the war in April 1861 by attempting again to resupply a fort that was militarily in-defensible—as his military advisers, who unanimously counseled withdrawal from it, had told him—and knowing full well that such re-provisioning would ignite a conflict. However, he mistakenly believed that any war to repress the rebellion would be short.

Democrat Buchanan, however, was not blameless for the start of the Civil War. Although he was from Pennsylvania, he had southern sympathies (the term at the time for northerners with southern sympathies was "doughface"). In the mini-civil war in Kansas over whether it would be admitted to the Union as a free or slave state, which preceded the cataclysmic national Civil War between North and South, Buchanan supported pro-slavery Kansans, which were a minority in the state. He thus helped fracture the Democratic Party, of which various factions in the 1860 election put up three candidates against Abraham Lincoln, a candidate from the new Republican Party.

At the time, the Republican Party was merely a regional organization from the North that was against slavery's expansion into Western territories, primarily because slaves competed with white workers—the principal voting base of the party. The southern states reacted viscerally to Lincoln's election, because he had in the past made uncompromising remarks that the country could not survive as half slave and half free. Lincoln had sown such disunity to make himself a serious contender for the Republican nomination and to sow dissention in the opposing Democratic Party.

In 1855, six years before he triggered the Civil War, Lincoln indicated that he didn't believe a peaceful way existed to end slavery. According to Bueno de Mesquita and Smith, in 1858, after the Supreme Court's horrendous Dred Scott decision of 1857—which, by erroneously ruling that Congress did not have the power to declare some territories "free," essentially ripped up the last vestiges of the Compromise of 1820 that had kept the nation at peace by geographically dividing territories with slavery from those that were free— Lincoln, in accepting the Republican Party's nomination for a US Senate seat from Illinois, purposefully tried to divide the Democratic Party for the 1860 presidential election. By sowing such Democratic divisions, Lincoln had a better chance of being selected as the regional Republican Party's presidential nominee and winning the presidency against a Democratic Party sectionally driven by the slavery issue. Lincoln's stance also made Civil War more likely if a Republican did win the White House in 1860. Lincoln prodded Stephen Douglas—Lincoln's opponent in the 1858 US Senate race in Illinois and also likely a Democratic presidential contender in 1860—to square his preference to let territories decide whether they would be slave or free (popular sovereignty) with the Dred Scott decision, which ruled against popular sovereignty and potentially opened all territories to slavery. Lincoln knew Douglas's stance would fracture the Democratic Party in 1860.

In his "House Divided" speech in June 1858, Lincoln essentially called for war or southern capitulation on the slavery issue. Against the advice of his advisers and friends, Lincoln declared, "In *my* opinion, it [slavery agitation] *will* not cease, until a *crisis* shall have been reached, and passed. A House divided against itself cannot stand. I believe this government cannot endure, permanently half *slave* and half *free*. I do not expect the Union to be *dissolved*—I do not expect the house to *fall*—but I *do* expect it will cease to be divided. It will become *all* one thing or *all* the other" [emphasis is Lincoln's].

In 1858, Lincoln's speech at the time was understood to be a call to Civil War. Stephen Douglas gave the following comments with Lincoln in the audience:

> Mr. Lincoln advocates boldly and clearly a war of sections, a war of the North against the South, of the free States against the slave States, a war of extermination to be continued relentlessly until the one or the other shall be subdued, and all the States shall either become free or become slave.[54]

That same year, during the senatorial campaign, Lincoln famously said, "The tug has to come and better now, than any time hereafter."[55]

During the four-month transition period between the Buchanan and Lincoln administrations, Lincoln repeatedly refused to indicate any willingness to compromise on the issue of expansion of slavery into the Western territories. William Herndon, Lincoln's law partner, summed up Lincoln's view on compromise with the South, "Away—off—begone! If the nation wants to back down, let it—not I."[56]

On the eve of his inauguration, Lincoln refused to see peace commissioners from the seceding states sent by Jefferson Davis, president of the new Confederacy. Davis had initially opposed secession, but because it was a done deal when he was selected to be president, he, trying to avoid war, sent the commissioners to propose assuming the seceding states' portion of the US national debt, and to offer to buy federal property in the South, for example Fort Sumter. Lincoln would have none of it. Furthermore, Lincoln's first inaugural address was regarded by the southern states as a call to war.

Lincoln had said that he would not touch slavery where it existed in the Southern states, but he didn't feel the need to compromise on the Republican

---

54. Quoted in Bueno de Mesquita and Smith, *The Spoils of War*, 114–15, 117–18, 120–22.

55. John Minor Botts, *The Great Rebellion: Its Secret History, Rise, Progress, and Disastrous Failure* (Charleston, SC: Nabu Press, 2010), 196.

56. Letter from William H. Herndon to Wendell Phillips, February 1, 1861, in Fehrenbacher and Fehrenbacher, eds., *Collected Works of Abraham Lincoln*, vol. 4, 172.

Party's "no expansion of slavery in the western territories" policy, because he felt the Republicans had won the election: [57]

> We have just carried an election on principles fairly stated to the people. . . . Now we are told in advance, the government shall be broken up, unless we surrender to those we have beaten, before we take the offices. In this they are either attempting to play upon us, or they are in dead earnest. Either way, if we surrender, it is the end of us, and of the government.

The Republicans had won a majority in the Electoral College but won only 39 percent of the popular vote against three candidates arising out of the split Democratic Party, which Lincoln had helped foster. So more than 60 percent of Americans had voted against Lincoln, which should have made him more willing to negotiate with his opponents. This Electoral College majority, however, made Lincoln and the Republicans unwilling to compromise on their no expansion of slavery platform. Lincoln believed Buchanan's moderate policy toward the South needed to be replaced with a hardline one. Thus, the Electoral College system had significant culpability in causing the greatest war in American history.

Not altering slavery in states where it already existed might seem to be throwing a bone to Southerners, but they could count. Because of industrialization of the Northern states and consequent population increases, the North had begun dominating the House of Representatives. Therefore, the last bastion of southern advantage in Congress was in the Senate, but if new states were added in the West as free states, eventually the slave-friendly majority would turn into a minority—thus potentially threatening slavery in southern states where it already existed.

Lincoln had turned down the best chance of averting war by rejecting the Crittenden Compromise, which proposed constitutional amendments guaranteeing slavery where it existed in southern states (Lincoln favored this part) and bringing back the Missouri Compromise of 1820, thus restoring slave and free territories in the West and therefore nullifying Southern gains from the Supreme Court's horrible and erroneous Dred Scott decision. The

---

57. Quoted in Bueno de Mesquita and Smith, *The Spoils of War*, 96.

seceding Southern states would have accepted the Crittenden Compromise. However, Lincoln believed he had won the 1860 election and would not compromise on the Republican electoral position of nixing all expansion of slavery into western territories. Yet, this compromise might have bought time for compensated emancipation of slaves without war, which is the route most slave-owning nations had taken to get rid of the abhorrent institution.

Lincoln cleverly notified the Confederates in Charleston that he was not reinforcing the federally held Fort Sumter in Charleston harbor but only sending "food for hungry men." By announcing the resupply, instead of attempting to do it in secret, Lincoln was inviting the South to fire on bread, so he could blame the South for starting the war—instead of withdrawing from a fort, which his military advisers correctly told him was indefensible, thus giving more time to peacefully avoid hostility.

After the hot-headed and foolish South Carolinian attack on Fort Sumter on April 12, 1861, Lincoln decided not to call Congress into special session until July 4 that same year, even though the monumental crisis fully warranted doing it earlier. He had learned from other presidents who had pressed executive powers farther than the Constitution's framers had envisioned— George Washington and Thomas Jefferson—that the president had more freedom in times of crisis when the Congress was out of session. However, unlike Washington, who was trying to stay out of a war between France and Britain, and unlike Jefferson, who feared Congress would push him into war over the *Chesapeake-Leopard* incident, Lincoln feared the Congress might impede his breathtaking—many historians have said dictatorial—use of executive power to send the country into war. Also, Washington's and Jefferson's abuses of executive power paled in comparison to Lincoln's. As an alternative, in the spirit of the Constitution, Lincoln could have called a special session of Congress immediately after the attack and then taken only defensive actions for several weeks until the Congress could have convened.

Showing that he was not naïve about the possibilities of war, Lincoln had once said, "Bring on a war . . . and . . . escape scrutiny by fixing the public gaze upon the exceeding brightness of military glory."[58] After South Carolina's firing on Fort Sumter, according to David J. Barron, "Lincoln was unafraid

---

58. Quoted in Bueno de Mesquita and Smith, *The Spoils of War*, 93.

of war, and even welcomed it now that South Carolina had attacked."[59] This view likely stemmed from the fact that the North had tremendous advantages over the southern seceding states in population, wealth, industrial arms production, technology, and thus the ability to wage war. Despite modern popular opinion to the contrary, New York University political science professors Bruce Bueno de Mesquita and Alastair Smith hint that the massive war should have been avoided: [60]

> Today he is remembered and revered because of what was accomplished in the Civil War. We will see, however, that all of it could have, and in all likelihood would have, been done without war. But had he not exacerbated the risk of war as the price for winning the presidency, his place in history might be minor. . . .
>
> With or without Lincoln, slavery would have been extinguished long ago. How long it would have taken is a question intensely debated among historians. Whether postponing the moment of liberation for nearly 4 million slaves would have been a better or worse outcome depends on who is answering; it is a question that cannot have a definitive answer.

Slavery had been in decline worldwide since the mid-1500s, when Spain freed slaves in its American colonies. Well prior to the American Civil War, most European governments had done away with slavery. Many nations in the world had used compensated emancipation, paying slave owners to free their slaves, as an alternative to war. Lincoln had advocated this earlier in his political career but only revisited when it was too late—during the war when things weren't going well for the North.

Even in the United States, after the American Revolution, as states in the North industrialized, slavery became economically non-viable.[61] The Civil War's arresting setback to industrialization in the South, when combined with white Southern bitterness from the war, counterintuitively dealt a blow to African American rights in the long term.

---

59. Barron, *Waging War,* 139.
60. Quoted in Bueno de Mesquita and Smith, *The Spoils of War,* 93–94.
61. Bueno de Mesquita and Smith, *The Spoils of War,* 99.

The worst war in American history—killing 850,000 Americans in internecine conflict, including about 40,000 African American soldiers—freed the slaves in name only. For a few years after the war, freed slaves made some progress. But then white Southerners, filled with war bitterness and taking it out on powerless African Americans, adopted abhorrently discriminatory policies and vagrancy laws that resulted in freed blacks being required to work off their jail time on trumped-up charges under such statutes. Discriminatory Jim Crow laws, separating the races, lasted until the civil rights movement 100 years later. Finally, in addition to such neo-slavery, the war brought hard feelings among southern whites, which in turn resulted in white terrorism against African Americans through the Ku Klux Klan and other white supremacist groups. Compensated emancipation may not have worked as an alternative to such carnage and suffering, but it was never tried as a way to avoid war (and thus its horrific aftermath).

During the War, Lincoln Was an Inept Autocrat

Lincoln ruled like a dictator during the Civil War, but that didn't make him efficient or competent. Prior to the war, he had almost no prior military experience—and it showed. Bueno de Mesquita and Smith concluded that Lincoln has been vastly overrated as a wartime leader: [62]

> Tragically, his contemporaries, who viewed him as a big-hearted but broadly incompetent leader, were probably closer to the truth than we are today. As we demonstrate, he neither worked masterfully to preserve the Union nor did he conduct the war against the Confederacy skillfully. Reasonable estimates suggest the Civil War should have lasted only about five or six months, rather than four years. Lincoln failed to win it quickly or efficiently, contrary even to the expectations of such major Confederate figures as Jefferson Davis or John Breckinridge. But for the long, costly war he instigated, in all likelihood

---

62. Quoted in Bueno de Mesquita and Smith, *The Spoils of War*, xi, 110–11. The authors used a model on the duration of wars by Professors Scott Bennett and Allan Stam, which takes note of the two sides' relative military and economic strength, number of allies, military strategies employed, terrain, and kinds of government.

we would remember Lincoln no better than such one-term presidents as Franklin Pierce or Rutherford Hayes. War made Lincoln—and Lincoln, with the help of short-sighted [Southern] fire-eaters, made the costliest war in American history.

Furthermore, like Hamilton before him, Lincoln believed in the inherent powers of the president as commander in chief in the Constitution. Unlike Hamilton, however, he felt much less constrained in using them. During the war, Lincoln ruled with an iron hand and justified it with the following convoluted reasoning: [63]

> I felt that measures, otherwise unconstitutional, might become lawful, by becoming indispensable to the preservation of the constitution, through the preservation of the nation.

Lincoln forgot to mention that he knowingly provoked a war over secession by trying to resupply a federal fort from which his military advisers had urged withdrawal because it was indefensible (which proved correct).

After the war started, Lincoln accumulated a long list of unnecessary unconstitutional actions. Lincoln exceeded the congressionally imposed personnel limits of the Militia Act of 1795 by using an executive order to quickly call up 75,000 militiamen and by pledging to retake Fort Sumter and other federal military installations that had been seized by the southern states in the fall and winter of 1860 and early 1861, which would have basically required an invasion of the South. There was never a congressional declaration of war during the Civil War, because Lincoln and the North did not want such a pronouncement to imply recognition of the Confederate States of America as a new, separate nation. Thus, Lincoln's unilateral executive pronouncement, without congressional approval, was all that was ever issued to take the nation into the most massive war it had ever seen—a war that cost 850,000 lives, destroyed much of the South, and ended up freeing the slaves in name only.

Lincoln undertook other unconstitutional moves while Congress was out of session, mostly by executive order. The Constitution implied that Congress

---

63. Letter from Abraham Lincoln to Albert G. Hodges, April 4, 1864, reprinted in Christopher Pyle and Richard M. Pious, eds., *The President, Congress, and the Constitution: Power and Legitimacy in American Politics* (New York: Free Press, 1984), 65.

had the right to defend federal forts, magazines, arsenals and naval ship yards that had been located in the states, and the original constitutional understanding surrounding the "Congress shall declare war" language allowed the president only to defend the country from an attack when Congress was out of session. However, a week after the Confederate attack on Fort Sumter, Lincoln unilaterally took the country into an offensive war by imposing, without congressional approval, a naval blockade on Southern ports. By this action, Lincoln was usurping Congress's war-making power, because imposing a blockade was traditionally regarded internationally as an act of war. Congress had earlier refused to allow Buchanan to establish such a blockade.

At the same time, ignoring the Constitution's stipulation that all monies expended by the US government be appropriated by Congress, Lincoln used private contractors as military recruiters and to buy war material (instead of calling Congress into special session to make the appropriations). This action followed Jefferson's earlier precedent of using non-appropriated monies to make defense preparations in the wake of the *Chesapeake-Leopard* affair without calling Congress back into session.

Lincoln's most controversial action was the suspension of habeas corpus—which enabled the government to hold prisoners indefinitely without the constitutionally guaranteed rights of being charged with a crime or having a trial. Initially, the suspension was in force from Washington to Philadelphia, but eventually, to suppress resistance to the military draft, it covered from Washington, DC, to Maine. Even Lincoln's fellow Republicans were uneasy about this action. The Constitution gave only the Congress this important power, and with the North's substantial military advantages over the South, the area of potential hostilities did not extend all the way to the northern reaches of the Atlantic seaboard. Lincoln ordered the military to arrest anyone it thought might be a threat to public safety and to defy writs of habeas corpus challenging such detentions coming from the courts, including the Supreme Court. Lincoln's actions set a (bad) precedent still cited today.[64] However, Lincoln's hypocrisy was bounded; the man who had protested James Polk's abuse of executive power during the Mexican War stopped a plan to arrest legislators in Maryland who were voting on whether to secede. Also, in 1864,

---

64. Posner and Vermeule, *The Executive Unbound*, 69.

to his credit, Lincoln did not suspend the election in the North using the Civil War as justification, even though he feared that he would lose.

The Constitution stipulates that Congress should raise armies and maintain a navy. Yet, in addition to calling out 75,000 militiamen, Lincoln unconstitutionally augmented the army and navy by calling up tens of thousands of volunteers for both services.[65] Also, the number of volunteers was much above Congress's established limit. Moreover, without congressional approval, Lincoln authorized the construction of new warships and sent weapons to Unionists in western Virginia.

Although Lincoln had purposefully waited more than two and a half months after the Southern attack on Fort Sumter to call Congress into a special session—in order to present Congress with a fait accompli of dictatorial war measures— he expected that the nationalist fervor would compel Congress to accept them after the fact. Yet of the five of his unconstitutional acts after the attack— calling up the militia, calling up volunteers, the blockade of southern ports, the suspension of habeas corpus, and the unauthorized spending on war materiel—the first three had already been previously rejected by Congress under the Buchanan administration.

Lincoln claimed authority under the Militia Act of 1795 to call out the militia to suppress an insurrection and the Insurrection Act of 1807 to blockade southern ports. However, these were prior congressional statutes of limited scope; in addition, the framers of the Constitution, intending to give Congress—not the president—the power to take the country to war, likely would have blanched at any offensive war-initiating blockade by the executive without congressional approval. However, once Fort Sumter had been attacked, Congress retroactively approved Lincoln's blockade and suspension of habeas corpus. Thus, Lincoln had been right in his prediction about the nationalist surge in the North pressuring Congress to approve his unconstitutional actions, including ones that had earlier been denied to Buchanan.

Lincoln admitted that he had acted outside the law by calling up regulars and volunteers, but said he was only undertaking what Congress likely would have enacted if they had been in session—forgetting to mention that he had intentionally waited months to call them into special session after the

---

65. Barron, *Waging War*, 132–37.

United States had been attacked. His defense of usurping the power to suspend habeas corpus in times of invasion or insurrection—clearly implied in the Constitution as a congressional power—became one of the most famous, but lame excuses in history. In excusing his arbitrary detention of potential traitors, he said, "Are all the laws, *but one*, to go unexecuted, and the government itself go to pieces, lest that one be violated?"[66] In other words, if the suspected rebels retained the right to challenge their detention, they would violate all other laws of the Union. He did not even attempt to justify buying war materiel without congressional approval, thus usurping Congress's power to spend federal monies.

Lincoln used executive orders to seize private property, declare martial law in areas far from combat, stifle opposition newspapers, censor the US mail, restrict foreign travel, and undermine Fourth Amendment protections against warrantless search and seizures. Stretching the Constitution beyond recognition, Lincoln justified many such wartime actions simply on his authority to ensure the laws were faithfully executed and on his inherent power as commander in chief. In 1863, in the middle of the war, the Supreme Court, in the Prize cases, approved his earlier blockade of Southern ports and seizure of foreign merchant ships, but did so using the thin reed of 1795 and 1807 laws and presidential constitutional authority to defend against attacks and invasions, rather than buying his attempt to stretch his commander-in-chief and law-enforcement powers. The glaring problem with that Supreme Court ruling was that the blockade was offensive in nature.

In *Ex Parte Milligan*, timidly decided by the court after the war was long over in 1866, the court rejected Lincoln's claim to emergency powers beyond the Constitution or law and the bypassing of open civilian courts to create kangaroo military commissions. Channeling the nation's founders, Justice Davis wrote this classic passage, which rejected the notion that the Constitution could be suspended by a "theory of necessity" and reiterated the need to uphold its principles especially during wartime:[67]

The Constitution of the United States is a law for rulers and people equally in war and peace. No doctrine, involving more pernicious

---

66. Abraham Lincoln, Message to Congress, July 4, 1861 (emphasis in original).
67. Quoted in Crenson and Ginsberg, *Presidential Power*, 327.

consequences, was ever invented by the wit of man than that any of its provisions can be suspended during any of the great exigencies of government.

Even after the secession of eleven states and an attack on a federal fort, bringing the possibility of a sizable Civil War, Congress was reluctant to permanently enlarge the regular army, although it did not rescind Lincoln's prior unilateral expansion. This reluctance shows that almost three-quarters of a century after the Constitution was signed, the tradition of American suspicion of standing armies still held sway. The Congress did grudgingly ratify most of Lincoln's other unconstitutional and dictatorial wartime actions. Unfortunately, this abdication by Congress of its constitutional powers, especially during wartime, would become a pattern as American history progressed and would quicken during the long Cold War, which began after World War II. Lincoln had justi-fied his unilateral actions on the basis of executive "war power" contained in his constitutional powers as commander in chief and executor of the nation's laws. Yet the Supreme Court, in the Prize cases, had rejected this rationale.

As the war progressed, Lincoln continued his unconstitutional acts. His Emancipation Proclamation freeing the slaves was clearly so, because slavery (unfortunately) was mentioned in the Constitution. In fact, slavery in the southern region had to be accepted or the thirteen original colonies would not have agreed to become the United States under that charter in 1788. Moreover, Lincoln's proclamation was a propaganda gimmick, because it only freed slaves in areas of seceding states not under Union military occupation. Therefore, slavery was still in effect in the Unionist state of Delaware; the border states of Maryland, Kentucky, and Missouri; and areas in seceding states under occupation by Union forces. Thus, Lincoln's famous proclama-tion freed no slaves.

During the war prior to the Emancipation Proclamation, Union armies had begun to confiscate southern property used in the war—including slaves —but these blacks were not freed and often later worked in menial jobs for Northern forces. Congress ratified Union field commanders' decisions on the battlefield by passing the First Confiscation Act, which avoided giving captured slaves, previously used in the Confederate war effort, their freedom but did not require Union armies to return them to their southern masters.

In fact, before Lincoln issued the Emancipation Proclamation, he rescinded one Union commander's permanent freeing of the slaves in his area of command, labeling it "simply dictatorship," because the commander had taken executive action that usurped Congress's legislative power by going beyond the First Confiscation Act. Then the hypocritical Lincoln later did the same thing by usurping such legislative power by issuing the unilateral Emancipation Proclamation without congressional consent.

In December 1861, a proposed Second Confiscation Act would have ordered Lincoln to warn rebellious slave owners that if they didn't stop their revolt, their slaves would soon be given their permanent freedom. During the congressional debate, as the war was going badly for the heavily favored North, Lincoln discussed the possibility of compensated emancipation of slaves and their migration to Africa.[68] (He did not think that whites and freed blacks could live in harmony together in the United States.) Most other major slave-holding nations, instead of becoming embroiled in cataclysmic civil wars, had done away with bondage by simply paying the masters to relinquish their slaves. Lincoln had advocated this superior solution in the 1840s. Unfortunately, Lincoln resurrected this otherwise plausible alternative, which might have avoided a massive war, much too late—only after his side was losing the grim meat grinder into which the conflict had morphed. By late 1861, war fervor on both sides would no longer have accepted this option, which would have been much less costly than the huge toll in blood, treasure, and long-lasting scars to the American social fabric that arose from the internecine slaughterhouse. The hair-brained voluntary migration scheme, also favored by Thomas Jefferson and Ulysses S. Grant, understandably did not appeal to African Americans, who shied away from essentially being off-loaded to much poorer countries, such as Haiti or those in Africa.

Taking advantage of the Congress's Second Confiscation Act, Lincoln issued, by executive order, the broader Emancipation Proclamation to allegedly carry out its provisions. However, in addition to standing under Congress's more narrow endorsement of emancipation, Lincoln's proclamation also claimed independent powers as commander in chief, which went beyond the narrow powers that the framers had envisioned for the president: merely

---

68. Barron, *Waging War*, 147–52, 156–59.

being commander of military forces on the battlefield. At any rate, both the law and the proclamation were likely unconstitutional, because slavery was recognized in the Constitution until the later Thirteenth Amendment legitimately freed the slaves. Because the Emancipation Proclamation was a wartime public relations gimmick, which freed slaves only in Confederate occupied territory as an attempt to induce slave rebellions within southern territory and as a gambit to prevent British and French recognition of the South as a separate nation, and because the Thirteenth Amendment—constitutionally requiring approval by Congress and the states, not the president—was ratified only after Lincoln's death, the Great Emancipator shockingly didn't free any slaves. (Lincoln did, however, help get the Thirteenth Amendment through Congress.

As the war dragged on, Lincoln perpetrated further unconstitutional acts, including military conscription (which Congress later put into law), expanded areas where habeas corpus had been suspended, and instituted nationwide trial by court martial for people accused of disloyalty—ignoring the constitutional requirement for a trial by jury. Lincoln jailed thousands of war critics for indeterminate sentences and looked the other way while mobs, led by Union troops, attacked and burned opposition newspapers.[69]

On non-martial issues, Lincoln was much more deferential to Congress than on matters related to the war. For example, because Congress had the power over whether or not to accept readmission of states that had been in rebellion, he failed to get Congress to readmit Louisiana to the Union on lenient terms, even after he won the 1864 election. Thus, Lincoln, had he not been assassinated, would have had to accommodate the Radical Republicans in Congress who wanted a harsher version of Reconstruction in the South than he did.

During the 1800s, and unlike the latter half of the 1900s, presidential independence was too linked to war to survive its end. The Civil War did not lead to permanent big government in the United States, because most of the powers granted to Lincoln were military ones that lapsed after the fighting ended.[70] Lincoln never had great power to intrude into the domestic economy

---

69. Fleming, *The Great Divide*, 269.
70. Crenson and Ginsberg, *Presidential Power*, 101–02.

to fight the war, as did Woodrow Wilson in World War I and Franklin Roosevelt in World War II. After the war ended, the era of nineteenth-century congressionally dominated government resumed.

Yet the Civil War, like many conflicts in American history, would set precedents that would disappear and recur later to ill effect. Copying the British during the Crimean war, the income tax was instituted to help fund the war. The tax lapsed after the war ended, but not until 1871, six years past the conflict's conclusion. However, the tax came back with a vengeance in the twentieth century and not only outstripped all other sources of federal revenue but expanded past just a tax on the incomes of the wealthy. The tax has provided fuel to the fire of expanding government down to this day.

Also, the Civil War eroded Congress's money power vis-à-vis the executive branch. During the latter part of the nineteenth century, Congress's money power was diminished by the splintering of the money committees in both houses and the annual appropriations bill into several pieces of legislation. Under the strain of massive Civil War financing, the money committees in both chambers—the Finance Committee in the Senate and the Ways and Means Committee in the House—were stripped of their authority over federal appropriations but retained their authority over taxes. Responsibility for appropriations in both chambers was parceled out to other committees, including new Appropriations Committees. Then, after the Civil War, the Appropriations Committees fragmented. Thus, by decentralizing congressional authority over money bills, the Civil War diminished Congress's money power relative to that of the president.[71]

Postwar Reconstruction

Lincoln had been ruthless in war—note his approval of Gen. William T. Sherman's unnecessarily brutal march to the sea after his key victory in Atlanta and Gen. Phil Sheridan's scorched-earth policy in the Shenandoah Valley—but lenient in peace. He transmitted this approach to his generals, including Sherman and his boss Ulysses S. Grant. Even before the war ended, Lincoln

---

71. Fisher, *Presidential Spending Power*, 19–21.

began implementing a Reconstruction policy that was generous to the South, which was popular among Southerners and even Northerners. After Lincoln was assassinated, Vice President Andrew Johnson, a southern Democrat who hadn't supported the South's secession, became president, but his attempted continuation of Lincoln's generous Reconstruction policy toward the South engendered the suspicions of radical Republicans in Congress, who wanted harsher military occupation of the South and hurdles for the southern states to be readmitted to Congress. Such differences on reconstruction, and Johnson's attempt to marginalize General Grant and oust Democrat Secretary of War Edwin Stanton, led to the first congressional impeachment of a president in American history; the Senate failed to convict Johnson by one vote.

After Lincoln's extralegal wartime presidency, Congress reasserted itself with a vengeance. This congressional resurgence would last almost 40 years and result in an era of peace and economic growth. Because Lincoln had delayed calling a special session of Congress after the war started so he could undertake many unilateral, unconstitutional acts, Congress passed laws in 1867 that allowed it to remain in continuous session, if it so desired. The legislative body also passed a law giving it the power to call itself into special session (this may have been unconstitutional).[72]

Even after the North won the Civil War, it faced a significant problem, which made fighting the bloody conflict even more questionable. The Thirteenth Amendment theoretically ended slavery, and the Fifteenth Amendment gave African Americans at least the legal right to vote. Before slavery had been abolished, the US Constitution allocated the number of representatives that states received in the House of Representatives based on the population of white voters and three-fifths of the population of slaves. Yet now that there were no longer slaves (legally, if not in practice), representation would be based on 100 percent of the entire population of voters, thus actually inflating the representation of southern states. Thus, although losers in the internecine slaughter, southerners and their Democratic northern allies might dominate a postwar Congress.[73] (If southern whites controlled the extra three-fifths

---

72. Fleming, *The Great Divide*, 385–86.

73. Crenson and Ginsberg, *Presidential Power*, 102.

votes in Congress allocated to slaves before the war, they were likely to try to more subtly disenfranchise the now free black voters, so they could control the added allocated votes they would get in Congress, which they eventually would do through extreme voter-suppression measures against African Americans.) Thus, the Republican-controlled rump Congress had to establish hurdles to the southern states returning to Congress. Thus, ironically, the North fought the Civil War to use military force to compel southern states to stay in the Union against their will, but once it won the war, barriers were put up for their readmission to that same Union.

Also, the Republican Congress believed that military occupation was needed to quell "bitter enders" in the South and safeguard voting and other rights of newly freed African Americans, who were much more likely to vote Republican than their white southern counterparts. In 1866, the Supreme Court, in *Ex Parte Milligan,* seemed to side with President Johnson's more lenient reconstruction when it nullified a military tribunal that had convicted Lambdin Milligan. The high court's decision—which banned the suspension of habeas corpus and military tribunals when civilian courts were open and no threat of attack or invasion existed, instead requiring civilian trials—threatened rule by the military in the South. The military occupation of Southern states had continued to arrest civilians far from any active battlefields—with the war over, there were none—and had transferred the suspension of habeas corpus and the use of military tribunals from wartime to peacetime. The court was correct, the insurrection was over and so should have been the suspension of habeas corpus. Yet unfortunately, the court ruled that in areas subject to martial threat during any war, the president had the power to suspend civil liberties. However, the Constitution implied that only Congress could suspend habeas corpus, because the provision was elucidated in Article I, which governs the powers of the legislature.

President Johnson got wind that General Grant—the chief general of the army, war hero, and likely president-to-be—was transmitting orders to his officers that contravened Johnson's predilection for a light military footprint in the South. As a result, Johnson started circumventing Grant in the chain of command, giving orders to Grant's subordinate officers. Johnson wanted to send Grant out of the nation's capital on a diplomatic mission and replace him with a more like-minded general. Afraid that if he left Washington, Johnson would seize dominance over the military aspects of southern Reconstruction, Grant, in an act of insubordination, refused to go on the mission.

To prevent Johnson from marginalizing Grant, Secretary of War Stanton asked Congress to pass the Command of the Army Act to create a legal penalty for any military officer carrying out orders not given by the chief general of the army and to keep that general's headquarters in Washington. The legislature did so, and Johnson signed it under protest. This legislation entered a gray area, because although the Constitution gave the president power as commander in chief to command military forces on the battlefield, it gave the Congress the power to regulate the army and navy. Since in general, the chief executive was supposed to enforce the laws passed by Congress, the commander in chief should thus acquiesce to Congress's regulations when commanding troops in the field. Thus, Congress had a better case than Johnson in this instance.

At the same time, Congress passed, over Johnson's veto, the Reconstruction Act of 1867, which replaced southern state governments established by Johnson using executive power with military-run governments, thus increasing, rather than diminishing, General Grant's power over Reconstruction. Although throughout American history, times of congressionally dominant government have been generally more peaceful than periods of executive dominance, during Reconstruction, the Congress advocated a harsher approach than did President Johnson.

The Command of the Army Act insulated the popular General Grant and the Tenure of Office Act sheltered the more politically vulnerable Secretary of War Stanton, a Democrat. The Act made it a "high misdemeanor" for Johnson to fire him without the Senate's consent. However, Johnson felt that this Lincoln-era holdover was conspiring with the Republicans in Congress against him and fired the secretary anyway.

Long after this incident, the Supreme Court eventually held the Tenure of Office Act to be unconstitutional, which was probably correct because the Constitution provided for a two-thirds vote in the Senate to confirm presidential appointees, but it didn't mention a Senate veto of appointees being removed by the chief executive. However, the Constitution did not speak on removing such appointees, except impeachment for wrongdoing. It may be a constitutional defect, but a literal reading of the document would imply that cabinet officials and other political appointees would serve until they quit, died, or were impeached. Thus, a strictly textualist reading of the Constitution wouldn't have allowed Johnson to remove Stanton in the first place.

After Johnson fired Stanton, the Congress became alarmed that he was going to circumvent both the Command of the Army Act and General Grant, using the Army to either launch a coup to take over the government or at least employ it to force Stanton out. Impeachment proceedings against Johnson began immediately. Yet in Johnson's trial in the Senate, it came out that Johnson had accepted the Command of the Army Act and consulted the military commander of local forces in the nation's capital only because he feared a military coup against him.

President Johnson was really impeached for his disagreements with the Republican Congress over Reconstruction policy. Thus, the standard interpretation of history is probably right here—the Congress overreached by impeaching Johnson just because it didn't like his lenient view of Reconstruction and because he took advantage of the Constitution's silence to remove a cabinet official who opposed his softer policy toward the defeated South.

However, proponents of executive power have overreached too, drawing the lesson that Congress cannot direct the president's conduct of wars once they are started. They inferred this conclusion from Chief Justice Salmon Chase's concurring opinion in the Supreme Court's Milligan decision in 1866—which outlawed military tribunals to try civilians during wartime when civilian courts were open and functioning—that Congress could not limit the chief executive's power as commander in chief in the "conduct of campaigns." Chase offered no prior court ruling to bolster his opinion, and this conclusion seemed to contradict previous Supreme Court rulings—for example, the *Little v. Barreme* case in 1804, which was left over from the Quasi War with France, the first war the new nation fought. In *Little v. Barreme*, the Supreme Court had ruled that even during wartime, the president had to follow congressionally passed laws, including those on the rules of engagement for the conduct of the war. Chase's conclusion had also contradicted prior practice, starting with that Quasi-War when President Adams had bowed to Congress's very restrictive limits about the conduct of the conflict.

Even worse than Chase's concurring opinion in the Milligan case, but much later, the Supreme Court's *United States v. Curtiss-Wright Export Corp.* case (1936) put forth a non-binding dictum that the president was the "sole organ of foreign policy." The Constitution's framers likely would have found such a finding appalling, because the document they wrote had given Congress, not the executive, most of the powers in foreign policy and defense. Thus, the Curtiss-Wright opinion helped provide the shaky legal foundation for presidents to unconstitutionally usurp congressional authority over war and foreign policy as American history progressed.[74]

Genocide and Ethnic Cleansing Against Native Americans

During and after Reconstruction until almost the Spanish-American War, a period of congressionally dominated government, smaller wars against various Native American tribes abounded. In fact, since the dawn of the republic, the US military had fought Native Americans to kill them and steal their land. As masses of white settlers moved westward to settle the nation from coast to coast, as miners swarmed to search for gold and silver, and as the railroads followed, the US government, using the military, kept breaking treaties with Native American nations, which guaranteed them specific lands, by slaughtering them, ethnically cleansing them onto undesirable reservations, and then letting them die of starvation and disease by allowing them inadequate food and medicine.

Unfortunately, both Congress and the executive were culpable in this sad chapter in American history. Congress never bothered to declare war on what were supposed to be separate nations, perhaps because the tribes were perceived as inferior peoples. This pattern would continue after the Spanish-American War when the executive fought unilateral wars against the poor, developing nations of Central America. The Native Americans had been "tamed" by 1890 and the American frontier was closed. It was now time for Americans to behave aggressively overseas.

---

74. Barron, *Waging War*, 54–55, 66, 168–69, 179–80.

US Stealing of Hawaii

The American representative had a role in overthrowing the native Hawaiian government to advance American business interests. Just before leaving office, Republican president Benjamin Harrison submitted the treaty of Hawaiian annexation to Congress. In addition, in what would become a familiar, but lame, excuse for American military interventions in foreign lands, he unilaterally sent US forces to "protect American lives and property." His Democratic successor, anti-imperialist Grover Cleveland, withdrew the treaty from Senate consideration, because he felt that the islands had been ill-gotten gains.

However, this shame was short-lived as Cleveland's successor, Republican William McKinley, took advantage of the juices of imperial acquisition that caused and were further enhanced by the Spanish-American War. McKinley used the war to dust off the treaty of Hawaiian annexation and get it ratified by the Senate. Hawaii, strategically located in the middle of the vast Pacific Ocean, was used as a coaling station and military base to enforce coercive trade with China.[75]

Congressional Government in the Late 1800s

Executives in the late 1800s were chary about expanding their power, because of the memories of Abraham Lincoln's excesses during the Civil War. For example, in 1866, after Lincoln had been assassinated and the Civil War was over, the Supreme Court rejected Lincoln's use of military tribunals to try civilians when civilian courts were in operation. In 1868, in a pushback against Andrew Johnson, Congress repealed statutes that allowed the transfer of appropriations from one federal department to another. In 1870 and 1874, Congress restricted the executive's use of appropriations not spent for the congressionally designated purpose. Between 1871 and 1898, Congress declined to ratify any treaties proposed by the president.

Despite some growth in the executive branch bureaucracy, with the creation of the Interstate Commerce Commission (ICC) and the Civil Service Commission, the White House staff remained tiny. Even in 1900, Congress

---

75. Eland, *Recarving Rushmore*, 174, 180–81.

allowed the president only one secretary, two assistant secretaries, two executive clerks, and four clerks.

Labor-management relations provided the only area in which the executive could expand power. Using a law from 1807, which allowed presidents to use force against "combinations" (read: unions) too powerful to be brought to heel in court, otherwise good presidents, Rutherford B. Hayes and Grover Cleveland, used troops to suppress worker strikes. Laissez faire is a wonderful doctrine, but when the government uses armed force to tip the negotiations for business over labor, such aggressive action becomes a perversion of the doctrine. In 1895, the Supreme Court backed Cleveland's busting of the railway strike, making presidents virtual dictators in the United States during "emergencies." The court said that Cleveland didn't even need statutory blessing to secure court injunctions against striking workers and to use force to end labor's freedom to walk off the job in protest.[76]

Conclusion

During the nineteenth century, presidents did unilaterally launch small military actions without congressional approval, but these were operations well short of general war, such as battling pirates, conducting small amphibious landings on foreign coasts, and pursuing criminals across the Mexican border. Nevertheless, they probably violated the framers' intent that even minor offensive military interventions should be approved by Congress—as demonstrated by the Constitution's requirement that Congress issue letters of marque and reprisal to commission privateers (private pirates) to attack and capture adversarial ships. Also, Congress heavily regulated the undeclared, limited, and seaborne only Quasi-War, which began only nine years after the new government under the Constitution was initiated and was the first war abroad after that framework was launched.

---

76. Patterson, "The Rise of Presidential Power," 47.

3

The United States as a Global Power

NEAR THE TURN of the twentieth century, despite the periodic expansions of executive power in the nineteenth century that were often later dissipated, the presidency looked much the same as the nation's founders had envisioned it more than a century before; it was limited to enforcing laws passed by the legislature at home and executing, narrowly, as commander in chief of US forces on the battlefield, any declaration of war by Congress abroad. As historian James T. Patterson concluded, during the nineteenth century the presidency was an "insignificant institution."[1] That state of affairs would change dramatically during the next century.

The Spanish-American War of 1898 and Gunboat Diplomacy

From 1898 to 1920, a period that uncoincidentally involved the Spanish-American War and World War I, the powers of the presidency expanded substantially. During that time a modern, institutional presidency would be created.[2]

Political scientists began noticing an expansion of presidential power around the time of the Spanish-American War. One of those academics, future president Woodrow Wilson, changed from lamenting congressional government in the 1880s to crowing, at the turn of the century, that the president was

---

1. James T. Patterson, "The Rise of Presidential Power Before World War II," *Law and Contemporary Problems* 40, no. 2 (Spring 1976): 39.

2. Patterson, "The Rise of Presidential Power Before World War II," 39.

at the front of the nation's affairs because of the rise of America to the status of a world power in the wake of the war. According to Wilson,

> When foreign affairs play a prominent part in the politics and policy of a nation, its Executive must of necessity be its guide: must utter every initial judgment, take every first step of action, supply the information upon which it is to act, suggest and in large measure control its conduct.[3]

In the depression of the 1890s, interest group pressure for government action increased in a society beset by industrialization, urbanization, and mass immigration, but it was the war that led to great expectations about what the government could do for society at home.

Although Ulysses S. Grant and Grover Cleveland (only two short years before) had avoided a war with Spain over its colony Cuba, William McKinley did not in 1898. A Cuban revolt against Spanish rule had been going on for a long time and so had Spanish repression. The Cuban rebels put out many stories of Spanish abuses. This propaganda fueled war fever by Assistant Secretary of the Navy Theodore Roosevelt, Sen. Henry Cabot Lodge, the Yellow Press, and others—all of whom wanted a European-like American Empire. Thus, the Spanish-American War was America's first overseas imperial conflict.

President McKinley claimed that he did not want war, but after the USS *Maine* blew up in Havana Harbor in 1898 (even back then, the top-ranking naval officer on the scene believed it had been an accident, which has been recently confirmed), he succumbed to the martial hysteria, blamed Spain for the explosion, and asked for a congressional declaration of war. McKinley could have continued to resist the pressure, however, and is therefore partially responsible for America's first imperial adventure. Like James Madison in the War of 1812, McKinley's reelection was threatened if he did not agree to take the country to war.[4] A hesitant McKinley eventually succumbed to intense heat from Congress to go to war with Spain, showing, as did congressional pressure on an unenthusiastic Madison in the War of 1812, that merely

---

3. Woodrow Wilson, *Congressional Government: A Study in American Politics* (Boston: Houghton, Mifflin and Company, 1901), xii.

4. Bruce Bueno de Mesquita and Alastair Smith, *The Spoils of War: Greed, Power, and the Conflicts that Made Our Greatest Presidents* (New York: Public Affairs, 2016), 240-241.

using constitutional processes requiring a congressional declaration of war is not a silver bullet to avoiding entanglement in ill-advised conflicts.

Once involved in the war, the "reluctant" McKinley demanded carte blanche in fighting it, without any congressional say. (He could have better used such assertiveness to stay out of this tawdry war in the first place.) He demanded $50 million from Congress for the task, but would put up with no congressional stipulations on the spending. Using his authority as commander in chief, he would not give the legislature any role in governing the Philippines once the war ended. In sum, McKinley had fewer constraints from Congress in running the Spanish-American War than Lincoln did during the Civil War.[5] Congress simply rolled over to McKinley's assertion of executive power.

Because the United States, in time of crisis, had always relied heavily on state militias, state governors and state politicians who were appointed as militia commanders could have great effect on any national war effort, as was the case during the Civil War. However, now that the United States would be fighting imperial wars overseas, it needed to get greater control over its military forces. Thus, at the start of the Spanish-American War, Congress passed the Volunteer Act of 1898, which required generals and the staffs of state militias (now renamed the National Guard) to be appointed by the president rather than the governors of the states. This law was in direct contravention of Article I, Section 8 of the Constitution, which clearly stipulates that the states would appoint the militias' officers. In 1903, the Dick Act further consolidated presidential control over state militias by authorizing the president to fold the state National Guards into the regular army during crises. (After World War I started, but before US entry, Congress passed the National Defense Act of 1916, which carried further the constitutional violation of the 1898 Volunteer Act by giving the president the power to appoint all commissioned and non-commissioned officers in the National Guard during time of war.)[6]

Imperialism is usually defined as conquering a territory, but not letting the population have a political voice in the metropolitan capital. Thus, despite the US government's brutal conquest of the Native Americans in the western United States and its violent coup against the native Hawaiian ruler,

---

5. Crenson and Ginsberg, *Presidential Power: Unchecked and Unbalanced*, 121–22.
6. Crenson and Ginsberg, *Presidential Power*, 247.

all these populations were eventually given rights, including voting rights in the United States. Therefore, these questionable acts should probably be called "aggressive nation building" rather than imperial conquests. In contrast, the people of "liberated" Cuba, the Philippines, Puerto Rico, and Guam did not get such political rights; thus, the Spanish-American War was therefore largely an imperial one. This small war was also a very important one in the history of US foreign policy and the American presidency.

The war marked the coming out of the United States as a world power. The American West had been won by 1890—with the closing of the frontier after all Native Americans had either been killed or confined to usually desolate reservations. Now, eight years later, America began to imitate the European powers by fighting wars to acquire colonies, both formally and informally.

Although the war started in Cuba, the previously mentioned four Spanish possessions were won by the United States after Adm. George Dewey destroyed the Spanish fleet in Manila Bay and US ground forces defeated Spanish forces in Cuba.

Cuba became an informal protectorate, ruled unofficially by the United States, but a rebellion by guerrillas broke out in the conquered Philippines. The United States had held out to Filipinos that if they helped the United States get rid of the Spanish rulers they would win their independence. Once the Spanish were gone, however, the United States reneged because it wanted the Philippine Islands as a coaling station and a naval base to be used in enforcing coercive trade with China (as the Europeans were also doing) and because it feared a rising Germany might grab them. Without a congressional declaration of war, McKinley proceeded to fight a brutal counterinsurgency against the Filipino guerrillas.

In 1900, McKinley, also without a declaration of war, sent 5,000 American forces to help other great powers put down a rebellion in China—the so called "Boxer Rebellion"—that was threatening the "Open Door" policy of Western exploitative, enforced trade with that nation.

These wars led to enhanced institutional power in the presidency. Until the late 1800s, presidents had few substantive advisers and had to pay them out of their own pocket. McKinley was the first modern president in terms of accruing more executive staff and power and using the new national media and the huge megaphone of the presidency to win popular support to pressure Congress to enact his policy desires.

After McKinley was assassinated, his vice president, Theodore Roosevelt, took over in time to continue the brutal US counterinsurgency campaign in the Philippines in which 200,000 Filipinos eventually died. The United States employed, by the same military officers, similar savage tactics used against Native Americans in the West, including burning villages and crops and torturing captives (using water boarding, to be replicated later in the US "war on terror" during the first decade of the twenty-first century). Anti-Imperialists in the United States publicized this carnage in their quest to show that Roosevelt's wielding of executive power was excessive. The war on Spain had been declared by Congress, but not the subsequent counterinsurgency war against Filipinos.

The Roosevelt administration—and specifically William Howard Taft, then the governor-general of the Philippines—tried to mislead Congress about Army's indiscriminate atrocities during the counterinsurgency war against Filipinos, which had turned the indigenous population from friend to foe. However, Roosevelt did not claim as commander in chief that he had the right to order torture and that Congress had no authority to rule certain methods in war off limits (as George W. Bush would later do when he said that the commander in chief had the right to ignore congressionally passed laws during national emergencies). Therefore, everyone in 1902 acknowledged that torture was wrong and thus the revelations of it were especially stinging to the Roosevelt administration.

Congressional hearings on the excesses of the Philippine counterinsurgency took the steam out of the American imperialist cause. When Roosevelt flexed US muscles by sending his "Great White Fleet" around the world on his own initiative, he got pushback from Congress, because relations with Japan were bad and Congress was afraid the cruise would ignite a conflict with the island nation. In the wake of congressional protests, Roosevelt said that he had the money to get the fleet to sea and that Congress could leave it abroad if it didn't want to fund its return. Although war did not result from this brash executive action, this instance is another example of the president abusing his power as commander in chief to potentially present Congress with the fait accompli of war by ordering US forces into dangerous situations without prior congressional approval or funding (as Polk did in the Mexican War, Lincoln did in the Civil War, Johnson did in the Vietnam War, and George H.W. Bush did in the first Gulf War).

Equally dangerous might have been Roosevelt's belief that war was a positive thing. However, to be fair to Roosevelt, he never ensnared the United States in any major war during his presidency and even won the Nobel Peace Prize for mediating an end to the Russo-Japanese War of 1905. In any case, Roosevelt understood that his presidential luster in history would be diminished if the nation was not involved in a major conflict during his tenure. Yet, the backlash from the brutal US counterinsurgency in the Philippines may have moderated the actions of the most inherently bellicose president in American history for the rest of his tenure in office.

However, with no prior congressional authorization, he "stole fair and square" from Colombia the territory through which the Panama Canal would eventually traverse by supporting a rebellion in the isthmus and then blocking, with US Navy ships, the Colombian government's effort to suppress it.

For the Monroe Doctrine, which allowed US military intervention in Latin America to keep foreign powers out of the Western Hemisphere, Roosevelt developed a corollary, which essentially said that the United States could meddle in the internal affairs of Latin American countries—especially their finances—to prevent outside powers from intervening (for example, to collect debt). This corollary has been used as an excuse by subsequent presidents up to the present day to intervene in Latin American countries to ensure "stability"—both political and economic. Using the corollary, Roosevelt set up a protectorate in Santo Domingo (now the Dominican Republic).

In general, Roosevelt had an expansive view of executive power. Roosevelt dangerously believed that if the Constitution or laws didn't specifically say the president couldn't do something, the executive could do it (he later called this the "Stewardship Doctrine," but it was really a rehash of Alexander Hamilton's vesting clause argument, which gave the president "inherent" powers not specified in the Constitution). This argument contradicted the framers' intent that the federal government's actions be limited to specifically enumerated powers, as enshrined in the Tenth Amendment. Roosevelt asserted that it was "not only his right but his duty to do anything that the needs of the Nation required unless such action was forbidden by the Constitution or laws."[7]

Taking after McKinley, Roosevelt used the new mass circulation (national) press and the president's unique "bully pulpit" to go over the heads of members of Congress to convince the public to pressure their representatives to favor his policies. He also withheld information from Congress about why he hadn't pursued an antitrust case against the United States Steel Corporation. Roosevelt's antitrust policy had been rather arbitrary, prosecuting some companies while leaving other favored ones alone.

In 1902, during the counterinsurgency campaign in the Philippines, Roosevelt was also employing troops at home. A violent strike had broken out among anthracite coal miners; the mine owners refused to negotiate with unions of mine workers. Previously, federal troops had been used to the benefit of crony capitalists to forcibly put down strikes—for example, during the Rutherford B. Hayes and Grover Cleveland administrations. Instead, the progressive Roosevelt inserted the federal government into a new role—coerced mediation of labor disputes—by inviting both sides to Washington to talk, while keeping 10,000 troops at hand, not to repress strikers but to threaten to confiscate the mines from their owners and put them under government operation. Upon hearing of Roosevelt's plan, a stunned congressional leader exclaimed, "What about the Constitution of the United States? What about seizing private property with no due process of law?" An exorcized Roosevelt responded, "The Constitution was made for the people and not the people for the Constitution."[8] In response to the government coercion, the mine owners and miners agreed to a presidential Coal Strike Commission, and the mines began to hum again.

In early 1909, congressional pushback on Roosevelt entailed nixing with contrary legislation his executive order to throw marines off navy ships. Although Roosevelt was the commander in chief of the military, the Congress reasserted its constitutional power to regulate the land and naval forces by requiring that 8 percent or more of officers on ships had to be marines.

---

7. Theodore Roosevelt, *An Autobiography* (New York: Da Capo Press, 1913), 372; and Fleming, *The Great Divide*, 387.

8. Crenson and Ginsberg, *Presidential Power*, 127.

Although Roosevelt was an assertive president, the balance between the executive and the legislature on the direction of the military had not yet changed in the president's favor. As with any other type of policy, the president was supposed to merely execute the will of the legislature.

Roosevelt's successor, William Howard Taft, had the opposite of Teddy's view of executive power—more akin to most of those at the Constitutional Convention rather than the outlier of Alexander Hamilton:

> The President can exercise no power which cannot be fairly and reasonably traced to some specific grant of power or justly implied with such express grant as proper and necessary to its exercise. . . . There is no undefined residuum of power which he can exercise because it seems to him to be in the public interest.[9]

Yet, even the restrained Taft was too generous about executive power. Article I, Section 8 of the Constitution allows only Congress to take actions—in its case, make laws—that are necessary and proper to carry into execution both its constitutional enumerated powers and the powers of other government branches, including any executive officers (including the president) and departments.[10] It does not give the president this implied power, as Taft claims. Therefore, if any branch of government has implied powers, it's Congress not the executive branch. In practice, even the legal-minded Taft deviated from his own ideal presidential model when he presided over undeclared unilateral executive wars that carried out "dollar diplomacy" in Latin America.

The federal budget had been in surplus for a twenty-eight-year run from 1866, the year after the Civil War ended, to 1893. Yet expenditures began increasing at the end of the 1800s because of the Spanish-American War, Civil War pensions, construction of the Panama Canal, and unconstitutional internal improvement boondoggles, such as harbors and rivers projects. From 1904 through 1909, under Theodore Roosevelt's administration, budget deficits resulted for six years. With the laudable goal of bringing the budget un-

---

9. William Howard Taft, *Our Chief Magistrate and His Powers* (1916) quoted in Christopher H. Pyle and Richard M. Pious, eds., *The President, Congress, and the Constitution: Power and Legitimacy in American Politics* (New York: Free Press, 1984), 70–71.

10. US Constitution, Article I, Section 8 in Linda R. Monk, *The Words We Live By: Your Annotated Guide to the Constitution* (New York: Hachette Books, 2015), 286.

der control, William Howard Taft proposed a government-wide president's budget (previously each executive agency had negotiated its budget with the corresponding congressional committee, with the congressional committees dominating the process). The Congress nixed Taft's proposal, in part because Taft had been more fiscally responsible than his profligate predecessor and in part because Congress feared enhanced executive budget power. Joe Cannon, the speaker of the House, worried that an executive budget would surrender the most critical part of representative government, stating that "I think we had better stick pretty close to the Constitution with its division of powers well defined and the taxing power close to the people."

The financial cataclysm of World War I would be needed to make the unified and consolidated executive branch budget a reality in 1921 under the postwar Harding administration.[11] During the war, federal government outlays ballooned 2,500 percent and the budget surplus of $48 million, before US entry into the conflict, had turned into a whopping deficit of $13.3 billion. The increases in government spending and resulting budget deficits, this time massive ones resulting from the war, led to one of the greatest expansions of executive power in American history.[12] In other words, the financial crisis induced by the war caused Congress to delegate much of its constitutionally given spending power to the executive branch.

Woodrow Wilson's Interventions in Latin America and World War I

Woodrow Wilson had been an academic before becoming president and had written books about American government. He believed that congressional government had the problem of fixing responsibility in a body of hundreds of legislators. Thus, he advocated a powerful presidency, the Constitution be damned. Wilson summed up his philosophy by saying, "The president is at liberty, both in law and in conscience, to be as big a man as he can."[13] Not only was this statement untrue, but it could well describe a king or dictator.

---

11. Fisher, *Presidential Spending Power*, 27–31, 33.

12. Mayer, *With the Stroke of a Pen*, 118.

13. Quoted in Fleming, *The Great Divide*, 387.

The Constitution's framers probably would have passed out at hearing such language.

Woodrow Wilson was the most interventionist president in American history and a key instrument in planting the seeds of big government in American society and in the expansion of executive power.

Before World War I, Wilson repeatedly sent troops into combat in Latin America without congressional approval for war—in Haiti, the Dominican Republic, and Mexico. He invaded Mexico several times. Wilson's actions left Congress little alternative but to approve the occupation of Vera Cruz and the failed expedition by Gen. John Pershing against the bandit Poncho Villa.

Making an enemy of Mexico also helped start World War I. In early 1917, in the secret Zimmermann diplomatic telegram, which was intercepted by the British and published, German foreign secretary Arthur Zimmermann proposed to give back what was then part of the American Southwest to Mexico in return for a Mexican alliance against the United States in the event of war between Germany and the United States. Had the Mexicans not grown tired of US forces invading their country and become hostile to the United States, Germany would never have been tempted to send the telegram urging Mexico to war against the Americans conditionally upon war between Germany and America. The revelation of the telegram stoked war fervor in the United States, because its conditionality was willingly overlooked.

Although Wilson was ostensibly reluctant to go to war and claimed US neutrality during the first three years of World War I, he showed once again in the American system that a president's actions as commander in chief can create the impetus for war. Although he won reelection in the 1916 election with the slogan, "he kept us out of war," after the poll was over he immediately commissioned, without congressional approval, a New York public relations executive, George Creel, to run a government-sponsored advertising campaign to convince a skeptical public that US interests required support of the British and French war effort. This campaign complemented a similar propaganda campaign in the United States by the British since the beginning of the war in 1914; Germany could mount no such campaign for the hearts of Americans, because Britain had cut the transatlantic communication cables. Although the German resumption of unrestricted submarine warfare against sea traffic around France, Great Britain, Italy, and the eastern Mediterranean

Sea in February 1917 triggered US entry into the war in April of that year, American entry was almost inevitable because of Wilson's prior actions.

Given Wilson's prior bad policy choices, it was a good bet that the United States would eventually abandon its faux neutrality to fight with the Entente against the Central Powers, Germany and Austria. Since the beginning of hostilities in 1914, Wilson and his primary aide, Col. Edward House, both anglophiles, had allowed huge US loans and arms sales to the allies. In contrast, few American loans were made to Germany and Austria-Hungary. The heavy lending to allies gave the United States a tremendous stake in an allied victory—to ensure repayment—thus making it more likely that the United States would not let the allies go under. As early as 1915, Colonel House, a manipulator of Wilson toward war, told Britain and France that the United States would not let them lose the war. Wilson's motivation for getting into the war on the allied side was to have a say in the reshaping of Europe and the world after the conflict ended, because he believed God had chosen America to show the nations of the globe the way to liberty. Even before US entry into the conflict, Colonel House had convinced Wilson that any US proposal that the allies didn't like would cause them to shut the United States out of the postwar peacemaking.

Wilson complained about Americans being killed when riding on British merchant ships (some armed) carrying munitions through a war zone, for example, in the sinking of the British ship *Lusitania* near Ireland's coast. However, he ignored the British "Hunger Blockade" by sea, which was strangling and starving Germany and which caused the Germans to resume unrestricted submarine warfare in desperation to gain leverage to get the blockade lifted. (Both the blockade and unrestricted submarine warfare went against international law.) That resumption was merely a German attempt to equalize the playing field and win the war before America almost inevitably jumped in and turned the tide—which it eventually did. William Jennings Bryan, Wilson's secretary of state and one of the few people who could disagree with the overbearing and vengeful Wilson, resigned because of Wilson's pro-allied "neutrality." Before that, he asked in April 1915, shortly before the sinking of the *Lusitania*, "why do Americans take the risk" of traveling on British ships carrying munitions through a war zone despite German warnings, and why should they "be shocked at the drowning of a few people, if there is no objection to starving a nation"?[14] Wilson even quashed a popular bill in Congress that would have warned Americans of the dangers of traveling on the ships of belligerent countries, because he thought it eroded his ability to make foreign policy unimpaired. The British even asked Colonel House when he was visiting if President Wilson wanted Britain to stop the starvation blockade against Germany, and House replied emphatically no.[15]

Thus, although Wilson did ask for a declaration of war from Congress in April 1917, the executive had tilted the playing field toward the Entente, and the United States had been hardly neutral when it professed to be so for almost three years. (In some sense, such executive creation of a fait accompli for Congress was foreshadowed by presidential conduct in the previously described Mexican and Civil Wars.)

World War I was a watershed, not only for the federal government assuming more functions in American society, which had traditionally been meager, but for the expansion of executive power in US foreign policy and defense. According to David J. Barron, an author who has detailed the conflict between the president and Congress over war,

> [Wilson] did believe in the untapped potential of the assertive exercise of executive power. And, from his studies, he knew how advantageous military action could be for a president determined to expand influence of the executive office. . . . Since his days as a doctoral student, Wilson had been convinced that, at least in the modern world, America could no longer afford for the legislative branch to be the locus of policy-making power. The old system [read: the legislatively led government of the nation's founders], which Wilson derisively called "congressional government," was intolerable now that America had become a great power, with a modern economy and a fate deeply entwined in world affairs. . . . That made all the more significant Wilson's observation as a scholar that, historically, it was war that provided about the only means by which presidents managed to loose themselves from the grip of Congress's control. . . . Keying off of Lincoln's stunning example during

---

14. Quoted in Healy, *The Cult of the Presidency*, 65–66.

15. G.J. Meyer, *The World Remade: America in World War I* (New York: Bantam Books, 2016), 120, 130.

the Civil War—which Wilson identified as the ideal of constitutional government—the Princeton professor had famously remarked that the presidency was only "as big" as the man in office chose to make it.[16]

Wilson's idea that the modern world and new role of the United States in it rendered anachronistic the ways of the founders' republic was resurrected later during the nuclear age of the Cold War and unfortunately had staying power, despite its dubious validity. The idea that the world's societies and their interrelationships were becoming so complex and fast-paced "in the modern world" that big government—read: expanding executive power—was necessary to control and direct them has had a poor track record. If societies were becoming so complex and fast-paced, perhaps slow-moving and stodgy governments should stand back and allow more agile market forces to take the lead in self-regulating them.

As war threatened, Wilson began abusing the power of the executive. After the Germans resumed unrestricted submarine warfare in waters surrounding Entente nations in late January 1917, Wilson went to Congress in late February and asked Congress to arm US merchant ships, essentially making them combatants in the war. Like the Bushes, who much later got congressional approval for their wars in Iraq only as a "courtesy," Wilson asked for congressional approval as a mere formality. When Congress did not authorize such armed neutrality, he implemented it anyway in March 1917.

This policy change from "neutrality" to "armed neutrality" would clearly make war with Germany more likely but was done without congressional sanction. In fact, armed merchant ships were regarded as warships. Under the framers' original vision, the president was the commander in chief of the armed forces only after a war had begun. Any defense policy matters before then were to be authorized by Congress. Wilson was again helping to create a fait accompli and implicitly taking the decision to enter the war away from Congress. Given the Supreme Court's post–Civil War rejection of Lincoln's assertion of extra-constitutional powers during that war, the consensus, up until World War I, was that war and emergency powers were lodged with the Congress rather than the executive. This tacit agreement was now becoming a little shaky. Nevertheless, during World War I, Wilson usually asked Congress

---

16. Barron, *Waging War*, 207–08.

for and was granted legal authority for the expansive wartime powers he exercised.

Despite a weakened position domestically after the 1918 elections—when despite the impending allied victory in the war, Wilson lost both houses of Congress to Republicans—he pressed ahead by spending months abroad at the postwar peace conference.[17] Without congressional input, Wilson had proposed favorable terms to Germany in his Fourteen Points, which had contributed toward that nation's capitulation. Yet at the peace conference, to get his pie-in-the-sky League of Nations, he allowed Britain and France to abuse the defeated Germany—a major cause of Adolf Hitler's rise and World War II—and expand their empires by taking over overseas possessions of defeated nations. The resulting Versailles Treaty containing these provisions was rejected by the US Senate, principally because the League's requirement for countries to engage in coercive acts to reestablish peace threatened the US Constitution's stipulation that the Congress must vote to take the United States to war. Also, Congress had repudiated Wilson's negotiation of a postwar world that envisioned an interventionist US foreign policy.

To attempt to stop the Bolsheviks from taking over Russia, Wilson, unconstitutionally and unilaterally, without congressional approval, sent 20,000 American forces to join British and French forces trying to help White forces against the Red Army in the Russian civil war, which followed the Bolshevik Revolution in 1917. The precarious post-czar Russian Provisional Government's decision to remain in the bloody World War I had contributed heavily to the Bolshevik Revolution in the first place, because the Bolsheviks were the only Russian political party that wanted to end the war. Wilson and the British and French had encouraged the Provisional Government—by making aid to that government contingent on staying in the war—to continue throwing Russians into the World War meat grinder, thereby sealing its fate. In the end, Wilson's blatantly Machiavellian effort to bribe the Provisional Government to stay in World War I and his unsuccessful meddling in the Russian civil war thereafter, which turned into a fiasco, merely helped sour relations with the new communist government in the Soviet Union for a long time.

---

17. Barron, *Waging War*, 214–16, 219–20, 223–27.

War at Home

At home, Wilson usually requested Congress for, and was given, statutory authority for the expansive wartime powers he employed. As soon as Wilson asked Congress for a declaration of war, he got Congress to delegate to him vast powers to run the war abroad and at home. He got the legislature to enact the Sedition Act of 1918 that made it illegal to make statements opposed to the American Army, the US government, or the cause of the United States; the Espionage Act of 1917 that would be used against people who discouraged the military draft; the authority for him to seize railroads for military use; the power for him to regulate food production and consumption; the authority for him to spend money; and the power for him to establish export controls. Wilson used such congressional authority to implement the worst suppression of civil liberties in American history. The government commissioned the Army to spy domestically and harass war dissidents and a vast vigilante organization, the American Protective League, to spy on and investigate their neighbors and harass and intimidate labor and antiwar groups.[18]

The National Defense Acts of 1916 and 1917 empowered Wilson to procure military weapons and equipment by requiring private companies to produce them. Wilson masterminded the War Industries Board (WIB), one of the most sweeping interventions of government into the private market ever in American history. The board regulated prices in key industries needed for the war, controlled war-related production, and had the power to commandeer and operate private factories. By executive order, Wilson nationalized the railroads and created the Railroad Administration to run them.

As noted earlier, the 1916 law violated the US Constitution by authorizing the president to appoint all commissioned and noncommissioned officers in the National Guard during wartime, which contradicted the Constitution's guarantee that the states would appoint officers of the state militias. The act also contravened the Constitution by creating national military reserves that would eventually compete with the state National Guard units in rounding out the US military during crises. Thus, the 1916 act further consolidated federal control over the military.

---

18. Healy, *The Cult of the Presidency*, 66–67.

The sweeping Lever Food and Fuel Control Act gave the executive the authority to confiscate food and fuel; to regulate mining, production, transportation, and storage of items vital to the war effort; and to requisition critical materials, take over the operation of mines and factories, and set prices.[19] To implement the Lever Act, Wilson created the Fuel Administration and the Food Administration, which rationed both items. The government controlled wages and prices during the war, mostly through indirect means.

The Selective Service Act of 1917 gave the president the power to coerce young men to serve in the military in "defense of freedom." The Trading with the Enemy Act gave the executive emergency economic powers and the ability to censor communications with foreign nations. The sweeping Overman Act allowed Wilson the autocratic power to reorganize government agencies without further congressional blessing. Essentially, to run the US war effort, Wilson sought and obtained unbridled authority from Congress to transfer functions and funding among executive agencies.

The Supreme Court blessed Congress's massive delegation of powers to the president during the war and in turn his actions. For example, the court approved conscription, the nationalization of the railroads, censorship, and limits on free speech by the Espionage Act of 1917 and the Sedition Act of 1918.[20]

Tellingly, Wilson beat back an attempt to create a joint congressional committee to oversee the war, much like the Joint Committee on the Conduct of the War that Lincoln had to deal with during the Civil War.

Prior to Woodrow Wilson, presidents occasionally recommended legislation to Congress, as permitted in the Constitution, but let Congress maintain its traditional dominance of the legislative process. However, Wilson regarded himself as also having the role of prime minister, shepherding his own legislative program through Congress. He often did so by using the presidential bully pulpit to go over the heads of the body's members to convince the public to pressure legislators to enact his program, just as William McKinley (the first modern president) and Teddy Roosevelt did. After US entry into World War I, Congress had given Wilson oodles of requested legislation filled with

---

19. Crenson and Ginsberg, *Presidential Power*, 19–20, 247.
20. Crenson and Ginsberg, *Presidential Power*, 221–24.

new powers. However, in the 1918 election, because of Wilson's overstretch in assuming executive power during wartime, the Republican opposition won majorities in both houses of Congress. This Republican victory was amazing, because it came just as the war was ending with America on the victorious side.

World War I Hangover and the 1936 *Curtiss-Wright* Supreme Court Decision

War often causes more war, revolution, civil war, civil unrest, xenophobia, and the abuse of civil liberties. World War I—the most important event that shaped the twentieth century and beyond—delivered on all counts. In 1919, anarchist bombings included the home of Wilson's attorney general A. Mitchell Palmer. The ensuing Red Scare and Palmer raids resulted in suspected communists being searched, detained, and deported without any legal due process.

Wilson's military and economic wartime powers, most of them given to him by the previous Congress, were so sweeping that the Republican-controlled Congress fortunately revoked many of them after the war was over. Even members of his own Democratic Party thought Wilson had gained too much power. The War Industries Board, the Railroad Administration, the War Finance Corporation, the Fuel Administration, the War Trade Board, the Shipping Board, the Grain Board, and other wartime agencies were dismantled.[21]

Despite this postwar revocation of powers, the war implanted the seeds of big government permanently in the American psyche. Progressives and academics, already promoting executive activism before the war, ramped up their advocacy during and after the war, eventually leading to the "war model" being pulled out and dusted off for future crises.

Some asked, if problems could be solved by federal government coercion during wartime, why couldn't this also be done during peacetime? For example, American farmers had prospered through US government intervention during the war, so why shouldn't the government act to ensure high prices during the lean years after the war when competing European agriculture had rebounded? During future crises, such as the Great Depression and World War II, the World War I model of government intervention would

---

21. Crenson and Ginsberg, *Presidential Power*, 228–29.

be revived and eventually become a permanent fixture in American life. For example, during the war, the Trading with the Enemy Act of 1917 allowed the president to declare a state of national emergency after Congress had declared war; yet, a state of national emergency was found nowhere in the Constitution, in wartime or peacetime. The law allowed the president to control economic transactions in which foreign property was involved. The act was used to seize property, suspend the gold standard, and even institute military conscription. During the Great Depression, Congress broadened the wartime state of national emergency to periods of peacetime crises. Franklin D. Roosevelt used this augmented emergency power during the economic crisis, suspending bank transactions during the 1933 "bank holiday."[22] The Espionage Act of 1917 also lingers to this day and is now being used to intimidate journalists who receive classified information from government sources.

And to pay for the expanded government, a golden source of revenue—the income tax—would be reinvigorated during the war. The income tax had originated during the Civil War, was discontinued after it ended, was brought back in the late 1800s, appropriately declared unconstitutional by the Supreme Court, and then officially blessed in 1913 with the ratification of a constitutional amendment allowing it. Yet the tax, then only on the wealthy, did not really take off and eclipse tariffs and excise taxes as the main source of federal revenue until World War I. The tax would be expanded to people of more limited means during World War II and has provided a cash cow for the expansion of the federal government ever since.

Like Wilson and prior presidents, Warren Harding, Wilson's successor, was too quick to use troops to bust labor unrest. Also, like Wilson and his predecessors, Calvin Coolidge, Harding's successor, sent troops to occupy Latin American countries without congressional approval.[23] More positively, in an attempt to smooth over domestic scars from the massive overseas conflict, Harding pardoned many whom Wilson had jailed for opposing the "Great War." Coolidge finished pardoning Wilson's prisoners of conscience and stopped the FBI from conducting domestic surveillance for political purposes.

---

22. Crenson and Ginsberg, *Presidential Power*, 340.
23. Patterson, "The Rise of Presidential Power," 52.

Also, the war made possible executive branch expansion that had been rejected prior to the conflict. Before the war, President William Howard Taft had asked Congress to allow him to create a unified executive budget. For most of American history, the budget was regarded as the purview of Congress, as specified in the Constitution, with the president as a mere bystander in a process by which each congressional committee negotiated a yearly budget for the executive agency under its jurisdiction. Regarding congressional control of the budget as a barrier against Prussian-style militarism and autocracy, House Speaker Joe Cannon had denied Taft his request. However, during the war, Woodrow Wilson also requested the authority to present a unified executive budget. Congress assented but imposed restrictions designed to retain congressional domination of the budget process; Wilson could not live with such limits and vetoed the bill.

Yet just after the war, Warren Harding persisted, convincing Congress to expand executive budgetary power the most since the beginning of the republic through the Budget and Accounting Act of 1921, which at last authorized a permanent unified executive branch budget to be created by a new Bureau of the Budget in the Treasury Department. However, Congress blunted the effect of this change somewhat by housing the bureau in the executive department most friendly to Congress rather than in the Office of the President, thus allowing other executive departments and agencies to continue to maintain some autonomy from the White House. (Although Congress avoided putting the bureau in the Office of the President, it was eventually moved by Franklin Roosevelt to a new Executive Office of the President, where it is today.)

Congress finally acquiesced to a unified executive branch budget, not fully grasping that it would significantly alter the balance of power between the two governmental branches, but instead thinking that it was only establishing some order to its own anarchic budgetary process. In a predecessor of presidential impoundment, the Harding administration even went beyond the new law and the Constitution, thus regarding congressional appropriations as a ceiling, spending only what was needed to keep federal agencies running and stashing the rest in a government "General Reserve." Harding's first budget director also went beyond the new law and attempted to have the budget bureau review all agency proposals for legislation that had budgetary implications but was rebuffed by cabinet secretaries, who jealously guarded their autonomy. After Harding died and Calvin Coolidge took over as president, however, such budget bureau clearance of agency legislative proposals was implemented.[24]

Therefore, the Bureau of the Budget not only presented a unified executive budget to Congress, but cleared all agency legislative proposals to Congress with budgetary effects. From then on, instead of creating the federal budget—the most important federal function after authorizing war and one that the Constitution had also assigned to Congress—the legislature now merely responded around the edges to the unified executive budget.[25] Nothing can be done in the federal government without money, and the financial strain of World War I—the war increased government spending from about $700 million prior to the war to $18.5 billion by 1919, while the national debt ballooned from about $1 billion in 1916 to $25 billion by 1919—was a major influence motivating Congress to delegate its dominance of this important function to the president after the war ended.

In response to their own approval of a unified executive branch budget in the 1921 law, the House and Senate consolidated appropriations authority, which had been spread out among various committees after the Civil War, into two appropriations committees. However, this attempt at recentralization did not last as appropriations power devolved to the committees' subcommittees because of the need for specialization.[26]

In increasing presidential budgetary power, Harding had good intentions and results. He and his successor, Calvin Coolidge, cut federal spending by almost half by 1924. Unfortunately, later presidents used the increased budget power less judiciously than Harding and Coolidge.

The unified executive budget and the increasing influence of the Bureau of the Budget follows the pattern in a number of episodes across presidencies and eras in American history. Political and societal pressure builds for a new government activity; in this case, the decisive impetus came from the huge financial costs of World War I. The president and Congress fight to control

---

24. Mayer, *With the Stroke of a Pen*, 112, 118–20.
25. Crenson and Ginsberg, *Presidential Power*, 20–22.
26. Fisher, *Presidential Spending Power*, 32, 36–39.

the activity, but Congress acquiesces to the chief executive, who uses the new facility in unexpected ways to grab even more power. Although initially contentious, the president's new powers eventually become established and even entrenched.[27]

Precedents of wartime expansion of executive power often either hang over in peacetime or lapse and are revisited at future dates. Both Republican Herbert Hoover and Democrat Franklin D. Roosevelt used the war mobilization model to attempt to combat the Great Depression. For example, Franklin D. Roosevelt, just after his first inauguration in 1933, used the Trading with the Enemy Act, passed during the world war to curtail trade with adversary countries, in peacetime to close all US banks during the worst of the great economic trough. Most new laws or agencies during the New Deal had roots in the war. Mimicking the government intrusion into the market during the war, the National Industrial Recovery Act (NIRA), the flagship of the first New Deal, established prices, wages, labor practices, and codes of fair competition for US industries. The National Recovery Administration (NRA), which administered the act, was modeled on the wartime War Industries Board (WIB) and the head of the new organization had been a WIB official during the war.

In 1936, reacting to totalitarian trends in Europe, FDR, not as much of a civil libertarian as Calvin Coolidge, reversed Coolidge's ban on FBI domestic political surveillance. J. Edgar Hoover, an authoritarian who headed the bureau for decades, interpreted FDR's domestic espionage authorization broadly. In 1939, Hoover created—from a list of subscribers to Italian, German, and communist publications—a manifest of people to be detained during any war. In 1940, FDR violated the Fourth Amendment of the Constitution, which requires warrants for government searches and seizures, by approving warrantless surveillance of suspected subversives. FDR even had Hoover spy on his political opponents and suspected government leakers of embarrassing information. Unfortunately, such illegal political espionage continued during future presidencies.[28] Congress didn't authorize or even know about any of these shenanigans.

---

27. Mayer, *With the Stroke of a Pen*, 121.
28. Healy, *The Cult of the Presidency*, 71–73.

In 1934, Congress had authorized the president to ban arms sales to Bolivia and Paraguay, which were at war, and FDR had issued a proclamation doing so. The Curtiss-Wright Corporation had been charged with illegally shipping machine guns to Bolivia. The company argued that Congress had unlawfully delegated its power to the president. In 1936, Supreme Court Justice George Sutherland, who wrote the court's opinion in the case, had an agenda of promoting an active American foreign policy made by the president and the judiciary, absent the allegedly narrow-minded perspective of Congress. Sutherland said that such delegation on a domestic matter would have been a problem, but in foreign policy, Congress could delegate as much power as it wanted—in this case to let the president decide when to execute a neutrality act banning arms sales to belligerents in a war. Using excessively broad language in a nonbinding dictum, Sutherland opined that in the area of foreign policy, the executive had "plenary and exclusive power," independent of any legislative power, as "the sole organ of the federal government in the field of international relations." Thus, the executive could act without congressional approval or even counter to the legally stated desires of Congress.[29]

Sutherland's "sole organ" language from the opinion, borrowing from John Marshall's speech in 1800, had no legal effect, and this broad opinion ran counter to even the text of the Constitution—the document gave Congress most governmental powers, even in foreign affairs and defense, and noted that the president's job was to execute Congress's wishes. Nevertheless, unfortunately, the Curtiss-Wright opinion has been cited ever since to justify executive power grabs in foreign policy. Yet many analysts question whether the framers wanted to give the executive exclusive control over any aspect of government.[30]

The executive's usurpation of congressional power occurred especially in the president being allowed to avoid the treaty ratification process in favor of executive agreements. In 1937, in *US v Belmont*, Sutherland again used his "sole organ" language for the court to give executive agreements with other nations, without congressional ratification, the same legal status as treaties ratified by a two-thirds Senate vote. Since that time, the courts have regarded

---

29. Crenson and Ginsberg, *Presidential Power*, 318–20.
30. Rudalevige, *The New Imperial Presidency*, 47–48.

executive-only (no congressional approval) and executive-legislative agree-ments (approval by only majorities of both houses of Congress) the same as treaties. They have ruled that such agreements, like treaties, preempt federal and state statutes at home, unless Congress overrides those agreements. If Congress takes no action on an executive-only agreement, the courts regard this as legislative deference to the president.[31] All of these judicial rulings are questionable, given the framers' requirement for arrangements with foreign nations to attain supermajority approval in the Senate.

The Constitution does not authorize executive agreements having a lower standard of, or no, congressional approval. The document clearly states that all treaties will be required to have a two-thirds vote in the Senate. The courts, recognizing such executive agreements is a classic case of legislating (or, in this case, "constitutionalizing") from the bench, which seems to directly con-tradict the Tenth Amendment, which states that if the Constitution doesn't enumerate a particular power for the federal government then it does not have it. Nowhere does the document mention executive agreements with other nations being in the federal purview. Yet many conservatives, interested in running an active foreign policy abroad, ignore this example of ill-advised executive and judicial law making.

World War II

Much, but not all, of Franklin Delano Roosevelt's expansion of executive power, like Wilson's during World War I, was a result of congressional passage of laws enhancing the presidential ambit, many times by delegating Congress's traditional powers.

FDR, after a landslide reelection win in 1936, became overconfident and tried to "pack" the Supreme Court with added justices friendlier to him and attempted to enhance the president's personnel and managerial powers, augment the White House staff, and authorize his reorganization of executive branch agencies. Such efforts failed because congressional fears of FDR's am-bitions for dictatorship prevailed. But in March 1939, with the start of another major war in Europe as Adolf Hitler invaded the remainder of Czechoslovakia,

---

31. Crenson and Ginsberg, *Presidential Power*, 321–22.

suddenly the Congress was more willing to compromise on the latter issues. As historian James T. Patterson concludes: "As the fascist menace developed in the late 1930s, the threat of war—historically the strongest force of all behind presidential aggrandizement—gave the President yet one more, ultimately unassailable, reason to provide energetic leadership."[32]

In the Reorganization Act of 1939, the legislature allowed FDR more staff and gave him, for two years and subject to congressional veto, the power to reorganize the executive branch. He used the power to sign an executive order that created the Executive Office of the President. Also, FDR transferred the Bureau of the Budget from the Treasury Department into the Executive Office and gave it more power to control the federal bureaucracy, by not just reviewing agency proposals that had budgetary implications (Coolidge had instituted this policy) but by reviewing all proposed legislation, presidential vetoes, and executive orders.

FDR's administration deliberately concealed the hidden expansion of presidential power in the executive order it drafted to create the Executive Office of the President (EOP).[33] After Hitler invaded the low countries in May 1940, the order was later used to create new wartime agencies used to run World War II, including the Office of Censorship, Office of Civilian Defense, Office of War Mobilization, Office of Production Management, War Food Administration, Office of Price Administration, and National War Labor Board. World War II expanded government intrusion into the marketplace and augmented presidential power even more than during the Civil War or World War I.[34] Yet neither Congress nor the Supreme Court was willing to challenge FDR's shenanigans during a time of perceived national crisis—probably what FDR was counting on. Thus, Congress approved funding for the questionable new wartime agencies. The establishment of the Executive Office of the President, when combined with increased presidential powers during World War II, would take the executive branch closer to the Cold War Imperial Presidency. The EOP was originally designed to help the president

---

32. Patterson, "The Rise of Presidential Power," 54.
33. Mayer, *With the Stroke of a Pen*, 110–12.
34. Crenson and Ginsberg, *Presidential Power*, 179–82, 194–95, 197, 224–25.

control the larger executive branch, which it did, but it has, over the decades, evolved into a large bureaucracy in its own right.

In the 1930s, FDR had signed neutrality acts, designed to keep the United States out of the brewing recurrent turmoil in Europe. The last of the four laws, enacted after World War II started in Europe in 1939, was designed to keep FDR from aiding democracies fighting against Adolf Hitler by banning any assistance to belligerent nations, stipulating that American provisions would be sold only on a cash basis, and preventing American ships from traversing any blockaded areas. Because of the massive carnage in World War I and the seeming folly of US wars for vague idealistic causes, even after Adolf Hitler's aggression in Poland in 1939 and in Western Europe in 1940, the American public remained overwhelmingly against getting involved in the new war in Europe. Therefore, FDR had to sneak his way into World War II.

Likely because of Woodrow Wilson's "modern, interwined world" arguments for expanded executive power (which really flowered during the later Cold War) and the non-legally binding and constitutionally indefensible Supreme Court dictum in the Curtiss-Wright decision of 1936, which labeled the president as the "sole organ of the federal government in the field of international relations," FDR and his advisers considered blatantly violating the neutrality laws.

After FDR's failed attempt to pack the Supreme Court in 1937 and the rise of dictatorships overseas, FDR decided instead to try to mildly loosen the neutrality provisions, which he was able to do after Hitler invaded Poland in 1939. Given that American public opinion still wanted to stay aloof from the European war, he billed the move as a way to keep the United States out of the war, not as a way to leap into it. Even as late as October 1940, a month before the US presidential election and after Nazi Germany had occupied France, the Netherlands, Belgium, Denmark, and Norway, about 83 percent of Americans wanted to remain aloof from World War II. FDR, like Wilson in the 1916 election when the world was at war almost a quarter century before, disingenuously ran for reelection on keeping the nation out of war. Mysteriously, the United States jumped into war in 1917 and 1941 after the elections were safely over. Also, FDR turned away hundreds of fleeing European Jews on the ship *St. Louis*. He was running for reelection and the American public was anti-immigrant, especially admitting large numbers of Jews, despite their known persecution in Nazi Germany. In this same vein, FDR's administration did not increase the quota for Jewish immigrants from Germany.[35]

America had conducted only a small military buildup before it officially entered the war in late 1941. In September 1940, the US Army was smaller than all the other major combatants already in the war and even many of the minor ones, with a ranking in size of only eighteenth in the world. From 1936 to 1940, US defense spending had declined as a percentage of the nation's economy.[36]

Although the War Department was nervous about giving scarce US arms to countries under threat from Hitler—which would undermine US security while the United States was trying to build up its forces—FDR found ways to do so. The laws blocking such transfers had criminal penalties, which Roosevelt apparently didn't mind violating. In 1938, FDR penned an executive order allowing the Army to sell older weapons to private companies, which then sold them to the desperate British.

In the spring of 1940, with Germany occupying France and threatening Britain, FDR arranged for new small "mosquito" boats to be secretly sent to Britain rather than to the US Navy. Congress began to investigate press reports of the transaction and was outraged when the administration admitted it. FDR had to cancel the mosquito boat transfer.

After the mosquito boat caper, Congress instituted two laws to prevent the transfer of outdated American World War I-era destroyers to the British. One statute said that Navy or Army materiel could be transferred to a foreign nation only if the top admiral or general, respectively, certified that such items were not essential to the defense of the United States. Another law, the Neutrality Act of 1940, expressly said that the administration could not send Navy ships to Britain unless the US Navy certified that the ships were no longer fit for use. Any such transaction would have also violated a 1917 statute, left over from the World War I era, prohibiting the transfer of warships to a belligerent nation.

---

35. Bueno de Mesquita and Smith, *The Spoils of War*, 164.
36. Bueno de Mesquita and Smith, *The Spoils of War*, 156.

With the fall of France in 1940 to the Nazis, FDR considered, but rejected, declaring that because of his inherent power as commander in chief, no congressionally passed law could stop him from donating military equipment to a foreign nation. (George W. Bush used the same legal theory to flout US laws after the 9/11 attacks.) In the end, however, FDR relied on a creative and suspect interpretation of the previously mentioned "unfit for service" statute. Thus, in circumvention of a congressional ban and in an unconstitutional executive power grab, FDR reached an executive agreement (unconstitutional when a treaty was required) that traded Britain fifty out-of-date US destroyers in exchange for British military bases in the Caribbean Sea.

Although in newspapers and in Congress some complaints about an autocratic power grab arose, public and congressional pushback on the president's action was generally muted. Thus, this incident is another example in American history of Congress's willing abdication of its constitutional power to the executive. The destroyer deal was important because it now put the United States on the side of supporting the Allies against the Axis powers, even though America had not yet entered the war. Even before a member of the Axis powers, Japan, had attacked the United States, FDR had effectively established an alliance with Britain, an active belligerent in the war, without Congress's approval.[37] In 1940, Congress had ratified no treaty of alliance and had not yet declared war on the Axis powers.

In March 1941, as a sequel to the destroyer deal, FDR more legitimately got Congress to give him great latitude in providing military aid to allied countries in Europe through the Lend Lease Act. However, in the spring of 1941, seven months before Pearl Harbor, Roosevelt declared a universal state of emergency to supplant the limited state of emergency he had declared in 1939 (the founders certainly did not mention either in the Constitution) and, without congressional approval, sent US troops to strategic Greenland to guard against a possible Nazi attack.

In the spring and summer of 1941, well before the Japanese attack on Pearl Harbor in December of that year, FDR effectively tried to bait Nazi Germany into war (in the fine tradition of James Polk, Abraham Lincoln,

---

37. Barron, *Waging War*, 284.

Woodrow Wilson, and later Lyndon Johnson), without congressional approval, by authorizing the US Navy to help British naval forces hunt and sink German U-boats and to "shoot-at-sight" any potential attackers.[38] FDR was hoping to provoke the Germans into an incident at sea that would then pressure Congress to formally declare war.

In the spring and summer of that year, FDR signed executive agreements with other nations to station US troops on Greenland and Iceland to defend the critical maritime choke point of the Greenland-Iceland-United Kingdom (GIUK) gap. The US Navy was ordered to protect supply convoys to those troops and sink Nazi U-boats threatening them. In September 1941, after a German submarine attacked an American supply ship, FDR ordered the Navy to shoot U-boats on sight. Although FDR told the American people the US ship just contained mail, it was really tracking the submarine and reported its location to the British before sinking. In October 1941, FDR escalated US "neutral" belligerency by arming US merchant ships and ordering the Navy to sink even German ships nowhere near US convoys. British documents released later showed FDR was actively trying to provoke the Nazis to start a war with the American colossus. For the moment, Hitler chose to pass on that invitation. All of FDR's shady executive overreach was retroactively justified by the Japanese attack on Pearl Harbor, Hitler declaring war on the United States in solidarity with its Axis ally, and the nastiness of the Axis powers before and during the war.[39]

At home, FDR also ran wild in expanding executive power. Wilson's "modern society and technology" argument for increasing presidential power, which gained traction during World War I, was resurrected and expanded by FDR in World War II. In both conflicts, the massive scale of modern combat resulted in the mobilization of entire societies for war, thus eroding the boundary between the home front and fighting front overseas. To execute both wars, the entire economy was mobilized for war production.

During World War II, technological advances made it feasible for long-range bombers to barely make it across oceans, and thus civil defense concerns arose. FDR also claimed that the conflict's worldwide battlefronts,

---

38. Crenson and Ginsberg, *Presidential Power*, 225.

39. Rudalevige, *The New Imperial Presidency*, 49.

representing total war, made the use of executive power more vital than in prior conflicts (this argument was a precursor to the case made for an imperial presidency after the dawn of nuclear weapons). Of course, the modern society and technology argument was inching toward being an excuse for both Wilson and FDR to try to become commander in chief of the country, instead of just the chief general on the battlefield, which the Constitution's framers had intended.[40]

Yet both Wilson and FDR flirted with, but did not directly invoke, their powers as commander in chief to run the country, as well as the wars they presided over. They coaxed as well as threatened Congress to pass laws allowing them sweeping powers at home. For example, FDR threatened to use his power as commander in chief to regulate wages and prices in the economy, but only to spur Congress to give him, by statute, the authority to do so. To avoid openly flouting congressional power, FDR reinterpreted statutes that Congress had intended to prevent him from doing something. Thus, FDR was less conscientious than Wilson was during World War I about staying strictly within congressional statutes, but Roosevelt nevertheless did not boldly claim extra-constitutional powers during an emergency.

As in the destroyer deal, FDR used creative interpretation of a congressionally passed law giving him the power to institute wartime rationing—the Second War Powers Act—to lower the farm price ceiling, which the Emergency Price Control Act had intended to subsidize farmers by holding agricultural prices high.[41] Although David J. Barron argues that such legislative acquiescence to executive circumvention of statutes is better than outright presidential claims of inherent power as commander in chief to disregard congressionally passed laws in time of emergency, it is still an abdication by Congress of its powers under the Constitution. Furthermore, a threat by the president to unilaterally use the power of commander in chief outside the battlefield to coerce Congress to pass legislation empowering him to do things was also an unacceptable erosion of Congress's constitutional power.

By threatening Congress that he would act on his own authority if Congress did not, FDR coerced the legislative body to pass the Emergency Price

---

40. Barron, *Waging War*, 259.

41. Barron, *Waging War*, 275–76.

Control Act of 1942. The law was an example of government regulation leading to the need for more government regulation: the government-imposed price controls so that it could buy needed war materials cheaply, but that increased demand, created shortages of goods, requiring the initiation of rationing.[42]

After Pearl Harbor, Congress delegated military and economic powers to the president by the shovelful. The first War Powers Act of 1941, like the Overman Act during World War I, gave the executive carte blanche authority to reorganize the government and authorized him to censor private communications and control international financial transactions. As a result of the law, FDR created, by executive order, many new government agencies to run the war. The Second War Powers Act of 1942 allowed the Federal Reserve to buy securities from the US Treasury to fund war budget deficits and permitted the president to regulate scarce materials.

Until the rise of aggressive autocracies in Europe prior to World War II and the war itself, the Supreme Court defended a non-delegation doctrine that prevented Congress from delegating its powers to the executive branch. With the Curtiss-Wright case in 1936 and the *Yakus v. United States* decision in 1944 during the war, respectively, the court threw that doctrine to the wind, first in foreign policy and then in domestic affairs, by letting Congress delegate to the president the establishment of maximum prices in the domestic economy.[43] The important effects of the destruction of the non-delegation doctrine, directly related to the rise of the fascist dictatorships and World War II, would contribute to the rise of the imperial presidency during the post-war Cold War period.

The original concept of constitutional checks and balances was that powers given to Congress by the document could not be delegated to the executive branch. Before World War II, the courts limited such congressional delegation to foreign affairs (see the 1936 Curtiss-Wright decision). However, because of the precedent of massive delegation for fighting the war, the courts relaxed their delegation doctrine during the postwar era. Such relaxation opened the way for the modern practice of Congress passing broad, vague statutes for popular acclaim (for example, achieving "clean air"), while leaving unpopular

---

42. Crenson and Ginsberg, *Presidential Power*, 227–28.
43. Healy, *The Cult of the Presidency*, 74.

detailed regulation to the unelected executive branch bureaucracies. Once again, wartime precedent hung over into peacetime.

Six months before FDR asked Congress for a declaration of war, he seized an airplane factory to prevent a strike from impairing bomber production. After the attack on Pearl Harbor, he seized more industries, but Congress only later passed the War Labor Disputes Act of 1943, which ratified FDR's seizure of private property for military purposes.

Also, after the attack on Pearl Harbor, FDR unconstitutionally used Lincoln's bad precedent from the Civil War to declare martial law in Hawaii, keeping it on long after the immediate threat had passed. Yet the Constitution implies that only Congress can suspend habeas corpus—and such suspension is far short of martial law.

In the spring of 1942, FDR, by executive order, cynically began rounding up about 100,000 Japanese residents and Japanese-Americans living on the West Coast and taking them to army-run prison camps. Congress later helped out by passing a law making it illegal to resist the relocation orders of the army.[44] Unbelievably (or perhaps believably), the Supreme Court validated, as it had largely done during past wars, horrendous and unconstitutional violation of civil liberties and many other executive constitutional usurpations.

Yet, two studies showed, including one by the White House, that Japanese residents and Japanese-Americans were loyal and posed little threat to the rest of the country. However, FDR perpetrated one of the worst thefts of civil liberties in American history anyway because of political pressure by Earl Warren, the governor of California, and other Californians to lock up the Japanese. Because German- and Italian-Americans were not also sent to prison camps en masse, one has to conclude that racism was a major factor in the sordid episode. Moreover, not one person in the 100,000 incarcerated was found to be disloyal.

FDR also followed Lincoln's unconstitutional precedent of establishing kangaroo military tribunals. The Constitution says that all people get a jury trial, unless they are in the US military in time of war—in which case, they get a military court martial. This requirement was the reason for the Supreme Court's post–Civil War *Ex Parte Milligan* decision, which ruled that the

---

44. Healy, *The Cult of the Presidency*, 253–55.

executive could not use his power as commander in chief to circumvent civilian courts if they were still functioning and no threat of attack or invasion existed, which Lincoln had unnecessarily and autocratically done during the war. FDR had even less reason to use these kangaroo military commissions than did Lincoln, because World War II was overseas, not here at home as was the Civil War. Therefore, all the civilian courts were functioning with no imminent threat of enemy attack or invasion. Yet the Supreme Court, in *Ex Parte Quirin* (1942) overruled the *Ex Parte Milligan* decision of 1866 and allowed FDR to name suspects as enemy combatants and to try them in military tribunals.

FDR used the unconstitutional military tribunals to try for war crimes two groups of German saboteurs who came ashore in the United States from a U-boat to attempt to damage US wartime industrial production. Kangaroo military tribunals are often used when successful prosecutions in civilian courts are hard to achieve or, even if attained, might result in sentences perceived as too lenient. In this case, military tribunals promised easier conviction for crimes during war and a stiffer penalty: death.

Although the Germans challenged their trial by military tribunal at the Supreme Court, FDR privately told the court that he would not release the defendants to civilian courts and might even execute them no matter how the court ruled.[45] Usually only dictators try to intimidate an independent judiciary in this manner, but FDR evidently figured he could get away with such shenanigans during wartime. Some of the potential saboteurs were eventually hung, including the leader of one of the groups who blew the whistle on the entire operation to authorities in the United States. And the Supreme Court blessed the president's use of the commander-in-chief power to create such kangaroo military tribunals, despite their bald unconstitutionality. As noted, the Constitution requires a civilian trial in all circumstances except for US military personnel charged with crimes during wartime.

During the war, FDR used what would become a routine practice among American presidents until Watergate brought down Richard Nixon in 1974: Using government agencies to spy domestically for political reasons, including on some political allies, despite little national security reason for doing so.

---

45. Barron, *Waging War*, 258, 262–63.

After the war was over, many wartime agencies were closed, and the system of production, wage, and price controls was dismantled, but conscription was retained. As important, the income tax was converted during the war from a class tax on only the wealthy to a mass tax on everyone, thereby doubling the number of people required to pay it. Federal income tax revenues jumped forty-five-fold from 1940 to 1945. The tax then stayed on after the war as a gold mine for revenues to fund bigger government in peacetime.

To get all the new taxpayers of more modest means to accept the broadened income tax system to fund the war, tax rates on the wealthy had to be jacked up. Yet to ameliorate political opposition from very powerful rich people, loopholes had to be established to relieve their tax burden. Thus, the war gave us not only a broader-based income tax but the "swiss cheese" tax code that endures to this day. High tax rates for the wealthy along with loopholes was just an illusion to make taxpayers of more modest means accept the new requirement to pay income tax.

The income tax and war had long been associated. To provide added revenues during the Civil War, the income tax was copied from the British funding of the Crimean War in the 1850s. The tax went away, but like many precedents during war time, resurfaced in the late 1800s. Although the Supreme Court correctly ruled it unconstitutional, the revenue stream was so good that in 1913, a constitutional amendment was passed to make it legal. Yet the tax really didn't take off again until revenues were needed to fight World War I, when the income tax replaced tariff and excise taxes as the dominant form of federal revenue generation for the first time in American history.

In addition, economist Milton Friedman during World War II helped institute the pernicious practice of government withholding of taxes from people's paychecks. Prior to that time, people just paid all the taxes they owed after the tax year ended. Periodic incremental withholding of pay allowed the government to conceal the taxpayers' full burden, ensured tax enforcement, and gave the government a steady inflow of funds during the year.

Today, people do not think that getting healthcare coverage through their employer is odd, but it is; it is also quite inefficient, as opposed to individuals just buying it themselves. The system originated in World War II, when wages were controlled, and labor shortages occurred because many workers were sucked into defense-related industries. In order to lure scarce workers, other businesses began offering "in kind" healthcare coverage, which did not count toward the wage ceiling. Thus, the inefficient healthcare system now used in the United States was born of war.

In the 1948 case, *Woods v. Miller*, the Supreme Court even used a war power justification to bless a postwar 1947 rent control law, saying, "The war power does not necessarily end with the cessation of hostilities."[46] This ruling again shows that some expansion of government during wartime usually hangs over into peacetime.

The crisis of World War II passed with the forms of the system of congressional regulation of war—instituted in America's first war, the Quasi-War—still clinging to life, but in practice being eroded significantly. (As a cautionary note, when the Roman Republic eroded into the Roman Empire, the old forms of the leader's deference to the Senate endured, but the real power had passed to the emperor.) Although in the lead-up to World War II, FDR had committed some constitutional violations and illegalities—for example, the Destroyer Deal and warrantless spying on Americans—he generally acted with restraint because Congress was suspicious and watchful that he did not violate the neutrality acts. As historian James T. Patterson noted, "In 1941 the foreign affairs presidency was far from the potent force it was to become in the post-war years."[47]

However, during the Cold War and the War on Terror, future presidents would throw such restraint to the wind, expanding the commander-in-chief role well beyond the framer's vision that the president would just command forces on the battlefield after the war began. Also, executives would take advantage of foreign wars and terrorist attacks to begin commanding the home front as well—without congressional authorization.

---

46. Crenson and Ginsberg, *Presidential Power*, 228–29.
47. Patterson, "The Rise of Presidential Power," 55–56.

4

The Rise of the Imperial Presidency

DESPITE THE US government participating in a huge Civil War and two massive world wars, at least the forms of congressional dominance in war had survived. During the 1800s and through the mid-1900s, executive aggrandizement during wartime tended to be temporary for only the duration of the war.

After each of these three massive wars, Congress, tired of the puffing up of presidential power, pushed back in a major way. During Reconstruction, the Congress impeached and almost convicted Andrew Johnson for trying to obstruct its plan for radical Reconstruction of the South. After World War I, Congress failed to ratify Wilson's Versailles Treaty and accompanying League of Nations scheme. After World War II, fed up with FDR's winning four terms, Congress passed and ratified the Twenty-Second Amendment, which limited the president to two terms. The legislature also trashed Harry Truman's domestic agenda and passed the Taft-Hartley Act in 1947 and the McCarran Internal Security Act of 1950 over Truman's veto.[1] Even so, at the start of the Cold War, the presidency had gained enough power to exceed even the very strong executive that Alexander Hamilton had hoped for at the Constitutional Convention.

However, the aggrandizement of presidential power did not end there. Writing in 2001, Kenneth R. Mayer concluded: "If the president's domestic policy power has grown steadily but incrementally since the 1930s, in foreign affairs it has grown explosively. Indeed, few dispute the pattern of increased

---

1. Crenson and Ginsberg, *Presidential Power*, 219, 229.

presidential power in foreign affairs over the past fifty years."[2] Similarly, David Gray Adler noted that:

> The unmistakable trend toward executive domination of U.S. foreign affairs in the past sixty years represents a dramatic departure from the basic scheme of the Constitution. . . . The president is vested with only modest authority in this realm and is clearly only of secondary importance.[3]

The long Cold War, with the advent of nuclear weapons, and the seemingly perpetual War on Terror would lead to the rise and sustenance of the imperial presidency, with its asserted "inherent"—and thus unconstitutional—executive powers, such as the inherent power as commander in chief to unilaterally make war without the consent of Congress. According to historian Thomas Fleming, "By 1964, Congress was considered an almost superfluous department of the American government."[4] During the Nixon presidency, historian Arthur Schlesinger, Jr. dubbed the near-monarchical powers in foreign policy, accrued to the executive since the beginning of the Cold War, the "imperial presidency" and argued that those powers were being used domestically, too. During the Cold War and beyond, sadly, even the forms of constitutional war power are almost extinct under the new way of unilateral presidential military action.

The modern Supreme Court, never one to stick up for the framers' original conception of the Constitution, has largely blessed usurpation by the executive of congressional power in foreign policy during the post-World War II era. The court has accepted that foreign affairs are mainly the purview of the president.

The imperial presidency is not just about the unconstitutional expansion of the executive's role as commander in chief; it is also about the presidency's institutional augmentation. Although Franklin Roosevelt had created the Executive Office of the President and transferred the Bureau of the Budget

---

2. Kenneth R. Mayer, *With the Stroke of a Pen*, 138.

3. David Gray Adler, "Court, Constitution, and Foreign Affairs," in David G. Adler and Larry N. George, eds., *The Constitution and the Conduct of American Foreign Policy* (Lawrence, KS: University Press of Kansas, 1996), 19.

4. Fleming, *The Great Divide*, 389.

from the Treasury Department into it, FDR still had an improvised decision-making style that he practiced during World War II. In 1946, the Congress made the president solely responsible for the economy and added the Council on Economic Advisers to the Executive Office to help him. In 1947, the passage of the National Security Act of 1947 created the National Security Council in the Executive Office, created a Central Intelligence Agency that would now report directly to the president instead of the Joint Chief of Staff, and consolidated the War and Navy Departments in the new Department of Defense, which would tighten the president's command over the military. All would help institutionalize the imperial presidency, thus providing more resources for policymaking.

The Employment Act of 1946, which created the Council on Economic Advisers, committed the government to manage the economy during peacetime by maximizing employment and production and reducing inflation. However, in American history, until Herbert Hoover battled the Great Depression and first accepted a federal role in combating unemployment, it was regarded as undesirable, or even counterproductive, for the government to manage the economy during peacetime. More important, over time, the president's National Security Council has become so powerful that the White House has eclipsed the Departments of State and Defense in driving national security policymaking.

The imperial presidency unconstitutionally shifted some legislative power to the president from Congress via executive orders, executive agreements, national security findings and directives, and signing statements. Some executive orders and national security findings and directives may be constitutional if they are only giving the executive branch instructions about how to implement congressional legislation. The problem is that many modern presidents now use them to "act when Congress won't," which is unconstitutional. Executive agreements with foreign countries are almost always unconstitutional, because they attempt to circumvent the two-thirds vote required in the Senate to ratify treaties. The Constitution doesn't mention executive agreements, only treaties. Presidential signing statements—first operationalized by Ronald Reagan to override the will of Congress and since growing in executive use—are unconstitutionally used as a way of nixing parts of congressionally passed laws, usually through executive branch non-enforcement, without the president needing to veto entire bills. Thus, Congress is never given a chance to override a presidential veto with a two-thirds vote. Unfortunately, courts now look at signing statements as part of the legislative history when interpreting laws.

Cold War

While it is still debated whether the Soviets or the Americans started the Cold War, it is known that President Harry Truman turned support for the Greek and Turkish governments against local communist insurgencies into a world-wide crusade against communism by taking the advice of Republican Sen. Arthur Vandenburg to scare the American people. Throughout the Cold War, the US government continued to exaggerate the threat from the Soviet Union, a country some experts in the national security field, including German chancellor Helmut Schmidt, called "Upper Volta with Missiles." The prospect of Communist takeover was most likely in poor developing nations, which had little strategic value to American security, but their fall instead would make the US empire look weak and ineffectual. Yet, the US government was able to exaggerate the threat from communism in backwater places, such as Korea and Vietnam—to get American public support for maintaining a worldwide informal empire of US-dominated alliances, overseas military bases to further those alliances, and numerous military adventures to police the vast semi-global realm. However, the greatest- and least-analyzed effects of the forty-five-year Cold War may have been at home.

The "modern, complex society" argument for the expansion of executive power—made by Wilson during World War I and refined by FDR's justification during World War II of technological improvements in warfare and the multifront war that had arisen—reached its pinnacle during the Cold War. Presidential scholar Richard Neustadt succinctly summarized the argument: "Technology has modified the Constitution."[5] The advent of nuclear weapons could require the president to decide rapidly whether the country would go

---

5. Richard Neustadt, *Presidential Power: The Politics of Leadership* (New York: Wiley, 1960), 167, 184–85; and testimony before the Senate Government Operations Committee, 1963, quoted in Arthur Schlesinger, *The Imperial Presidency* (New York: Houghton, 1973), 166.

to war, but the same logic was also applied to conventional war and military actions short of general war, such as the need for the rapid use of force without congressional approval based on the inherent power of the executive as commander in chief. Because the original conception of the Constitution's framers could still hold during the nuclear age, this unconstitutional expansion of the executive's power as commander in chief and the retraction of the congressional war power was unneeded. (Even at the dawn of the republic, when the constitutional framework for war was established, great threats to the new, weak nation existed—the French, British, and Spanish great powers didn't retract from US borders until the first decades of the 1800s.) Although nuclear war could arise quickly because of technical advances in long-range missiles and bombers, the framers always allowed for the president to take military action in self-defense of the nation without congressional approval; in the nuclear age, only the president's response time might be reduced. If the president believed the country was under nuclear attack, he could constitutionally retaliate rapidly in self-defense without congressional authorization. Thus, slow congressional action would not need to impede a presidential response. In fact, because the United States has led the world in nuclear, missile, and long-range bomber technology, such advances likely have deterred other countries from attacking the United States—either with conventional or nuclear weapons—actually rendering rapid presidential self-defense situations much less, rather than more, likely.

Therefore, expanding presidential authority as commander in chief during the Cold War to rapidly and unilaterally launch an offensive conventional military action—large or small—was still unconstitutional and even more unneeded for the nation's security. Furthermore, congressional action could be much faster than at the nation's founding. If more rapid action was needed by Congress during the Cold War or nuclear age, improvements in transportation and communication had allowed Congress to be in almost permanent session during the year (in contrast to the limited sessions held during the framers' era in an agricultural economy) and had allowed members of the legislative body to reassemble much more quickly if a declaration of war had been needed. Thus, the need for unconstitutional and unilateral exercise of executive war making even during the Cold War was a red herring.

Korean War

Even Franklin D. Roosevelt, during World War II, for the most part, had only creatively interpreted congressionally passed laws and threatened Congress that he would act unilaterally as commander in chief if the legislative body did not pass statutes giving him the authority to run the war the way he wanted. In contrast, Harry Truman, FDR's successor, simply ignored the Constitution's requirement that Congress declare war after North Korea invaded South Korea in 1950. Instead, citing only the Senate-ratified United Nations Participation Act, Truman unilaterally launched a US-led UN "police action" to save the South Korean dictator Syngman Rhee without any prior congressional declaration of war. Thus, Truman flouted American tradition for major wars, invoked just nine years before, after the Japanese attacked Pearl Harbor. Truman purposefully ignored congressional leaders' offers to pass a resolution approving the war, because Dean Acheson, his secretary of state, had advised him that accepting it would allow Congress to undermine his authority as commander in chief. This instance was the first time this dubious rationale was ever invoked for a major American war and was an important factor in Truman being labeled as the first "imperial president" by many historians.

Equally important, Congress, nervous about the need to push back against the communists, did nothing to hold Truman to account for his blatant autonomous action in violation of the constitutional requirement that only the Congress could declare war; in fact, the legislature implicitly approved of it by appropriating funds for the conflict and voting to extend conscription. (Such implicit approval by funding is a poor substitute for explicit congressional approval of the war in advance, because legislators are usually reluctant to shut off funding for troops when they are under enemy fire.) Yet, a full-blown war that killed 37,000 Americans was not merely a "police action."

In any event, the requirement in the Constitution that even letters of marque and reprisal to authorize privateers (private pirates working for the government in times of conflict) to attack and capture enemy ships seems to indicate the nation's founders intended that Congress should approve even minor uses of force. The experience of the Quasi War with France (during the late 1790s)—which was not only the first limited war since the Constitution was ratified but also the first conflict of any kind—indicates that even limited military actions without declarations of war were intended to be heavily regulated by Congress.

Unfortunately, for executive aggrandizement of Congress's constitutional war power, Truman's ignoring the need to get congressional approval for a major war was a watershed. After this bad precedent, presidents felt free to abuse the framers' original constitutional framework, which ensured that one leader, like the kings of Europe, could not take the nation to war, thus inflicting costs in blood and treasure on the common people, who had no voice through their representatives in the matter. During the ensuing Cold War and thereafter in the War on Terror, presidents might ask for some type of congressional approval for the occasional bigger wars, but only as a political insurance plan in case something went wrong—still failing to obtain a formal congressional declaration of war required by the Constitution. For smaller wars and military actions—of the undeclared Quasi War variety—the executive felt free to send troops anywhere in the world where a superpower's seemingly unlimited interests were perceived to be threatened without any congressional approval at all. For example, the United States invaded or attacked many countries without any congressional approval—Lebanon in 1958, the Dominican Republic in 1965, Granada in 1983, Panama in 1989, Bosnia in 1995, Iraq in 1998, Serbia in 1999, and Libya in 2011.

Truman even claimed the power, as commander in chief, to send US forces anywhere in the world he wanted, even if no war existed. After he had unilaterally committed forces to Korea, he sent four army divisions into a peaceful Europe to reinforce those already serving there under the newly created NATO alliance. This deployment, also under his alleged authority as commander in chief, caused more congressional debate than had his insertion of US troops into the hot Korean war zone. Truman's secretary of state, Dean Acheson, also claimed that once the president deployed forces overseas, Congress had no right to recall these forces. Thus, the Truman administration made the breathtaking claim that the president could make unilateral long-term military deployments that could be provocative to a US adversary (the Soviet Union) and that Congress could have no power to object.[6] Congress backed down in this confrontation.

---

6. Barron, *Waging War*, 302, 304–05.

For an imperial power, it was argued that the image of national strength, prestige, and "credibility" was everything and that rapid military action to combat communism, and later terrorism, required the rapid deployment and employment of armed force to even remote areas of the world to avoid the perception of weakness. Congress should have challenged this questionable troop deployment logic, but instead rolled over for executive aggrandizement. Unfortunately, this timid congressional behavior would become a pattern during the post–World War II era of the United States as the dominant superpower. As with ancient Rome centuries before, creating an overseas empire—even the more informal one possessed by the United States—leads to the erosion of the republic.

Yet Truman eschewed the lessons of ancient Rome and that of the nation's founding, deciding to run a never-ending worldwide Cold War crusade to contain communism, as explicated in the National Security Council's planning document, NSC-68. The document formalized the "domino theory" of advancing communism by ludicrously saying that a defeat of free institutions anywhere is a defeat for them everywhere.

NSC-68 called for a massive military buildup and that is what Truman and Congress agreed to after North Korea invaded South Korea. A prominent principle at the nation's founding was the constitutional framers' suspicion of a standing army during peacetime, due to its deleterious effect on the maintenance of liberty. One hundred seventy-six years into the nation's history, Truman threw that venerable tradition to the wind and for the first time created a large peacetime military (not just in the theater of limited war in Korea), which endures to this day. By 1952, the United States had tripled its military spending, doubled its Army and Marine Corps, augmented its Navy, begun deploying long-range bombers with the mission of striking the USSR, and increased its nuclear weapons programs. Also, the Universal Military Training Act of 1951 expanded the conscription originally reinstated in the Selective Service Act of 1948. Finally, Truman created the permanent peacetime military-industrial complex by augmenting and instituting FDR's defense contracting system, which originated in World War II. Even after the much smaller Korean War, Dwight Eisenhower, Truman's successor, did little to dismantle the peacetime military-industrial complex that he would famously criticize, in his farewell address, as being a threat to liberty.

Truman fired Gen. Douglas MacArthur, the American military commander in Korea, for insubordination in running a public campaign for an all-out war against China after that country entered the war. Truman's necessary action reinforced republican civilian control over the military and was the last time that a US military commander tried to use Congress against the president. Truman consolidated the president's role as commander in chief by getting Secretary of Defense George Marshall, the Joint Chiefs of Staff, and the secretary of state to support his firing of the insubordinate MacArthur. Also reinforcing his power as commander in chief, Truman fired Navy admirals, who had pressured him for excessive naval spending by launching an "admirals' revolt."

Yet even as Truman unilaterally undertook this jarring precedent of stretching his power as commander in chief by rejecting the constitutional requirement to get congressional declaration of war for the first time in American history for a major overseas war, the Supreme Court at home was rebuking his attempt to become commander in chief of the country, rather than just of the military. The court said that Congress still had some role in determining how the war was managed—at least on the home front.

Truman wanted to stop a nationwide strike by workers in the steel industry in 1952, because he felt it threatened the US military effort in the Korean War. He asked Congress to give him the authority to resolve the work stoppage. Congress did nothing. Laws authorizing the seizure of private property for government use during World Wars I and II had been repealed, and the Taft-Hartley Act, passed by Congress in 1947, said the government could not expropriate private industries. Nevertheless, Truman, by executive order, directed the government to seize private steel mills to end the labor dispute on favorable terms to steelworkers, asserting that his role as commander in chief gave him the power to commandeer steel for the war effort. The president made matters worse at a news conference when asked if, by his legal reasoning, he believed he could seize private newspapers or radio stations if he thought it necessary to win the war. When he wouldn't say "no," a furor ensued.

The Truman administration argued that the president determined when a state of emergency existed, that the courts could not review that designation, and that the president had unlimited power during the emergency. It was difficult to find a precedent for such an extreme legal view. The Constitution does not speak of the federal government, executive branch or Congress, having the power to declare a general state of emergency but does imply that only the Congress can authorize a more limited suspension of habeas corpus in times of invasion or insurrection. Furthermore, in arguing the case before the Supreme Court, the Truman administration argued that the president's inherent power gave Congress and the public only the remedies of impeachment and election loss, respectively, to discipline executive actions that were not desirable. (Nixon later used the same illegitimate argument.)

Supreme Court Justice Robert Jackson, FDR's appointee to the court, in a concurrence to the court's *Youngstown Sheet and Tube Co. v. Sawyer* decision, reiterated a principle he had championed to reject FDR's attempt to send small "mosquito boats" to the British as part of a destroyer-for-bases deal prior to World War II—by saying that the executive could not take an action expressly forbidden by Congress, even during times of emergency. Truman was not executing Congress's wishes or even taking advantage of Congress's silence on an issue. In other words, the court ruled that the president's power as commander in chief did not override a congressionally passed law to the contrary. In other words, the president could not seize private property just because he did not want to follow a labor arbitration law passed by Congress. Essentially, Jackson repudiated Alexander Hamilton's original "vesting clause" argument, which has not faired that well over time in American courts. Jackson also noted that the Constitution's framers realized the real possibility of the usurpation of liberty during crises and so declined to give the federal government the general power to suspend liberties, but instead gave Congress the power to suspend habeas corpus only in the event of an invasion or insurrection. Justice Hugo Black's majority opinion also rejected Truman's conception of unlimited power during an emergency, saying that the president was only supposed to execute the laws Congress had passed, not legislate himself. Unfortunately, the Youngstown case proved somewhat of an anomaly in the post–World War II era, because most federal court decisions during the period have supported the aggrandizement of executive power during wartime and national emergencies. This unconstitutional use of executive orders to make policy—legislating from the executive branch—has only increased since the ruling. Conservatives hate when the courts legislate from the bench, but those on the right spouting executive primacy don't seem to have the same concern when a powerful president does the same thing.

Truman's antics against the steel strike in 1952 had been foreshadowed by his interference in the nationwide railroad strike of mid-1946, which did not even have the excuse of being during wartime. Truman declared that he would bust the strike using the military and attempted to get Congress to allow him to draft the strikers into the military if they did not go back to work. When his own attorney general brought up the questionable constitutionality of the latter action, Truman angrily replied, "We'll draft them and think about the law later."[7] Such intimidation guaranteed the strike would be settled quickly.

In contrast to Truman's unconstitutional policymaking executive order in the steel strike, which the Supreme Court rejected in the Youngstown Steel case, his lawful executive order, as commander in chief of the armed forces to desegregate the military was merely his enforcing of the Fourteenth Amendment to the Constitution, which required all persons to have equal protection under the law but which had not been theretofore enforced in the armed forces.

The Korean War brought another red scare at home, this time with demagogue Republicans in Congress, such as the House Committee on Un-American Activities, conducting loyalty investigations of executive branch employees. Although Truman believed that charges of disloyalty in the US government were a political "red herring" in an attempt to show his administration was "soft on communism," he attempted to forestall even more draconian congressional action by establishing, through an executive order, loyalty investigations of every government employee, regardless of whether their jobs dealt with national security issues. (The precursor to this loyalty program and that of FDR's during World War II was Woodrow Wilson's confidential executive order to department heads to fire anyone who had sympathies against US involvement in World War I.) Truman's loyalty program ended up stoking the "anti-red" hysteria in the country that he wanted to avoid. Many innocent government employees—who had to prove they were loyal rather than the government being required to prove they were disloyal—were persecuted

---

7. Quoted in Healy, *The Cult of the Presidency*, 98.

unfairly using insufficient or secret evidence.[8] Truman could have just vetoed any drastic congressional "loyalty" bill and invited the Republican-controlled legislature to override it, but politics dictated a race to be more "patriotic" in usurping the country's unique civil liberties originally enshrined by the nation's founders.

Republican Sen. Joe McCarthy also conducted a witch hunt to try to find a communist behind every bush. Truman did push back some against McCarthy. Also, in a rare instance of eschewing executive aggrandizement, Truman vetoed the congressionally passed McCarran Internal Security Act of 1950, which permitted the president, during a security emergency, to detain anyone he thought likely to commit espionage or sabotage. However, Congress, not to be denied in its delegation of power to the executive branch, overrode Truman's veto.

Although Dwight Eisenhower did not push back publicly against a member of his own party, his strategy was designed to let McCarthy shoot himself in the foot. The senator eventually did that by trying to find communists in the US Army. Although his motives were good, Ike tried to invoke unconstitutional "executive privilege" across the entire executive branch, so that the Army could withhold information from McCarthy's investigative committee. Previously established practice, also of questionable constitutionality, had allowed presidents to shield from Congress only internal consultations with their closest advisers in the White House. However, Ike's government loyalty inquisition was even more harsh than Truman's. Despite a Soviet espionage program against the US government during this time, such "red baiting" by these two presidents and Congress didn't significantly enhance the government's security against communist subversion.

In another form of government oppression, the temporary income tax hikes to fund the Korean War largely became permanent in peacetime. The added revenues could be used for the first large, permanent standing army during peacetime in American history and expansion of government intervention into the economy and society at home.

Although Arthur Schlesinger, Jr. coined the phrase "imperial presidency" to push back against Richard Nixon's aggressive use of executive power during

---

8. Mayer, *With the Stroke of a Pen*, 149–56.

the Vietnam War, Harry Truman's blunt and novel expansion of his power as commander in chief to include ignoring Congress, both overseas and domestically during times of crises, was the first example of the phenomenon. Truman took advantage of augmented, institutionalized, and unilateral presidential power in foreign policy given by the National Security Act of 1947's creation of the National Security Council in the White House, consolidation of the military services into the Department of Defense thereby enhancing the presidential chain of command over the armed forces, and the creation of the CIA under the president's authority. During World War II, the Office of Strategic Services, then the US agency in charge of intelligence and covert operations, reported to the Joint Chiefs of Staff. Now the president had his own national security bureaucracies reporting directly to him.

In the mid-1950s, Dwight Eisenhower, following in Truman's footsteps, demanded carte blanche in advance from Congress for military action in the Taiwan Strait and the Middle East—to deploy forces as he saw fit with no enemy listed nor any other restrictions on their use. Congress supinely obliged. The only overt overseas military action of Ike's eight-year presidency was in 1958, when he sent Marines to hit the beaches in Lebanon, without congressional approval, to encounter only bewildered sun bathers on the sand. Truman's precedent of unilateral executive war making was taking hold.

At home, in 1957, Eisenhower used the army to desegregate schools in Little Rock, Arkansas, by invoking the Insurrection Act of 1807, which allowed the executive to use the army to repress rebellion or lawlessness. Ike's goal was laudable—to enforce the equal protection clause of the Fourteenth Amendment. Yet the law used may be of questionable constitutionality, because the Constitution gives Congress the power to provide for calling out only the militia, not the army, to suppress an insurrection or invasion. In fact, the Constitution doesn't even authorize a permanent standing army.

Although at the end of his eight-year tenure as president, Ike noted that the "conjunction of an immense military establishment and a large arms industry" was new to the country during peacetime (Truman had created it during the Korean War), Eisenhower thought its retention was necessary to fight the Cold War and so did little to dismantle it. However, he warned in his farewell address of this "military-industrial complex" gaining "unwarranted influence" in circles of power. He believed the complex to be a threat to liberty and democracy, but his only solution was to lamely call for an alert citizenry to ensure that "security and liberty may prosper together."[9] Throughout American history, the nation's economic incentives had favored peace, but beginning with the Cold War, crucial parts of American industry and whole areas of the country now depended on military contracts to maintain their prosperity.[10] Economic incentives at home were now advantaged by US military action abroad. (Even after the Cold War ended, the military-industrial complex and its poor incentive structure remained.)

Covert Actions During the Cold War

The CIA, created after World War II, was supposed to be an agency gathering intelligence on foreign threats to the United States. It quickly evolved into an agency whose main function was instead the conduct of covert military and political operations—and not all of these "dirty tricks" were confined to foreign shores. Harry Ransom, a leading scholar on intelligence matters, concluded that nothing in the public record "nor in such archives as are accessible (for example, in the Truman Library) suggests that Congress ever intended to create or knew that it was creating an agency for para military operations and a wide range of foreign political interventions." Similarly, in 1974, Sen. John Stennis, who was elected to the Senate shortly after the original CIA bill was enacted, said, "There was nothing clearer around here, not anything that sounded louder, than the fact the CIA act was passed for the purpose of foreign intelligence." He added that he was "shocked and disappointed and considerably aroused" when he got wind of the agency's involvement in Watergate.[11]

Furthermore, the Central Intelligence Act of 1949, governing the new agency created by the National Security Act of 1947, authorized the CIA to hide its budget by receiving money from other federal agencies, such as the Department of Defense. After the chairpersons of the congressional appropriations committees inform the White House's Office of Management and

---

9. Dwight D. Eisenhower, Farewell Radio and Television Address, January 17, 1961.

10. Christopher Preble, "The Founders, Executive Power, and Military Intervention," *Pace Law Review* 30, no. 2 (Winter 2010): 697–98.

11. Fisher, *Presidential Spending Power*, 215–16.

Budget what the CIA budget is for the year, the money is transferred from the Defense Department to the CIA. This process upends the Constitution's requirement that "a regular Statement and Account of Receipts and Expenditures of *all* [author's emphasis] public Money shall be published from time to time" because not only is the CIA budget a secret, but therefore the public does not know the amount of the real budget of the Department of Defense either. In addition, following the early, but questionable, accounting practice allowed by Congress for the use of hidden funds in the 1790s, the CIA director is allowed to simply certify, with no documentation or congressional audit, that public funds have been spent properly.

Eisenhower decried Truman's bald attempt at usurping power in the steel case as reminiscent of that by the fascists he fought against in World War II. Yet Ike found his own way to abuse his power as commander in chief. Instead of starting small or large conventional wars to foil communist expansion around the world, which could have led to escalation to nuclear war, Eisenhower began to use covert action by the CIA (created during the Truman administration) to blunt Soviet momentum. He successfully overthrew governments in Iran, Guatemala, and Laos. Another of Ike's purposes in using covert action was to avoid the constitutional conflicts with Congress and the courts that Truman's publicly blunt unilateral war making abroad and at home, as commander in chief, had provoked.[12] Eisenhower may have avoided conflict with Congress, but undeclared secret mini-wars, initiated on executive authority alone, were hardly constitutional either. (Congress did little oversight of Ike's or his successors' use of covert action until the Church committee hearings on the abuses of US intelligence agencies led to the creation of the congressional intelligence committees in the late 1970s.) JFK also augmented the executive's capability to launch secret wars by establishing the military's Special Forces and using them secretly to assist the South Vietnamese government without sounding out Congress.

Richard Nixon used the CIA to help General Augusto Pinochet overthrow President Salvador Allende, the elected left-leaning leader of Chile. The coup resulted in Allende's murder and many years of dictatorial rule under the brutal Pinochet. Jimmy Carter and Ronald Reagan used the CIA to funnel

---

12. Barron, *Waging War*, 306–11.

money and arms to radical Islamist Mujahedeen fighters in Afghanistan during the 1980s. In doing so, they inadvertently helped create the greatest threat to the US mainland since the War of 1812: al Qaeda.

Waging small secret wars by CIA covert action or by using US military "advisers" to "advise and assist" the forces of indigenous governments also robbed the Congress of its constitutional war-making power in the name of the American public. In fact, Congress and the public did not even know about most such unilateral war making, some of it with severe consequences for the republic. For example, the secret massive escalation of the Vietnam War by Lyndon Johnson originated in initial covert action and military "advise and assist" missions started by Eisenhower and continued by JFK and LBJ.

Cuban Missile Crisis

John F. Kennedy helped generate this crisis in 1962 by unilaterally supporting an invasion of Cuba by US-trained Cuban exiles at the Bay of Pigs in 1961 to try to overthrow the communist regime of Fidel Castro. The CIA had also made numerous attempts to assassinate Castro. The next year after the failed invasion, the Soviets and Cubans agreed to place offensive nuclear missiles on the island nation to ward off another US attack. (Unbelievably, even after the Bay of Pigs debacle, the United States continued to plot the demise of the Castro regime and the assassination of Castro.) Besides, the United States previously had installed nuclear-tipped Jupiter missiles right on the Soviet border in Turkey. The Bay of Pigs fiasco shows how unilateral executive covert action, unbeknownst to Congress and the public, can lead to immense unintended consequences—for example, a potential nuclear war between the superpowers.

In early September 1962, meeting with US Attorney General Robert Kennedy, Soviet Ambassador Anatoly Dobrynin falsely assured him that no offensive missiles, especially surface-to-surface missiles, were based in Cuba. Trying to toughen his image before the 1962 congressional elections, and with the Soviet assurance in his pocket, JFK took a bombastic public stance against any such missiles being installed.

When US intelligence discovered Soviet offensive nuclear-tipped surface-to-surface missiles had been placed in Cuba, JFK was then forced to do something about it. The administration realized that in the nuclear age, with no missile defenses, the emplacement of such missiles did not alter the strategic balance between the superpowers, because it only shortened the time that missiles could reach the United States; the nuclear destruction would be the same as if they had been launched from the Soviet Union. Robert McNamara, JFK's secretary of defense, admitted the Soviet missiles did not amount to "a serious change in the balance of power. A missile is a missile." Retaliation by the massive US nuclear arsenal likely would have deterred a Soviet first strike nuclear attack, no matter whether its missiles originated from Cuba or Soviet territory.[13] Also, JFK admitted privately that if he hadn't previously delivered such a tough speech on the missiles, he wouldn't have had to do anything about them.

In his October 22, 1962, speech, in which he demanded that the Soviet missiles be withdrawn, he blatantly focused on the unilateral, presidential Monroe Doctrine and broader American credibility in the world during the Cold War:[14]

> This secret, swift, and extraordinary build-up of Communist missiles—in an area well known to have a special and historical relationship to the United States and the nations of the Western Hemisphere, in violation of Soviet assurances, and in defiance of American and hemispheric policy—this sudden, clandestine decision to station strategic weapons for the first time outside of Soviet soil—is a deliberately provocative and unjustified change in the status quo which cannot be accepted by this country if our courage and our commitments are ever to be trusted again by either friend or foe.

In short, JFK almost got the United States embroiled in a nuclear war over nonstrategic issues just to look macho for upcoming congressional elections and because he feared impeachment if he didn't look tough enough. (Soviet leader Nikita Khrushchev had made him look weak at the Vienna summit of 1961 and the failed US-sponsored Bay of Pigs invasion the same year had made him look incompetent.) His generals wanted to invade Cuba and take out the

---

13. Quoted in Healy, *The Cult of the Presidency*, 95–96.
14. Quoted in Bueno de Mesquita and Smith, *The Spoils of War*, 230–33.

missiles, but he instead unilaterally decided to blockade Cuba (he euphemistically called it a "naval quarantine"), which is technically an act of war, without any congressional input. A recent discovery indicates that the world came even closer to nuclear war than was previously thought. Had JFK chosen to invade Cuba, US forces would have been met by tactical short-range nuclear weapons, which could have rapidly escalated the conflict to all-out nuclear war between the superpowers. And all this without any congressional say.

Finally, the broader US national credibility argument in JFK's speech has been shot down by well-known international relations specialists, whose research has shown that in a potential conflict, to determine its actions, a country usually looks at factors in the specific situation rather than at an adversary's general reputation for weakness or strength (at least one other analyst argues against their view). However, this fallacious broader national credibility argument also was a factor in LBJ's escalation of the Vietnam War, because Vietnam and Indochina were hardly strategic areas to the United States.

In the end, JFK managed to hide that he had risked nuclear war—he himself estimated the chances were one-in-three to even—for political reasons by negotiating an executive agreement that made him look like the winner of the altercation. The Soviets withdrew the offensive missiles from Cuba in exchange for a US pledge not to invade Cuba. However, unbeknownst to the world, an accompanying secret agreement may actually have tipped the balance toward the Soviets. JFK had secretly agreed to take Jupiter nuclear-tipped US missiles out of Turkey and Italy.

JFK—like other presidents, such as FDR, Harry Truman, LBJ, and Richard Nixon—relied on national security excuses to use the FBI and intelligence agencies to spy on political opponents. JFK wiretapped journalists and, citing the Cold War crises in Berlin and Southeast Asia, went after the executives of steel companies that had raised prices, wiretapping them and conducting FBI raids on their houses. His administration even wiretapped government employees and civil rights leader Martin Luther King to learn about his sex life. LBJ used the CIA to carry out surveillance on the campaign of Barry Goldwater, his Republican opponent for president, and to obtain advance copies of his campaign speeches, while he had the FBI bug Goldwater's campaign plane. Richard Nixon was forced to resign for doing similar things during Watergate.[15]

In the age of the imperial presidency, JFK also circumvented congressional legislation by using an executive order to create an agency that did a lot more for middle-class kids in the United States than it ever did for poor countries—the Peace Corps. Like the space program and race to the moon, the Peace Corps was primarily designed to be used in the propaganda war against communism.

In the spring of 1965, LBJ, JFK's successor, unilaterally used force without prior congressional approval to prevent a rebellion from restoring Juan Bosch, the Dominican Republic's democratically elected leader. Bosch had earlier been ousted by a coup, and LBJ believed he had suspect anticommunist credentials. Alleging that foreign nationals were in danger and that the communists backed the rebellion—neither was ever proved—Johnson invaded the country with 25,000 troops. Belatedly, Congress passed a resolution supporting armed US military interventions to prevent communist overthrow of governments in the Western Hemisphere.[16]

Vietnam War

Similar to the Mexican War and the Civil War, the Vietnam War was another case where executive actions caused adversary reactions, which created a fait accompli that undermined Congress's constitutional authority to decide whether to take the nation to war.

The roots of the war began when, as a barrier to communism, Harry Truman unfortunately agreed to help the French regain their colonial empire in Indochina after World War II. However, Dwight Eisenhower refused to bail out the French at the battle of Dien Bien Phu in 1954, which they lost and exited Indochina. Ike then also declined to support the Vietnam-wide election promised in the peace treaty of that same year, for fear of communist victory, and then began to aid the South Vietnamese government with money

15. Healy, *The Cult of the Presidency*, 102–04.
16. Rudalevige, *The New Imperial Presidency*, 79.

and US military "advisers." John F. Kennedy increased the number of those advisers. Some analysts say the war was lost before Lyndon B. Johnson, JFK's successor, even escalated it because JFK, in a unilateral executive covert action, was complicit in a successful coup against South Vietnamese president Ngo Dinh Diem, who was replaced by a South Vietnamese general. This coup forever destroyed the legitimacy of the South Vietnamese government, which is usually the most critical factor in winning any counterinsurgency war.

In the spring of 1964, US military planners had created a detailed plan for major attacks on North Vietnam, but Lyndon B Johnson did not think the American public would support an expansion of US involvement in the war for South Vietnam between the South Vietnamese government and North Vietnam and its Viet Cong guerrilla force in the South. By the summer of 1964, the forces of the North had occupied one-half of South Vietnam and LBJ was being criticized by Republican Barry Goldwater, his opponent in the 1964 presidential election, for this loss. LBJ needed a cause for escalating the war to burnish his image as tough on communism. Also, LBJ feared Robert F. Kennedy, a Democratic political foe, would also criticize him for being soft on communism. Thus, despite that LBJ could have avoided escalating the Vietnam War—fewer than 20 percent of Americans thought that the conflict in Vietnam was an important issue and even LBJ thought the conflict likely would become a quagmire—he nevertheless reluctantly plunged into a predictable disaster for the aforementioned political reasons.

Unbeknownst to the American public, LBJ ordered the US Navy to support secret raids on the North Vietnamese coast by South Vietnamese patrol boats and commandos. The South Vietnamese raids were designed to light up North Vietnamese radars, so that the United States could map them. In retaliation for these raids, the North Vietnamese allegedly attacked US destroyers in the Gulf of Tonkin. LBJ reported to Congress and the public about this alleged North Vietnamese "aggression," but Robert McNamara lied to Congress that the North's attacks were unprovoked and that the US Navy had nothing to do with prior South Vietnamese actions, if any existed. LBJ was in such a hurry to get on television to announce US retaliatory bombing against North Vietnam that he announced it completed before it had begun. Unfortunately, the North Vietnamese had TV sets and trained their antiaircraft weapons on US aircraft, resulting in needless American casualties. Also, LBJ was in such a rush that he did not confirm that the North Vietnamese attacks on US destroyers actually had happened. Historians now think that the first one may have occurred, causing only one small bullet hole in a US ship, but that the second one may have been a false alarm on the destroyer's radar, as even LBJ suspected at the time. These niggling facts did not impede LBJ's request for a broad congressional resolution to wage war in Southeast Asia.

Some days later, although Congress did not declare war (this constitutional requirement had fallen out of favor during the Korean War), it passed the excessively broad Gulf of Tonkin Resolution, which allowed the president, as commander in chief, to take

> all necessary measures to repel any armed attack against the forces of the United States and to prevent further aggression. . . . The United States is, therefore, prepared, as the President determines, to take all necessary steps, including the use of armed force, to assist any member or protocol state of the Southeast Asia Collective Defense Treaty requesting assistance in defense of its freedom.[17] [These protocol states included South Vietnam, Laos, and Cambodia.]

Members of Congress later said that, with this vote, they did not think they were endorsing a massive escalation of the war, but they had endorsed the wide-open delegation to the executive of authority over the war. LBJ and Richard Nixon took advantage of this opening and both drove a truck through it. The Gulf of Tonkin Resolution was not drafted by the LBJ administration in response to the aforementioned Gulf of Tonkin incidents of August 1964, but drafts go back as early as May 1964. Like James Polk's request for a declaration of war with Mexico in 1846, the resolution was ready to go pending a US provocation of war with an adversary. Such a blank check resolution was not new either; the Gulf of Tonkin Resolution was modeled on Congress's broad authorizations for possible use of force by the Eisenhower administration— the Formosa Resolution of 1955 and the Middle East Resolution of 1957.[18]

---

17. Transcript of Tonkin Gulf Resolution (1964), 88th Congress of the United State of America, 2nd Session, ourdocuments.gov.

18. Rudalevige, *The New Imperial Presidency*, 77.

In July 1965, LBJ requested $700 million in supplemental funding for the war, a clear referendum on his policy, and both chambers of Congress passed it nearly unanimously. LBJ then secretly escalated the war, so as not to imperil his domestic Great Society program then going through Congress; at one point, LBJ deployed more than a half million US forces in Vietnam. In 1968, the war became very unpopular, because LBJ had been telling the American people that the United States was winning the war, but then the North Vietnamese and Viet Cong launched the massive Tet Offensive into South Vietnam. US and South Vietnamese forces eventually beat back the onslaught and effectively eradicated the Viet Cong. Nevertheless, LBJ's credibility on the war had been destroyed. After military success in repelling the communist offensive, despite five more years of fighting, America really had no chance to win the war politically. The conflict became unpopular because it was dragging on, middle-class young men were being shanghaied into the US military via the draft to fight and die for "freedom," and LBJ paid for the war by raising taxes.

Although Nixon ran a campaign in the 1968 election that promised to end the war, he, as president, further escalated the conflict as he claimed to be deescalating it by "Vietnamization"—reducing US ground forces and turning the war over to the Vietnamese. He thus launched secret wars into enemy sanctuaries in neighboring Laos and Cambodia to make Vietnamization possible. In 1970, Nixon used American ground forces to invade Cambodia, despite a CIA analysis that concluded that such an incursion would not prevent further use of the Cambodian sanctuary by the North Vietnamese; the analysis never reached his desk because it was slow-rolled by his CIA director. Nixon later came clean about inserting ground forces into Cambodia, triggering a new wave of protests on college campuses about the unpopular war. All the while, Congress implicitly blessed these unilateral executive actions of the commander in chief by funding all such activities.

Thus, to deescalate the war by Vietnamization, Nixon felt he had to escalate in the neighboring countries of Laos and Cambodia and increase bombing to force the North Vietnamese into a negotiated settlement of the war. By such escalation, Nixon was trying to get the North Vietnamese to believe in his "madman theory"—that he would be crazy and ruthless enough in his use of deadly force to gain "peace with honor"—yet the North Vietnamese knew that antiwar sentiment in the United States was strong, thus undermining this image. After all, Nixon had been elected in the 1968 election on a platform of ending the unpopular war, and Vietnamization had been the result.

Although opponents of the war called Nixon's expansion of war making in Southeast Asia illegal, he, with some justification, pointed to the broad Gulf of Tonkin Resolution—although the Cambodian government, which was looking the other way despite secret US air and ground incursions, as long as they were not publicized, certainly did not request US armed assistance, as the resolution required. The initial articles of impeachment against Nixon had mentioned the illegal undeclared war in Cambodia, but tellingly this article was removed from the final version. However, despite the argument that the resolution covered Nixon's wars in Laos and Cambodia, it is never a good idea in a democracy to run such secret wars. Furthermore, since the resolution passed in 1964, the Congress had allowed both LBJ and Nixon a free hand in Southeast Asia by not cutting off money for the war. That lassitude was about to end.

When in 1970, Nixon finally revealed the existing air and planned ground war in Cambodia publicly, already increasing antiwar protests reached a fever pitch and Congress began to push back. In 1971, the Cooper-Church amendment to the Foreign Military Sales Act was introduced to stop funding all US land combat in Cambodia by a statutory deadline but allowed Nixon to use air power only on missions not in support of the Cambodian government. However, the amendment contained language that stated that Cooper-Church did not take away any of the executive's power. The amendment passed in the Senate and failed in the House, but it had the desired effect; Nixon withdrew US ground forces from Cambodia by the amendment's deadline. Although Congress was only pushing back around the perimeter of Nixon's war in Southeast Asia, Cooper-Church destroyed the consensus of unilateral executive war making that had held for a generation since the Korean War. It was the first time in U.S. history that Congress sought to restrict, against the president's wishes, the deployment of US forces during a war. After passing Cooper-Church in 1971, Congress then finally repealed the Gulf of Tonkin Resolution of 1964.[19] Unfortunately, after the resolution's repeal, Nixon merely continued

---

19. Barron, *Waging War*, 318–31.

the war in Southeast Asia unconstitutionally under the inflated conception of his role as commander in chief.

Just before the 1972 election, Henry Kissinger, Nixon's national security adviser, had declared that "peace is at hand." Therefore, after his reelection in November of 1972, the nation was surprised to learn, in December 1972, that Nixon had begun the most massive bombing campaign of the war—the Christmas bombing of North Vietnam. As a result, legislation to end the war began making its way through Congress as soon as it convened in early January 1973. By the end of that month, Nixon finally announced a peace agreement with the North Vietnamese.[20] Congress's pushback had seemed to quicken the war's end.

However, even though Congress had disapproved of further bombing in Cambodia, Nixon continued to bomb there. Congress attached a ban on further funding for bombing to a critical debt limit bill, and Nixon was forced to end military operations in the region by August 1973.

After Nixon had signed the peace accord with North Vietnam in the summer of 1973, Congress cut off funding for US activities in the entire theater of Indochina, over Nixon's veto, so that he could not resume bombing if a violation of the peace agreement occurred—which Nixon intended to do. Nixon had made a secret promise to South Vietnam that if North Vietnam violated the peace accord, which it was doing by the spring of 1975, the United States would use military force to beat back any attack. Due to the congressional funding cut off, Gerald Ford, Nixon's successor, could do nothing to stop the North Vietnamese from taking over South Vietnam. Ford asked for a resumption of such funding, but the nation's legislature, tired of endless futile war, declined. Congress was even afraid that the president would restart the war with any new statute that merely authorized evacuation of Americans and friendly South Vietnamese, so it passed no law allowing it. Congress thus taught the president a needed lesson about secret, unilateral, and unconstitutional executive war making.

Congress also cut off the Ford administration's funding of Angolan rebels trying to overthrow the country's government because the administration had

---

20. Rudalevige, *The New Imperial Presidency*, 82.

failed to report this covert action to Congress, as required by the Hughes-Ryan Amendment. This was an extraordinary time of congressional pushback against executive action in foreign policy, made tenable by the most unpopular war in American history. Congress in the future would be reluctant to use funding cutoffs to end presidential military action once begun, thereby risking being accused of putting America's armed forces in danger while in battle.

Congressional Resurgence After Vietnam and Watergate

The Great Depression, which greatly increased the federal government's intrusion into the American economy and society in the form of a newly created welfare state, and World War II, which created a national security state, both vastly expanded the executive branch and thus made congressional control over it much more difficult. After the abuse of executive power during the Vietnam War and Watergate, Congress passed a web of laws meant to both constrain the now-imperial presidency and rejuvenate its own institutions, processes, and influence. For a time, the legislative body did restrain the executive, but the constraint began to erode with the Reagan presidency, beginning in 1981, and then almost collapsed after 9/11, when the George W. Bush administration purposefully tried to roll back the Vietnam/Watergate constraints and substitute an imperial presidency on steroids—using the Unitary Theory of the Executive as justification.

Over Nixon's veto, Congress passed the War Powers Resolution, which attempted to limit the president's ability to commit the US military into armed conflict without the approval of Congress. In its statement of purpose and policy, the resolution stipulated that the executive could only commit American forces to combat by a congressional declaration of war, legislative statutory authorization, or in the event of a national emergency created by an attack on the United States, its territories or possessions, or its armed forces. The resolution required the president to "consult with Congress" before the use of force "in every possible instance." In the last scenario of national emergency, the resolution required the president to notify Congress within forty-eight hours of introducing US forces into hostilities, or situations in which imminent hostilities might occur, and to automatically withdraw them within sixty to ninety days if the Congress had not voted to approve of the intervention via a statutory authorization or declaration of war. At any time before that period was over, Congress could vote to end the military action.

Although presidents and some proponents of executive power have argued that the resolution is unconstitutional because it constrains the unilateral executive power as commander in chief to make war, the resolution generally followed the framers' intent at the Constitutional Convention to require offensive war to be approved by Congress in advance but to allow the president to take rapid action in self-defense. As legal scholar Bruce Fein has noted, both the text and legislative history of the law indicate that the resolution should not be interpreted as altering the original constitutional war powers.[21]

If the resolution is unconstitutional at all, it might be because it expanded the definition of self-defense to include US forces—most likely overseas nowadays—which is much past merely an attack on the United States or its territories and possessions, or because it contains a legislative veto, which was later ruled unconstitutional by the Supreme Court in an unrelated case. However, the statement of purpose and policy as a statement of legislative intent is clearly mostly constitutional. However, if this statement is not legally binding, the remainder of the resolution seems unconstitutional because it allows the executive to commit the US military to offensive military action without prior congressional approval.

Post-resolution presidents, if they did not just flout the resolution, they incorrectly applied the forty-eight-hour notification and ninety-day withdrawal provisions to offensive, unilateral military adventures they had undertaken, rather than only to military actions in self-defense as the resolution intended. In other words, they latched onto the aforementioned unconstitutional interpretation of the resolution. After all, the framers at the Constitutional Convention and the authors of the War Powers Resolution both required advance congressional approval for offensive military actions but allowed the president to take self-defense actions. After the executive abuses during the Vietnam

---

21. Fein, Comments at the "Debate Between John Yoo and Bruce Fein on the War Power."

War, the resolution was meant to restrict even executive military actions over-seas taken after an adversary's initial attack.

In general, the War Powers Resolution failed to curb unconstitutional unilateral executive war because of presidential flouting of the law and judicial non-enforcement. Presidents often carefully did not start the ninety-day clock running when they reported to Congress that they were sending troops into hostilities or situations in which hostilities were imminent. Congress has been negligent in enforcing the War Powers Resolution either by declaring that the law's clock had started when the president made the initial troop deployment or by simply cutting off funding for the particular military action. Also, the modern-day judiciary has been reluctant to insert itself into political battles between the legislative and executive branches, especially when national se-curity is claimed.

After Vietnam and Watergate, Congress became more active in foreign pol-icy. Disgusted by presidential dealings with repressive regimes, Congress began to use foreign aid and trade as weapons to prod such countries to improve their human rights records. Congress set up an office in the State Department to monitor the human rights records of countries asking for US military aid. Congress then cut off aid to some nations perpetrating human rights abuses. In 1974, Congress passed the Jackson-Vanik Amendment requiring the Soviet Union to increase the emigration of Jews in order to get Most Favored Nation trade status with the United States. Also, Congress cut funding for the United Nations.[22]

US intelligence agencies had tried to assassinate foreign leaders, and despite finding no links to foreign communists, had illegally spied on American anti-war and civil rights groups (including Martin Luther King), kept dossiers on them, and attempted to sabotage their efforts using dirty tricks—all of which congressional investigations in the mid-1970s uncovered. To head off con-gressional legislation, President Ford issued an executive order banning CIA assassinations. Also, Congress rebelled against the assumption for decades that the president had the inherent power to conduct intelligence operations without congressional oversight; Congress created intelligence committees

---

22. Rudalevige, *The New Imperial Presidency*, 126.

and an independent oversight board, in 1976–1977 and 1980, respectively, to monitor those agencies and their covert operations.

The Nixon White House voraciously wiretapped and claimed inherent executive power to wiretap at will domestically in cases where national security was involved. Yet there is no executive power not enumerated in the Constitution, and there is no national security exemption in the document's Fourth Amendment, which requires a judicial warrant based on probable cause that a crime has been committed for searches against citizens and non-citizens. For these reasons, in 1978, Congress passed the Foreign Intelligence and Surveillance Act (FISA), which was designed to end spying by intelligence agencies on people in the United States without court-approved warrants, as the Fourth Amendment requires. The passage of this law showed that Congress could limit the executive's power of surveillance, and the president would acquiesce to it. Ford's attorney general, with Ford's approval, helped Congress write the statute, and Jimmy Carter, Ford's successor, signed it into law.

Arthur Schlesinger, Jr.'s "imperial president" was not confined to national security. Once a president like Nixon decided he could run unconstitutional unilateral wars, he then began to think that he had the power to do anything. In the book, *The Imperial Presidency*, Schlesinger concluded the president now resorted to

> the all-purpose invocation of "national security," the insistence on executive secrecy, the withholding of information from Congress, the refusal to spend funds appropriated by Congress, the attempted intimidation of the press, the use of the White House as a base for espionage and sabotage directed against the political opposition—all signified the extension of the extension of the imperial presidency from foreign to domestic affairs.[23]

Schlesinger thus tied the domestic abuses of the Watergate scandal to such executive aggrandizement in the national security arena. And the facts of the Watergate scandal bore out Schlesinger's connection. Nixon originally ordered the creation of the "plumbers" dirty tricks squad, a group of ex-CIA operatives

---

23. Arthur M. Schlesinger, Jr., *The Imperial Presidency* (New York: Houghton Mifflin, 1973).

controlled by the White House to "plug leaks" associated with the Pentagon Papers and secret war in Cambodia, the existence of which was slowly bleeding to the media. J. Edgar Hoover's FBI traditionally had done illegal political spying for presidents, but had grown cautious during the LBJ and Nixon administrations out of fears of bad publicity; Nixon's plumbers, directed from the White House, filled this void. In 1973, John Ehrlichman, Nixon's top domestic adviser, testified that the plumbers' roguishness, including their burglaries, were "well within the President's inherent constitutional powers," because they were done for reasons of national security. Attorney General John Mitchell came up with a similar rationale.[24] The plumbers eventually broke into the Democratic National Headquarters to plant listening devices to get potential dirt on the opposition's weak 1972 election effort.

When the Watergate burglars were caught red-handed by police, one of many presidential tape recordings showed that Nixon tried to cover up the White House connection to the dirty tricks squad by attempting to get the CIA to stanch the FBI investigation into the burglary by telling the bureau that investigators had just run across a CIA national security operation. Although the CIA ultimately refused to do so, public release of the "smoking gun" tape of Nixon talking about such a cover up fueled the House's impeachment proceedings against Nixon and also led to his quick resignation. (Conservatives have made the argument, not without merit, that Nixon was forced to resign for conducting surveillance of opponents, which Democratic predecessors had also undertaken: FDR and Truman had illegally ordered the FBI to snoop on their political opponents, JFK illegally wiretapped businessmen and even raided their houses, and LBJ illegally installed listening devices on the campaign plane of Barry Goldwater, his Republican opponent in the 1964 election.)

Yet the central issue was not Watergate, but the expansion of executive power, according to historian Arthur Schlesinger and political scientist Andrew Rudalevige. People had lost confidence in unilateral executive government. In 1960, more than 70 percent of Americans believed that the government did "what is right" all or most of time, but less than 30 percent thought so in 1980. The rapid decline in trust of the federal government led to the success

---

24. Quoted in Rudalevige, *The New Imperial Presidency*, 68–69.

of presidential candidates espousing anti-government rhetoric—for example, Jimmy Carter and Ronald Reagan.

Running covert operations out of the White House usually generates catastrophic outcomes—as Watergate and Reagan's Iran-Contra scandal proved. Such operations done by the unaccountable CIA are risky on a good day, but when they become "politicized" by being run by the White House or National Security Council staff, disaster becomes even more likely. During the Nixon administration, the staffs of the White House, National Security Council, and Executive Office of the President grew rapidly. The paranoid Nixon believed that because Democratic presidents had controlled the huge executive branch bureaucracy for eight years (ignoring that the Eisenhower administration, in which he was vice president, had controlled it for the eight years before that), the federal bureaucracy would try to thwart his initiatives. He therefore wanted to build up the presidential bureaucracy that he controlled to counter the larger executive branch bureaucracy. For example, the National Security Council under Henry Kissinger, not the State Department, ran Nixon's major foreign policy initiatives.

George Washington had questionably withheld information from Congress on a catastrophic military campaign against Native Americans in 1792 and on the negotiation of the Jay Treaty in 1796, and Dwight Eisenhower dressed up the suspect practice by calling it "executive privilege" and applied it to policy deliberations for the entire executive branch (based on the model of lawyer-client privilege). However, Nixon tried to expand it further and claim it shielded what turned out to be criminal conduct, revealed in his White House tape recordings, from being subpoenaed by Congress and the special prosecutor. All such claims are based on the fictitious "inherent power" of the president. The Supreme Court unanimously recognized the constitutionally questionable, previously informal doctrine of executive privilege, especially in cases of alleged national security, but excluded from it shielding potential presidential criminal conduct. Nixon's inclination was to resist the court's ruling and not turn over the tapes, but the unanimous decision discouraged that course of action.

Unfortunately, future presidents would exploit this court-made, out-of-whole-cloth law to make wide claims of executive privilege. Initially, after the darkness of Watergate, executive privilege got a bad name and was seldom used during the "open presidencies" of Gerald Ford and Jimmy Carter. But the executive practice of withholding information from Congress came back—even if the term "executive privilege" was sometimes avoided.

Congress did occasionally push back in cases of the executive withholding of information. In 1973, the Congress wanted to know if the confidential funds for White House Special Projects had been used to fund the plumbers in their dirty tricks campaign. When the White House refused to produce the requested vouchers and expenditures for the account, Congress deleted all funds for the account.[25]

In 1971, in the case *New York Times Co. v. United States*, the Supreme Court rejected Nixon's attempts—under his alleged constitutional power as commander in chief and his authority to conduct foreign policy—to stop the *New York Times* from publishing the Pentagon Papers, a secret government history of the Vietnam War, thus upholding the First Amendment right of free speech over government "prior restraint" of publication. Furthermore, the Constitution's framers intended to restrict the president's powers in foreign policy, as well as to limit his authority as commander in chief to being the chief general on the battlefield. In another case, the court also rejected Nixon's claim of authority to conduct warrantless wiretapping on anyone suspected of being a danger to domestic national security.

Congress also pushed back against civil liberties violations by passing the Non-Detention Act of 1971, a repeal of the McCarran Internal Security Act of 1950, which allowed the president during internal security emergencies to lock up likely subversives. The Non-Detention Act prohibited the president from detaining citizens unless Congress passed a law. Nixon was motivated to sign this law because of revelations of government domestic spying and dirty tricks by security and intelligence agencies against antiwar groups. Also, Congress passed the National Emergencies Act of 1974 putting a time limit on all future executive emergency powers and permitting Congress to terminate them earlier with a concurrent resolution. Furthermore, the law ended, by 1976, the four lingering states of emergency.[26] Such vast emergency powers, according to a Senate committee, would have allowed the president to rule the country

---

25. Fisher, *Presidential Spending Power*, 211–12.
26. Healy, *The Cult of the Presidency*, 112.

without going through normal constitutional procedures; the executive could declare martial law, seize property, nationalize industries, limit communications or travel, or order the detention of various groups (as FDR did during World War II with Japanese-Americans). The International Emergency Economic Powers Act of 1977 was designed to restrict executive emergency powers to control international and domestic financial transactions, limiting strictures on domestic transactions to the time period of declared war. However, the executive has abused the law to declare at least thirty states of emergency since 1979 to terminate trade with or freeze assets of unsavory countries, sometimes unilaterally acting when Congress didn't—as Reagan did against Nicaragua.[27]

Although a laudable clawback of congressional delegation of power, the Constitution never authorized any general states of emergency imposed by the president, because the founders feared the federal government would abuse such broad powers. The Constitution only allowed Congress to suspend habeas corpus in times of invasion or insurrection.

Despite the rising protests when Nixon announced his invasion of Cambodia in 1970, Congress nevertheless approved his proposal that the Bureau of the Budget be replaced by the Office of Management and Budget, which the Senate Government Operations Committee later said had morphed into a "super department with enormous authority over all of the activities of the Federal Government. Its Director has become in effect a Deputy President who exercises vital Presidential powers." Furthermore, whereas the Bureau of the Budget had always been perceived as staffed by highly qualified nonpartisan professionals, the Office of Management and Budget began to be deemed populated with highly politicized political hacks.

By 1973, because of Nixon's excessive use of the impoundment of congressionally appropriated funds, Congress was ready to take back some of its lost budgetary authority.[28]

Although presidential authority to impound congressionally appropriated funds is not found in the Constitution, Congress had tolerated a very limited use of it for decades, beginning when Teddy Roosevelt was president, because a few changes in circumstance could occur during any budget year,

---

27. Rudalevige, *The New Imperial Presidency*, 113–14, 172.
28. Fisher, *Presidential Spending Power*, 46–56.

requiring corresponding executive financial adjustment. Then LBJ had begun impounding funds that Congress had appropriated but that he just did not want to spend—about 6.7 percent of the federal budget. Claiming inherent executive power to impound funds, Nixon even more ruthlessly resorted to an unprecedented level of impoundment—a whopping 20 percent of federal discretionary spending—prompting a suspicious Congress to refuse to adopt his unilateral budget ceiling for lack of agreement on how to limit executive discretion. Nixon was basically saying that if Congress failed to agree to his views on the budget, he had the unilateral power to act on his own—exercising "inherent" executive authority over federal spending not in the framers' original basic law.[29] This action was an unconstitutional line-item veto by another name and threatened to allow a president to nullify Congress's constitutional appropriation power. Nixon was essentially refusing to execute congressionally passed law with which he disagreed. Some in the legislature warned that such executive usurpation of the power to legislate would render Congress an empty branch of government.

Consequently, in 1974, to reclaim lost congressional budgetary power, Congress passed the Congressional Budget and Impoundment Control Act and the Congressional Budget Act, which limited the president's power to impound funds and also set up a unified congressional budget process to compete with the unified executive budget process that had been instituted by Warren Harding in the early 1920s. Each house of Congress set up a budget committee to create a budget resolution to set congressional spending limits and priorities.

Also, Congress passed the Federal Election Campaign Act of 1974, which was supposed to take big money out of presidential politics, but failed. In 1978, The Ethics in Government Act authorized special prosecutors to investigate senior officials of the executive branch.[30] The Freedom of Information Act (FOIA) Amendments of 1974, Presidential Records Act, and the Presidential Materials and Preservation Act were designed to make executive branch activities more transparent to the public. The Privacy Act of 1974 protected citizens

---

29. Fleming, *The Great Divide*, 389; and Fisher, *Presidential Spending Power*, 176–77.

30. Jeet Heer, "Don't Just Impeach Trump. End the Imperial Presidency," *New Republic*, August 12, 2017, https://newrepublic.com/article/144297/dont-just-impeach-trump-end-imperial-presidency.

from government abuse of data they collected from the public.[31] Finally, the Congress began televising its floor debates to counter presidential dominance of the media and thus public opinion.

Congressional Resurgence Did Not Last

Much of the reassertion of congressional authority in the 1970s did not last. The bald assertion of executive power during the Vietnam War and Watergate scandal had resulted in pushback from Congress, but as those crises faded in memory, congressional checks on the executive waned; so did those of the judiciary and the media on the president.

In 1975, although Gerald Ford, Nixon's successor after he resigned, followed the War Powers Resolution during the attempted rescue of crew of the ship *Mayaguez* who were kidnapped by communist Cambodia, it was only because the law was new. Subsequent presidents have not followed the resolution very closely or at all. This problem of compliance will be discussed later. After the 9/11 attacks, intelligence agencies once again got out of hand and spied on Americans unconstitutionally without warrants—violating the 1978 FISA law because President George W. Bush believed congressionally passed laws could not interfere with his power as commander in chief during wartime. The legal regimes on campaign finance and special prosecutors have since been modified.

In 1973, because Nixon believed that conscripting middle-class kids into the military had generated most of the virulent opposition to the Vietnam War (and he was likely correct), he ended the draft and went to an all-volunteer professional military. The military, trying to avoid another quagmire like Vietnam, put many key support functions into the reserves, which both LBJ and Nixon had been reluctant to call up during the war for fear of disrupting the civilian economy and society and exacerbating already strong opposition to the war. Unfortunately, this migration of functions to the reserves did not keep the United States out of future wars, and an eventual reversal of this transfer by the George W. Bush administration once again made it

---

31. Rudalevige, *The New Imperial Presidency*, 7.

much easier for politicians to involve the US military in many more overseas misadventures.

The Case-Zablocki Act of 1972 required the president to give Congress every year a list of new international agreements. Presidents have never fully complied with this law, unilaterally exempting national security directives and other national security arrangements.

Although Congress in 1974 set up its own budget process and created its own Congressional Budget Office to provide non-partisan budget information, the president has nevertheless dominated the federal budget process ever since the unified executive budget was created in the 1920s. Each year, because the executive branch has become so massive, Congress usually only incrementally changes the massive president's budget on the margins. The new congressional budget process worked for a time but later was manipulated by the Reagan administration and then broke down all together. Many times, budget resolutions and appropriation bills are not passed in time for the start of a new fiscal year, necessitating continuing spending at the prior year levels until an omnibus bill combining most or all appropriations is passed. The must-pass omnibus bill gives the president greater leverage over what budget becomes law. The Congressional Budget and Impoundment Act of 1974 was designed to instill budget discipline in Congress, so that it could push back against presidential domination of the budget process. However, beginning with the Reagan administration hijacking the congressional process, the framework led to an era of budget indiscipline, large annual fiscal deficits, and massive public debt accumulation that began in 1982, Reagan's first budget year in office, and continues to this day.

After Nixon's aggressive unconstitutional impoundments of congressional appropriations, the 1974 budget and impoundment law was supposed to rein in the practice. However, Gerald Ford, Nixon's successor, somehow found new impoundment authority in the act; to test the new law, attempted presidential impoundments spiked to levels even above those of Nixon.[32] However, Congress was able to beat back most of Ford's impoundment attempts.

This episode shows that clear legislative intent—in this case, even the word "control" in the title of the new law—is no barrier to the imperial president

---

32. Fisher, *Presidential Spending Power*, 200–01, 262.

in attempting to further aggrandize power. To this day, Congress has never formulated a means by which to counter executive budgetary impoundment, reprogramming, fund transfers, unauthorized funding commitments, and covert financing. Thus, sometimes Congress authorizes and appropriates funds that the president never spends; other times Congress can discover that it is required to pay for executive branch commitments that it never authorized.

Not only did most of the legislative pushback of the 1970s wane, congressional oversight of executive branch activities actually declined. A study by one political scientist showed that congressional committees convened only half as many days in 1997 as they did in 1975 and that fewer of those days were spent conducting oversight. Congressional reauthorization of executive branch activities went from an agency-by-agency basis to an omnibus bulk basis, or sometimes was even put on autopilot with recurring waivers of authorization provided during the annual appropriations process.

One factor leading to reduced oversight may have been a ruling by the Supreme Court in 1983 (*INS v. Chadha*) declaring unconstitutional the legislative veto, which affected 200 statutory provisions. Congress had been trying to lasso the monstrous executive bureaucracy by reviewing regulations and vetoing them by a majority vote of one or both chambers. These laws were designed to monitor the powers it had delegated to the executive branch. The court ruled that laws with legislative vetoes violated the presentment clause in Article I of the Constitution, which governs how a bill becomes law. The basic law says that both chambers of Congress need to pass the bill, and the president needs to sign rather than veto it, but it doesn't say anything about a congressional veto of executive enforcement of the bill without the possibility of an executive veto. (Of course, the court said nothing about the president's similar evasion of the proper process by using funding impoundments, attaching signing statements to laws, and issuing executive orders and proclamations not grounded in congressionally passed laws.) However, some analysts convincingly argued that Congress never had the will to veto many executive regulations anyway, since the legislative body had delegated broad regulatory authority to the executive branch in the first place to avoid political responsibility for hard decisions.[33] The solution to the problem of congres-

---

33. Rudalevige, *The New Imperial Presidency*, 177–78.

sional oversight of executive branch actions was not inserting a legislative veto into laws but instead not delegating the congressional responsibility for detailed law making to the executive branch in the first place.

Donald R. Wolfensberger, former staff director of the House Rules Committee, best summed up the result of the parchment barriers that Congress erected after Vietnam and Watergate to attempt to rein in the executive branch:

> Despite all of the congressional muscle flexing in the 1970s in response to the imperial presidency, close observers have argued that Congress is just as deferential and acquiescent to the president today on foreign policy matters as it was pre-Nixon.[34]

This summation could apply almost as much to the domestic sphere as well.

The Cold War Comes to a Close

As Vietnam and Watergate drifted into memory, presidents resumed their unconstitutional executive war making, which had started with Truman's unilateral war making in Korea. At first, this was done in circumstances that might be excused. In his four years in power, Jimmy Carter conducted only one direct military intervention—the military's botched attempt to rescue hostages taken at the US embassy in Iran. Technically, overseas embassies are the territory of their home government, and Iranian "students," backed by the new radical ruler Ayatollah Ruhollah Khomeini, in response to America's long support of the brutal ruler there, seized the embassy and held hostage American diplomats. Negotiations failed to get them out. Under the framers' original conception of the constitutional war power, Carter could claim that he was taking action in self-defense of the territory of the United States when he, without notifying Congress, sent a justifiable helicopter mission to rescue the diplomats, which ultimately failed.

In another ambiguous episode, Carter did abrogate the mutual defense treaty with Taiwan and instead recognized its nemesis, the Peoples Republic of China, completing the rapprochement with communist China that Nixon

---

34. Donald R. Wolfensberger, *A Brief History of Congressional Reform Efforts*, Bipartisan Policy Center, February 22, 2013.

had started but had since lapsed into a moribund status. The Supreme Court refused to stop this nixing of a congressionally ratified treaty. The Constitution is clear on the requirements to approve a treaty but is silent on how to get rid of one that has outlived its usefulness. (This problem is similar to the Constitution's silence on how to get rid of presidential appointees once Congress has confirmed them.) Thus, if the Constitution were to be strictly followed, a new treaty should probably be ratified that abrogates or changes significantly the prior one, but this route was not taken in this case, thus setting a precedent for future scrapping of unwanted treaties. Using this precedent, George W. Bush scrapped the Anti-Ballistic Missile (ABM) Treaty in 2001 to pursue missile defenses in an unbridled way. In neither case did Congress reverse executive action.

In general, Ronald Reagan, Carter's successor, was much less deferential to congressional power than Carter had been. Reagan was a zealous rhetorical proponent of small government who contradictorily strengthened executive power. Yet the executive branch already was overwhelmingly the largest branch of the massive federal government.

Accordingly, Reagan set about ignoring the War Powers Resolution. In 1981, just after Reagan took office, he began inserting the US Navy into waters claimed by Libya to attempt to provoke Muammar Gaddafi into a conflict. Reagan regarded Gaddafi as a stooge of the Soviet Union and may have been trying to create an active enemy to justify his massive peacetime defense spending increases (so much for small government). He got one. Gaddafi had theretofore sponsored terrorist attacks mainly in Europe. Throughout the 1980s, Reagan continued provoking Gaddafi with military actions, and Gaddafi continued responding with surreptitious terrorist attacks—now against Americans—which culminated with the Pan Am 103 bombing over Lockerbie, Scotland. Reagan was good at putting forces in harm's way without congressional approval and good at creating new enemies for the United States. In 1986, responding to Gaddafi's La Belle disco bombing of US servicemen in Germany, which in turn was a response to Reagan's military provocation of Gaddafi, Reagan launched a bombing raid on Libya that ignored the War Powers Resolution's requirement that he notify Congress within forty-eight hours of taking military action. Instead, Reagan invoked his supposed inherent constitutional power as commander in chief to wage unilateral executive war.

In 1982, claiming authority under the Constitution as commander in chief, Reagan sent US Marines into harm's way as a peacekeeping force in Lebanon to secure Israel's gains from invading the country. Clearly, this deployment of forces was to an area of "imminent hostilities" and thus was covered by the War Powers Resolution.

Like many peacekeeping missions, this one got sucked into the conflict, hardly as a neutral party. US Marines were essentially operating with the Christian forces in the Lebanese civil war. In response to the bomb planted by Islamist forces that killed 241 US service members in a barracks in Beirut, Congress passed a law that confined the mission to a defensive nature and set the War Powers Resolution clock running. Reagan eventually ignominiously withdrew the forces from a nation in chaos before the congressionally imposed, but extended, deadline. According to Osama bin Laden, this episode taught him that killing a few Americans could motivate the United States to withdraw from an overseas occupation. After bin Laden became enraged by the later US military presence in the holy land of Saudi Arabia, Reagan's prior withdrawal under fire from Lebanon motivated him to wage war against the United States to try to compel its ultimate exit from the Middle East. Thus, Regan would have been better not to have initiated the unilateral executive military mission in the first place.

Two days after the barracks bombing in Lebanon, Reagan unilaterally, without notifying Congress or getting its approval, ordered an invasion of the island nation of Grenada after a pro-Cuban coup. Reagan claimed that this distraction was done to rescue American medical students who had never appeared to be in danger. Although the United States won the war against the tiny country, it faced unexpected resistance from Cubans there and experienced infamous communication failures among US military services that required calling back to the Pentagon on a pay phone to coordinate interservice operations. Congress threatened to invoke the War Powers time clock, but Reagan withdrew US forces before the legislature could act.

Later, capitalizing on the ineptitude of military communication and coordination during his invasion of Grenada, Reagan tightened and unified control over the US military by congressional passage of the Goldwater-Nichols Act of 1986. The law eliminated the chiefs of the individual military services (the Joint Chiefs of Staff) from the chain of command, thereby strengthening direct control by the president and the secretary of defense over US forces in various military theaters around the world.

Illustrating how a president's inflammatory rhetoric and actions can erode Congress's constitutional responsibility to decide on whether the nation will have war or peace, Reagan, in November 1983, decided to conduct the most massive nuclear command and control training exercise in American history. Known as Able Archer 83, this exercise not so secretly simulated a NATO nuclear war with the Soviet Union. When combined with Reagan's dangerously bellicose anti-Soviet rhetoric since taking office in 1981, the Soviets thought US leaders moving to secure locations for the simulation might be more than just an exercise. In the second closest nuclear war scare after the Cuban Missile Crisis of 1962, the alarmed Soviets made unexpected war preparations, including putting their nuclear forces on alert. Reagan found all this appropriately alarming but was in denial that he had contributed heavily to Soviet nuclear angst. He incredulously asked Bud McFarlane, his national security adviser, how the Soviets could possibly believe that he wanted to start a nuclear war: "Do you suppose they really believe that? I don't see how they could believe that—but it's something to think about."[35] However, to his credit, Reagan was scared enough by this episode, and influenced by a fictional movie he watched around the same time about the massive effects of a nuclear war, that he began overtures to the Soviets in nuclear arms control that would eventually result in the Intermediate Nuclear Forces (INF) Treaty, which eliminated intermediate-range nuclear weapons from Europe. At this writing, President Trump seems to be heading to unilateral abrogation of this pact.

In the worst constitutional scandal so far in American history, Reagan tried to nullify Congress's most important remaining constitutional power of funding activities of the federal government in the Iran-Contra affair. After the Reagan administration's evasion of the first Boland Amendment, which banned the CIA or Defense Department from using any funds to overthrow the Sandinista government in Nicaragua, Congress tightened strictures on aid to the opposition Contras, who were trying to oust that government. In October 1984, Congress passed the second Boland Amendment, which prohibited any US funds from being used to assist the Contra rebels. The

---

35. Quoted in Suri, *The Impossible Presidency*, 247–48.

law prohibited the use of funds by any government agency "which would have the effect of supporting, directly or indirectly, military or paramilitary operations in Nicaragua by any nation, group, organization, movement, or individual."[36] The statute dictated that no money available to "the Central Intelligence Agency, the Department of Defense, or any other agency or entity involved in intelligence activities" could be employed to support the Contras.[37] But that was only one-half of the Iran-Contra scandal.

Reagan administration officials in the National Security Council, including two national security advisers, helped violate the Arms Export Control Act, a criminal statute, to sell weapons to terrorist-sponsoring Iran at inflated prices. They did so in the hopes of freeing hostages still held in Lebanon by Iranian-sponsored terrorist groups in retaliation for the Reagan administration's ill-fated meddling in Lebanon during the early 1980s. (Knowing that the United States would ransom hostages, the terrorists simply kidnapped more people and even murdered one hostage—why it is not a good idea for governments to pay such ransoms.) These administration officials then used the profits from the illegal weapon sales to Iran to illegally and unconstitutionally fund the ineffective and thuggish Contras in Nicaragua. Reagan clearly knew about the Iran part of the Iran-Contra scandal, but it is unclear whether he knew about the diversion of the profits to the Contras. However, even if he did not know about this part of the caper, he helped National Security Council officials raise money for the Contras from wealthy individuals and other countries, such as Taiwan and Saudi Arabia. Even this violated the second Boland Amendment, because the salaries of Reagan and his aides, who were indirectly funding the Contras, were paid by the federal government. Therefore, if nothing else, Reagan knew that US officials were indirectly supporting the Contras in violation of a congressionally passed statute. Even more important, denying the US Treasury the profits from the Iranian arms sales and sending them directly to the Contras and soliciting money from private donors and other governments for the Contras violated the Constitution's stipulation that all monies for federal activities are required to be appropriated by Congress.[38]

---

36. Quoted in Healy, *The Cult of the Presidency*, 122.
37. Quoted in Mayer, *With the Stroke of a Pen*, 175–76.
38. Rudalevige, *The New Imperial Presidency*, 157.

According to Malcom Byrne, "The president approved every significant facet of the Iran arms deals, and he encouraged conduct by top aides that had the same aim and outcome as the diversion—to subsidize the Contra war despite the congressional prohibition on U.S. aid."[39] Reagan's aides believed they were carrying out the intent of his policies—his fixation on freeing hostages in Lebanon and assisting the Contras in overthrowing the Nicaraguan government—and had his consent.

After the second Boland Amendment passed, the Reagan administration transferred control of the Contra-aid covert operation from the CIA to the National Security Council and later argued that the Boland Amendment didn't apply to that White House organization because it wasn't in the intelligence community, as defined in other statutes and executive orders. However, as noted, the Boland Amendment referred to any "agency or entity involved in intelligence activities." The National Security Council may not be an agency in the intelligence community, but that is irrelevant because it was an entity involved in intelligence activities before and during the Iran-Contra affair, especially after control of the Nicaraguan covert action was transferred to it from the CIA.

The Hughes-Ryan Amendment of 1974 required that no funds could be spent on a covert activity unless the president issued a finding that the operation is important to the national security of the United States and reported a description and the scope of the activity to appropriate congressional committees in a "timely fashion." The Intelligence Oversight Act of 1980 also stipulated that the president had to report covert operations to congressional intelligence committees in a "timely fashion." In the Iran-Contra affair, Reagan's findings were either nonexistent or retroactive for covert operations that were already underway. The findings were not reported to Congress.[40] Reagan's aggressive CIA director, William Casey, a veteran of the swashbuckling Office of Strategic Services during World War II, was more than happy to dispense with all these congressional restraints on covert operations.

This secret war in Nicaragua in violation of a congressional prohibition was constitutionally more suspect than Nixon's secret wars in Laos and Cam-

---

39. Malcom Byrne, *Iran-Contra: Reagan's Scandal and the Unchecked Abuse of Presidential Power* (Lawrence: University Press of Kansas, 2014), 42, 44.

40. Mayer, *With the Stroke of a Pen*, 174–76.

bodia, because at least Nixon could initially fall back on the broad Gulf of Tonkin Resolution authorizing US military action in Southeast Asia. The violation of Congress's most important remaining power to appropriate federal funds (as I have shown, the war power has become defunct) was probably more severe than Nixon's obstructing of justice to cover up petty illegal campaign dirty tricks during Watergate. Therefore, Reagan administration officials had gone to the core of the US Constitution and violated one of the major checks and balances.

In addition, to support his policies in Central America, Reagan began using domestic spying to further his policy agenda by using FBI surveillance against groups in the United States that opposed such policies, despite the publicized abuses of such conduct in the 1970s. As with Vietnam-era antiwar groups, his administration hoped to discover that these groups were either violent or controlled by foreign powers. However, as occurred during the Vietnam War, the government could find little such evidence.[41]

Although Richard Nixon had rhetorically started the "war on drugs," Reagan took advantage of the Military Cooperation with Law Enforcement Officials Act in 1981 to get the military involved in training and equipping local police forces in combating commerce in illegal drugs. During the 1980s and 1990s, the war on drugs began the militarization of the police, which now use military equipment and tactics for ordinary law enforcement. Politicians used such visible measures to show they were serious about battling illicit drugs, but civil liberties suffered while the drugs continued to flow into the United States to satisfy insatiable demand.[42]

Congress's budgetary power was further eroded when trying to combat the huge budget deficits arising from Reagan's fraudulent tax cuts (a playbook he imitated from what Nixon did prior to the 1972 election). Reagan's tax cuts were combined with federal spending increases, which included unprecedented and unneeded massive defense spending hikes during peacetime, accelerated spending on the elderly, and ballooning farm price supports. The government's national debt tripled during Reagan's presidency from $1 trillion to $3 trillion and thus federal intrusion into the economy increased, especially

---

41. Rudalevige, *The New Imperial Presidency*, 180.
42. Healy, *The Cult of the Presidency*, 226–28.

for future generations who had to pay back the principal and interest on the massive federal borrowing.[43] The federal government actually increased as a percentage of the value of the economy (GDP) during the Reagan's two terms as a "small government" president. The budget deficits and accumulating debt became so yawning that Reagan had to raise taxes in six out of his eight years as president, thus giving him the lowest net tax cut of any Republican president since World War II.

As a result, Congress restrained its own power over spending by enacting deficit-reduction targets, caps on spending, and "pay-as-you-go (PAYGO) rules," which required equivalent spending reductions or tax increases if new spending programs or tax cuts were adopted. Such accounting restrictions would be needed to deal with budget deficits, first during the Reagan administration and continuing during the terms of many presidents. For example, George W. Bush followed Reagan's bad precedent by creating big deficits by similar fake tax cuts accompanied by spending increases. Barack Obama, his successor, had to grapple with Bush's deficits and didn't excel at budget restraint until he proposed "sequestration"—automatic, across-the-board cuts in spending—which he didn't think would ever be activated. Sequestration was indeed triggered when the Democrats and Republicans couldn't agree on a budget and did restrain growth in the federal budget—thus, eventually reducing George W. Bush's huge budget deficits but not eliminating them. Meanwhile, through the terms of most post–Nixon presidents—except for that of Bill Clinton—federal spending increased as a percentage of GDP. Congress's budget process, enacted in 1974, eventually broke down and was a factor in this out-of-control federal spending.

Overall, Reagan—with his unilateral military interventions against Libya, in Lebanon, in the tanker war against Iran, and against Grenada in violation of international law and the US Constitution—unfortunately ended the "Vietnam Syndrome" of the Ford and Carter administrations, which had been leery of ambitious US military interventions overseas in favor of a more restrained US foreign policy. Thus, after the foreign policy of restraint of Gerald Ford and Jimmy Carter, Reagan put the United States back on the road to expanding government meddling overseas. Reagan, despite his "small

---

43. Suri, *The Impossible Presidency*, 253.

government" rhetoric, enlarged the size of the federal government—both absolutely and as a portion of GDP—expanded its intrusion into the private economy, and aggressively sought to inflate executive power (already by far the largest and most powerful branch of government), including gross violation of the Constitution's checks and balances during the Iran-Contra affair. Reagan continued Nixon's transfer of power from the larger executive branch into the president's personal bureaucracy that tries to control it—the White House staff, Executive Office of the President, and National Security Council. In short, like George W. Bush who would come later, Reagan purposefully wanted to reverse the post–Vietnam/Watergate congressional pushback against the executive and allegedly make the presidency great again. They both overstated the reach and success of post–Vietnam/Watergate congressional pushback on the executive during the 1970s and thus merely further enhanced the power of the imperial presidency.

Post–Cold War Interventions

Although the Cold War ended with the demise of the Soviet Union, which was the rationale for the informal American Empire (American security commitments around the world, armed interventions globally, overseas military bases from which to conduct them, and a massive defense budget to fund it all) and the imperial presidency, the use of unconstitutional executive power on steroids did not. George H.W. Bush, Bill Clinton, George W. Bush, Barack Obama, and Donald Trump have continued to take unilateral offensive military actions without proper congressional approval. Also, because of the influence of the American military-industrial complex, about which President Eisenhower had spoken, the US military budget declined only by a quarter, US security commitments were expanded and strengthened, many overseas bases were retained, and the weakened threat of nuclear escalation by its Russian adversary allowed the lone remaining American superpower to run wild with military interventions worldwide.

George H.W. Bush, Reagan's successor, unilaterally on his alleged authority as commander in chief and without congressional approval, invaded Panama for reasons that are still hazy. Perhaps Panamanian leader Manuel Noriega's drug running had become too embarrassing to the former Reagan

vice president in charge of drug policy. Despite this unconstitutional unilateral executive war making, Congress passed a non-binding resolution of
acquiescence to it.

Bush also sent hundreds of thousands of soldiers to Saudi Arabia without prior congressional approval after Iraqi ruler Saddam Hussein invaded
Kuwait. Like the Mexican War and the Gulf of Tonkin, Bush's presidential
assertive force deployments made war much more likely. Yet the framers
intended that the president's commander-in-chief powers applied only to the
command of military forces once the war had already started. Thus, Congress
would be responsible for *prior* approval of overseas troop deployments and the
initiation of hostilities. Congress did pass resolutions, unrequested by Bush,
to endorse the troop buildup as it was already proceeding.

Bush did eventually get Congress's approval to use these forces offensively in
Operation Desert Storm to kick the Iraqis out of that small Persian Gulf nation,
but he insisted that he had the authority to do so anyway as commander in chief
and only got a congressional vote as a courtesy. (His son, George W. Bush, used
the same reasoning before he invaded Iraq to depose Saddam Hussein in 2003.)
His administration also adopted Harry Truman's fallacious posture that getting
a United Nations Security Council Resolution was a substitute for congressional
approval. However, the elder Bush had effectively usurped Congress's power
to decide whether the nation would go to war or not by placing huge forces in
the Saudi desert in the first place without advanced congressional blessing. It
is difficult for a large army to maintain its readiness to fight for long in such
harsh conditions, so eventually taking the offensive in an attack was almost
inevitable once the troops were placed in the desert near Kuwait and Iraq.
Bush justified this massive deployment by alleging that Saddam had amassed
250,000 troops and 1,500 tanks on the border with Saudi Arabia for yet another
invasion—this time of the crown jewel of the Organization of the Petroleum
Exporting Countries (OPEC) cartel. Yet commercial satellite photography
showing empty desert, commissioned by Florida's *St. Petersburg Post*, exposed
this lie as yet another abandonment of truth when war was afoot.[44] George W.
Bush would learn from his father's lying to fabricate imaginary threats from
Saddam to justify his invasion of Iraq in 2003.

---

44. Healy, *The Cult of the Presidency*, 123.

After the Vietnam War, the military had placed many key support functions for the active forces in the reserves in the hopes of inhibiting politicians from using armed force excessively in major wars (LBJ and Nixon had been reluctant to call up reserves during the war); however, post–Cold War presidents had no problem mobilizing the reserves for their military adventures.

As Eisenhower did in 1957 to desegregate schools in Little Rock, Arkansas, George H. W. Bush invoked the Insurrection Act of 1807, which allowed the executive to use the Army to repress rebellion or lawlessness, to suppress riots in Los Angeles. Yet that act may be of questionable constitutionality, because the Constitution gives Congress the power to provide for calling out the militia (now the National Guard), not the Army, to suppress an insurrection or invasion.

The first Bush also sent troops to Somalia on a peacekeeping mission, probably the only real post–World War II humanitarian US military mission. Because it was a peacekeeping mission, Bush, like Reagan in Lebanon, decided the War Powers Resolution didn't apply, even though US military personnel were sent to an area with hostilities or imminent hostilities. And like the Lebanon peacekeeping mission, ostensibly neutral US forces were dragged into fighting on one side of the conflict. Mission creep was already beginning when Bush left office and turned the operation over to Bill Clinton. Clinton continued the mission creep and began chasing around Somali warlords, instead of merely safeguarding humanitarian food shipments, the original purpose of the US mission. In 1993, one of the warlords, with Osama bin Laden's help, attacked US forces and killed 18 of them in the now famous "Blackhawk Down" episode. Congress mandated a vote by mid-November 1993 on whether to authorize the mission or order a US withdrawal. Under such congressional pressure, Clinton agreed to such a withdrawal by March of 1994, and a Democratic Congress cut off funding by that time to make sure he did. As in the Vietnam War, congressional and public pressure, if the political will exists, can make a difference in pushing the executive branch to end a failing military action.

Clinton's other military interventions were disguised efforts to oust unfriendly governments. In most cases, Congress enacted laws limiting the operations' scope and timelines. In 1994, although Congress protested, Clinton planned to invade Haiti and overthrow a coup-installed dictatorship and "restore democracy" by reinstating Jean-Bertrand Aristide as president. Clinton, using a United Nations Security Council resolution and claiming he did not need legislative approval to invade another country, called off the invasion at the last minute when the dictator fled. Nonetheless, without consulting Congress, Clinton sent 10,000 troops into Haiti to bolster Aristide's corrupt government. Many pundits said Clinton's real motive was to stanch the heavy flow of refugees from Haiti to Florida, an important state during American presidential elections.

In Bosnia in 1995, Clinton unilaterally ordered air strikes, but Congress prohibited the use of ground troops. Clinton signed these statutes. Yet Clinton, using his alleged "inherent" power as commander in chief, inserted US ground forces into the country as a peacekeeping force under the Dayton Accords after hostilities ended, over incessant objections by the House of Representatives.[45]

In 1998, Clinton had two unilateral air campaigns that coincided with problems at home, lending credence to the notion that they were to divert attention from these domestic troubles. Coinciding with his admission of an affair with Monica Lewinsky and her second testimony before a grand jury were Clinton's cruise missile attacks on a terrorist training camp in Afghanistan and an alleged chemical weapons plant in Sudan. The strike missed killing Osama bin Laden at the training camp, and a soil sample later indicated no chemical weapons were being manufactured at the factory. Coinciding with his impeachment over lying and obstructing justice in the Lewinsky affair was his Desert Fox air campaign against Iraq. The campaign claimed to be aimed at motivating Saddam Hussein to better cooperate with international arms inspectors, but really just caused such inspectors to leave Iraq before the bombing started and then get locked out until late 2002.

In the US offensive air war against Serbia over Kosovo in 1999, which contravened international law, Clinton claimed that he wasn't introducing US troops into an area of hostilities or imminent hostilities, which would have triggered the War Powers Resolution (WPR). Also, Congress didn't officially

45. William Michael Treanor, "Fame, the Founding, and the Power to Declare War," *Cornell Law Review* 82 (1997): 704–05.

start the WPR clock ticking. The Republican House of Representatives, as the ninety-day limit of the WPR was about to expire, declined to approve a Senate-passed authorization for continued air strikes. (At the same time Congress failed to pass a concurrent resolution terminating the conflict, refused to limit the potential use of US ground forces in the conflict, and provided twice as much funding as Clinton requested for the ongoing operation.) Clinton, blatantly violating the WPR's requirement to end hostilities without both houses authorizing a continuation of them within ninety days of the conflict's initiation, used the lame excuse of continued congressional funding as a justification to continue the war.[46] Congress was too timid to cut off that funding or affirmatively vote to end the war. Like Harry Truman, Clinton refused to call this major military operation a "war." Despite the WPR's requirement that both houses of Congress must approve a military intervention before the ninety-day period ends or the operation must be terminated, the courts ruled that because Congress had not nixed the president's war, no role existed for the judiciary in the matter. This episode is said to finally have killed the War Powers Resolution.[47]

After an investigation by Independent Counsel Ken Starr—who started out investigating the Clintons' involvement in the Whitewater episode but ended up entrapping Bill Clinton into perjuring himself in the Lewinsky Affair—Democrat Clinton was impeached by the Republican House of Representatives despite public opinion adverse to it and midterm Republican congressional losses anticipating it. Unlike Watergate, the Clinton impeachment politicized the impeachment process and discredited the independent counsel regime. There are signs that if the impeachment process is ever justifiably needed again, politicization may render it ineffective. Instead, if Clinton was going to be impeached for anything, he should have been for the worst violation of the War Powers Resolution since Congress passed it in 1973.

In 1994, after a Democratic Congress had rejected his rescue package of loans for Mexico to prevent the collapse of its currency, Clinton authorized, by executive order, loans of $43 billion. Executive orders are constitutional

---

46. Barron, *Waging War*, 379–83, 411.
47. Posner and Vermeule, *The Executive Unbound*, 10–12.

only if they provide specific guidelines for the executive branch to implement Congress's legislative wishes. If no congressional legislation exists or the executive order contradicts Congress's will, the order is unconstitutional rule by presidential fiat.

Clinton, despite multiple limited military interventions overseas, avoided getting involved in episodes that required large numbers of US ground forces, especially after the small-scale debacle in Somalia. Despite his high-flying moralistic rhetoric, surprisingly Clinton even avoided getting involved in the Rwandan genocide, which killed 500,000 to a million people, because he didn't want to incur US military casualties. Clinton's successor, George W. Bush, was not so cautious and ended up getting the United States involved in two larger quagmires on the ground.

Also, Clinton was the best president since Truman in budgetary restraint. Unlike Reagan, with his largely empty small government rhetoric, Clinton "walked the walk" and cut federal government spending as a portion of GDP (even beating out Dwight Eisenhower, the only other president during that period to do so, in magnitude of the reduction). Although Clinton experienced an economic boom during his term and had to raise taxes to deal with the humongous budget deficits left over from the Reagan/George H.W. Bush era, he also was the only executive since Truman to cut federal spending per capita in the United States. Clinton thus turned these huge deficits into a budget surplus. (Although Speaker Newt Gingrich and congressional Republicans helped Clinton's budget restraint, Clinton cut the budget at a greater rate before that when he had a Democratic Congress in 1993 and 1994.)

Unfortunately, George W. Bush, his successor, learned from Reagan that "deficits don't matter," in the words of his powerful vice president, Dick Cheney. With Bush's war on terror, protracted war in Iraq, other unneeded defense spending increases, creation of a new entitlement program (Medicare prescription drug coverage), and generally large domestic spending increases, he turned Clinton's surplus into even bigger deficit spending than in the Reagan/George H.W. Bush era. Bush had created the largest peacetime deficit in history to date in inflation-adjusted terms.[48]

---

48. Rudalevige, *The New Imperial Presidency*, 149–50.

Global War on Terror

Other presidents had expanded executive power in the course of promulgating their policy agendas. However, as a top priority in and of itself, the George W. Bush administration attempted to restore what Bush's vice president believed was the executive's rightful, but diminished, dominance. Dick Cheney ignored the text of the Constitution and the framers' original intent that Congress would have most of the powers in defense and foreign policy, and he had lived through Congress's already reversed pushback against executive aggrandizement during the Vietnam and Watergate era. Yet Cheney was a believer in the Unitary Theory of the Executive, a view of immense executive power, especially during wartime. The theory essentially brings back the royal prerogatives of the British king, as elucidated by John Locke in the 1600s. Even Alexander Hamilton, an extreme proponent of executive power at the nation's founding to the point of being a near monarchist, was more moderate than the Bush administration—believing that the decision to go to war was the Congress's and that the executive would merely execute any war after Congress approved it. Thus, the Bush administration had likely the most expansive conception of executive power in American history to date. And the 9/11 attacks provided the assertive administration a perpetual war to justify yet another period of executive aggrandizement.

After 9/11, the Bush administration sought to construe the "War on Terrorism" as broadly as possible—targeting not only al Qaeda, but "every terrorist group of global reach." However, the administration really wanted an even broader authority: congressional authorization not only to use force against those entities and nations responsible for the attacks, but also "to deter and preempt any future acts of terrorism and aggression against the United States." Congress was dumbstruck by Bush's open-ended request for authorization to attack any entity that might be contemplating terrorist attacks or any country that might be weighing attacking the United States. As one participant in the negotiations later concluded, "Given the breadth of activities potentially encompassed by the term 'aggression,' the President might never again have had to seek congressional authorization for the use of force to combat terrorism." Also, the Bush administration unsuccessfully tried to insert the words "in the United States" in the resolution to allow domestic surveillance and perhaps the use of military operations against terrorists inside the country.[49] Finally, the administration asked that Congress give it standing authority to appropriate whatever funds it needed to fight terrorism.[50]

Congress balked at giving the administration these legislative blank checks. The legislature only authorized the use of force against the perpetrators of the 9/11 attacks and those that harbored them—really the main al Qaeda group and their Afghan Taliban hosts. Yet, the Authorization of the Use of Military Force (AUMF 2001) has been used by the Bush and subsequent administrations (Obama and Trump) to attack many groups that had nothing to do with the 9/11 attacks. Such groups included the Pakistani Taliban, al Qaeda in the Arabian Peninsula in Yemen, al Shabab in Somalia, and ISIS in many countries. During the negotiations over the resolution, the congressional representatives vowed not to have it become another broad authorization such as the Gulf of Tonkin Resolution, but because Congress then failed to police the more restrictive AUMF 2001, presidents similarly ran wild with it.

The most dangerous part of Bush's broad War on Terror—even more so than its likely indefinite length, which predictably would become a problem for civil liberties, as happened during the long Cold War—was the inclination to regard the battlefield as being at home too. After 9/11, congressional creation of the Department of Homeland Security and the military's Northern Command, with jurisdiction over North America, turned the externally focused national security machine inward. Furthermore, flouting the omission of the wording "in the United States" from the AUMF, Bush claimed "inherent" authority as commander in chief to disregard the Posse Comitatus Act of 1878 in order to use military force within the United States to prevent or deter terrorism. That statue restricts the military's use in domestic law enforcement unless authorized by the Constitution or congressional statute. If the president can violate such congressionally passed laws restricting the use of the military for law enforcement, the fears of James Madison about wars leading to tyranny at home become very real. (Later, after the failed federal

---

49. Quoted in Barron, *Waging War*, 387–88.
50. Posner and Vermeule, *The Executive Unbound*, 45.

response to Hurricane Katrina, the then-very-unpopular George W. Bush got Congress to weaken the Posse Comitatus Act, allowing more dangerous presidential discretion to use the army for enforcing the law at home, during natural disasters and epidemics, over the objection of state governors—a seeming violation of the Constitution.[51] Thus, even federal government failure generates more federal power.)

Members of Congress, fearing that the Bush administration would regard the battlefield against terrorists as also including the home front (which his Justice Department later did), inundated the *Congressional Record* with restricted parameters of the AUMF 2001's purpose: if the government's powers of domestic surveillance or covert action needed to be augmented, the administration would need to return and get that approved.[52] (During the hysteria after the 9/11 attacks, the Bush administration rammed through Congress without the members even reading the bill, the USA PATRIOT Act, which vastly increased the government's domestic surveillance and curtailed judicial review of it.)

However, in arguing to the Supreme Court in favor of the president's power to designate "enemy combatants," the administration stated:

> The court of appeals' attempt to cabin the Commander-in-Chief authority to the conduct of combat operation on a traditional battlefield is particularly ill-considered in the context of the current conflict. . . .
> The September 11 attacks not only struck targets on United States soil; they also were launched from inside the Nation's borders. The "full power to repel and defeat the enemy" thus necessarily embraces determining what measures to take against enemy combatants found within the United States.

The problem with this argument is that the framers did construe the commander-in-chief authority narrowly in terms of battlefield command of military forces once Congress approved any war, as demonstrated by the aforementioned early history of the nation: Under the constitutional frame-

---

51. Healy, *The Cult of the Presidency*, 218–19.
52. Barron, *Waging War*, 390, 392–94.

work a self-defense action by the executive is allowed only in an emergency situation before the Congress can authorize war. As noted earlier, to the extent that Congress, in the AUMF 2001, authorized a war on terror, it confined it to overseas by omitting the words "in the United States" from the authorization. Domestically, countering terrorism required treating it as the crime that it was and is.

Yet the legislative intent of the AUMF was ignored, as Bush used his "inherent" power as commander in chief to violate the Fourth Amendment and the Foreign Intelligence and Surveillance Act (FISA) of 1978 to spy on Americans without judicially approved warrants. Normally, the FBI would request those warrants, but the administration went outside the law because it wanted to use the superior electronic snooping capabilities of the National Security Agency (NSA), whose charter allowed operations only outside the United States. However, Bush, by executive order, used the NSA to spy, without warrants, on those in America who were calling or emailing people outside the United States who were suspected of links to al Qaeda or organizations that supported the terror group. Alberto Gonzalez, Bush's attorney general, testifying at a congressional hearing, hinted that the president even had the inherent authority to conduct warrantless surveillance of calls or emails between Americans in the United States. It was later learned that Bush had the NSA conduct massive data-mining operations on all Americans by sifting through data on all their calls and emails, looking for signs of the miniscule few who might possibly be linked to terrorism. The data mining clearly violated the Constitution's prohibition on general warrants, which requires government snooping to be specific in the persons, places, and information sought.

Even though Congress had refused to insert in AUMF 2001 approval to use military operations within the United States to fight terrorists, the US Department of Justice argued that the law allowed it. However, even if it did not, the department argued, the FISA statute's restrictions on warrantless surveillance were unconstitutional anyway because the president's power as commander in chief could overrule such pesky laws during wartime. According to Jonathan Yoo of the Justice Department's Office of Legal Counsel, the government's legal adviser, no law by Congress "can place any limits on the president's determinations as to any terrorist threat, the amount of military force to be used in response, or the method, timing, and nature of the response."[53]

The Democratic Congress complained loudly about NSA's unconstitutional warrantless spying on Americans and then in 2007 promptly passed the Protect America Act, which just as unconstitutionally made it legal. The act removed the FISA court from individually approving warrants for the wiretapping of Americans' emails or phone calls when the government reasonably believes that the targeted person at the other end of the call is outside the United States.[54]

Other internal Bush administration legal memos argued that as commander in chief, Bush had the power to not only ignore any legislatively passed statutes on assessment of threats or restrictions on presidential responses using force, but could ignore congressionally passed laws on torture, rendition of captured terror suspects to other countries where torture was practiced, and the use of kangaroo military tribunals. In the case of torture, the United State was a party to the United Nations Convention Against Torture, federal law prohibited torture inside and outside the United States, and the Uniformed Code of Military Justice barred using threats, assaults, or cruel treatment of detainees under the military's control. The Bush administration's astonishing initial legal determination—similar to Nixon's appalling post-resignation statement that "if the president does it, it's not illegal"—was that the president's authority as commander in chief "could render specific conduct, otherwise criminal, not unlawful." In the administration's view, international and national legal strictures banning torture were unconstitutional, because they interfered with the president's dictates as commander in chief during wartime.

This line of reasoning was a variant of Alexander Hamilton's dubious argument that the vesting clause of executive power in Article II of the Constitution—despite the very limited enumerated powers directly given the president in the document—permitted the executive broad action in "traditionally understood" executive functions (as identified by British and European constitutional theorists before the time of American independence)—including

---

53. Quoted in Crenson and Ginsberg, *Presidential Power*, 202–03.
54. Healy, *The Cult of the Presidency*, 214.

defense and war—unless an enumerated constitutional power is specifically given to Congress. This interpretation turned on its head the founders' intent to break from European tradition and strictly enumerate, and thus limit, the powers of the federal government, and especially the executive branch. However, the vesting clause thesis provides an easy solution in squaring the limited executive powers listed in Article II and more numerous congressional powers enumerated in Article I with executive dominance of the federal government in practice during the Cold War and beyond.[55]

Even when Congress passed a provision banning cruel or inhumane treatment of detainees held by the US government, Bush, who had opposed the amendment, signed it but issued a signing statement that the law would be enforced "in a manner consistent with the constitutional authority of the president to supervise the unitary executive branch and as commander in chief and consistent with the constitutional limits on judicial power." As conservative Sen. Lindsay Graham cogently concluded, this language meant that to protect us "during war," the president, as commander in chief, could disregard any law in the land.[56] The Bush legal team bought into exactly that analysis.

Bush also unilaterally issued an executive order that noncitizens suspected of terrorism, even those with permanent legal residency in the United States, could be detained and tried in a kangaroo military tribunal rather than getting the civilian trial guaranteed by the US Constitution to all "persons" (not just US citizens). With the initial indefinite detention of José Padilla, a US citizen, as an enemy combatant under Bush's commander-in-chief authority, the Bush administration even ignored the Non-Detention Act of 1971, which prohibited the government from detaining citizens without an act of Congress. Padilla was held for three and a half years without being charged, until he was transferred to the civilian court system, because the Bush administration feared losing the Padilla case in the Supreme Court. As conservative Judge Antonin Scalia said, "The very core of liberty secured by our Anglo-Saxon system of separated powers has been freedom from indefinite imprisonment at the will of the Executive."[57]

---

55. Bradley and Flaherty, "Executive Power Essentialism and Foreign Affairs," 549–50.

56. Crenson and Ginsberg, *Presidential Power*, 204.

57. Antonin Scalia's dissenting opinion in *Hamdi v. Rumsfeld*, 542, U.S. 507, 554-55 (2004).

Usually only dictators ignore habeas corpus, but Lincoln did during the Civil War and was later overruled by the Supreme Court if civilian courts were operating, and FDR did during World War II with the Supreme Court's blessing, despite the fact that civilian courts were open. The Bush administration was relying on the second, more pernicious precedent, even though the Constitution implies that only the Congress can suspend habeas corpus—not the executive using his authority as commander in chief—and then only during times of invasion or insurrection (implying that civilian courts would not be functioning). The 9/11 attacks were neither.

Gene Healy perceptively noted that the Bush administration's claim of inherent executive power as commander in chief, during wartime, to indefinitely detain American citizens on American territory without a judicial review of their detention, was worse than Nixon's claim after leaving office that "When the president does it that means it is not illegal." In fact, Nixon had signed the Non-Detention Act of 1971, which forbade such detention without the passage of a congressional statute. Yet Bush's Justice Department would argue that during wartime, the president could ignore this law.[58]

The nation's founders would have passed out at this claim of executive rule by fiat without any checks and balances. In fact, Article 1, Section 8 of the Constitution gives Congress the power to "make Rules concerning Captures on Land and Water" and to "define and punish . . . Offenses against the Law of Nations."[59] The Bill of Rights has no national security exception and requires, for example, the use of judicially approved surveillance and civilian trials for citizens and non-citizens alike, even during wartime.

Showing that unconstitutional precedents from previous wars resurrect themselves during later conflicts, the Bush administration argued that the 1942 *Ex Parte Quirin* Supreme Court decision during World War II allowed the president to designate terror suspects as enemy combatants and try them before military tribunals, even though the civilian courts were functioning, and no threat of enemy attack or invasion was imminent.

Pushing back on these outrageous claims of presidential authority, the Congress and Supreme Court only lamely limited the extent of executive

---

58. Healy, *The Cult of the Presidency*, 175.
59. US Constitution, Article I, Section 8.

power's expansion. Throughout American history, possessing legal authority but little political legitimacy, the Supreme Court's cautious pushback on the expansion of executive power during any emergency usually happens after the crisis is long over, thus ameliorating the court's impact.[60]

The Supreme Court ruled that the president could not continue using his kangaroo military tribunals—which are nowhere mentioned in the Constitution and were created by Bush's executive order in disregard of congressionally approved limitations—unless they were established by a new congressional statute or followed legal procedures used by the US military for courts martial of American service personnel. Bush then asked Congress to approve his tribunals, which the legislative body did through passage of the Military Commissions Act of 2006. Congress also approved torturing detainees and allowing the admission of evidence obtained from torture to be introduced in the tribunals. Shockingly, the Supreme Court even allowed the administration to torture an innocent man and then use the state secrets privilege—nowhere to be found in the Constitution—to shield the government from the wronged victim, who was demanding restitution in the courts.

Yet, the administration was restricted on who could be detained as "enemy combatants," a designation that it had purposefully used to simultaneously remove both detainee rights under the Constitution and rights as prisoners of war under the Geneva Conventions. Also, the Supreme Court allowed prisoners to at least challenge their detentions under habeas corpus petitions. After Congress and the Supreme Court resisted mildly, even the Bush administration, which was likely the most aggressive administration in American history in asserting executive war power, realized it needed to retrench to save some of its expanded ambit. For example, Department of Justice legal memos backed off on their contention that the president's power as commander in chief precluded Congress from having any say by statute concerning the detention, transfer, interrogation, and prosecution of terror suspects.[61]

The Bush administration cynically used the 9/11 attacks to try to link Osama bin Laden and al Qaeda to Saddam Hussein's Iraq and its alleged weapons-of-mass-destruction programs (nuclear, biological, and chemical

---

60. Posner and Vermeule, *The Executive Unbound*, 52–54.
61. Barron, *Waging War*, 397–403, 423–24.

weapons). Bush used popular thirst for revenge, against even Islamic people unassociated with the attacks, to drum up support for an invasion of Iraq. After 9/11, Bush issued many executive orders, including unconstitutionally creating a new Office of Homeland Security in the Executive Office of the President and authorizing the CIA to use all methods to overthrow Saddam Hussein in Iraq. (During the Clinton administration, the Republican Congress had passed a vague bill promoting regime change in Iraq, but although Clinton signed it, he was wisely unenthusiastic about effectuating that goal.)

In a replay of the Iran-Contra affair, during the summer of 2002, much before Congress's October 2002 approval of the invasion of Iraq, Bush clandestinely began a series of military projects in Oman, Qatar, and Kuwait that would be needed to pursue an invasion of Iraq and had no other purpose. Congress had not approved the money for these projects, as required under the Constitution. The only difference with the Iran-Contra affair is that the Reagan administration was circumventing a congressional ban on assisting the Nicaraguan Contras. In this case, Congress had not spoken on the military projects being funded. Yet both efforts were kept from the Congress and the American public and the ramifications of Bush's circumvention of Congress's constitutional appropriation power were much more disastrous than Reagan's—laying the groundwork for what would turn out to be a long and grueling major war versus providing military assistance to Contra rebels, who had no chance of ever overthrowing the Nicaraguan government. Bush's actions were one more episode of presidents being able to create facts on the ground that erode Congress's constitutional function of deciding whether to go to war.

When it eventually came to an overt invasion of Iraq in early 2003, like his father in the first Gulf War, Bush believed he had the constitutional authority to take the country to war without congressional approval, but he asked for a vote just as a courtesy. After 9/11, because the Congress was so eager to pass approval of an unrelated invasion of another Islamic country—the very US military interventionism in the Middle East that spurred Osama bin Laden to attack the United States on 9/11—it breezed by evidence from Bush's own intelligence agencies that severely undermined Bush's case for war. In a letter to the House and Senate Intelligence Committees two days before Congress took up the war resolution, George Tenet, Bush's intelligence chief, reported, "Baghdad for now appears to be drawing a line short of conducting terrorist attacks with conventional or chemical or biological weapons [no one in the intelligence community thought Iraq had nuclear weapons]." Yet Tenet said that if Saddam Hussein believed a US attack was imminent, "he probably would become much less constrained in adopting terrorist action." The letter also said that "a senior intelligence witness" at a recently closed congressional hearing told the committee that absent an imminent US invasion, "My judgment would be that the probability of [Saddam Hussein] initiating an attack—let me put a time frame on it—in the foreseeable future given the conditions we understand now, the likelihood would be low." Therefore, Bush's own intelligence community was telling the world that the threat from Saddam attacking the United States with alleged weapons of mass destruction or giving them to terrorists—the major alleged threat the invasion was supposed to eliminate—would actually grow if the end of Saddam's regime was near and he had nothing to lose.[62]

Instead of approving or disapproving the invasion of Iraq directly, Congress passed the responsibility onto Bush in case things went wrong (and things did go wrong). Congress authorized Bush to "use the Armed Forces of the United States as he determines to be necessary and appropriate . . . against the continuing threat posed by Iraq." This is just one more historical case of Congress abdicating or slighting its most important responsibility—the war power.

Nonetheless, everyone in Congress knew what Bush was going to do with the authority. Congress was implicitly authorizing a preventive war—a war not in self-defense when under attack or even a preemptive attack to crush an imminent threat. The international community had traditionally frowned on preventive wars as dressing up aggression. The same was true, at least rhetorically by the US security community. NSC-68, the US blueprint for the Cold War, stated in 1950 at the beginning of the Cold War:

> It goes without saying that the idea of "preventive war"—in the sense of a military attack not provoked by a military attack upon us or our allies—is generally unacceptable to Americans.[63]

---

62. Quoted in Healy, *The Cult of the Presidency*, 155, 158–59.
63. Rudalevige, *The New Imperial Presidency*, 271–72.

During the Cuban Missile Crisis in 1962, a preventive first strike to take out Soviet missiles being assembled in Cuba was rejected by JFK because the United States was not that kind of country. Yet three decades later, in the case of invading Iraq, the Congress willingly accepted the expansion of executive power that preventive war entailed.

Sometimes war is used to bludgeon Congress to agree to unrelated policies at home. After the Iraq War began in March 2003, Republican leaders of the House argued that members of Congress should not pull the rug out from under Bush during wartime and thus should vote for his $726 billion tax cut. They characterized members who voted against it—because they were concerned with ballooning federal budget deficits—as unpatriotic.[64] Yet perhaps the opponents were the true patriots, because this was the first time in American history that a president irresponsibly cut taxes during wartime. Meanwhile Bush was spending like a drunken sailor domestically and racking up soaring expenses for what became two protracted counterinsurgency wars. Record peacetime budget deficits resulted. Bush's vice president, Dick Cheney, told everyone that Ronald Reagan had taught everyone that "deficits don't matter." That conclusion may be true politically, because many people love both tax cuts and government programs and don't mind sticking their children and grandchildren with the outrageous bill; but it's not true economically because resultant government borrowing crowds out critical private-sector borrowing, driving up interest rates and perhaps inflation. Tax cuts are good, but spending must also be cut and that is difficult during wars—both domestic spending and defense spending tend to rise during conflicts.

As the war dragged on and disaster ensued, with the creation of what would become ISIS using guerrilla tactics against the invaders, Congress did have a role in pressuring Bush to come up with a timetable for US withdrawal by 2011, which Barack Obama eventually carried out. Congress attached a requirement to a war-spending bill that would have required withdrawal by 2008. Bush vetoed that bill but was alarmed enough by it to create his own timetable for US withdrawal ending in 2011, after he would have left office.

---

64. Quoted in Rudalevige, *The New Imperial Presidency*, 3.

To implement such a timetable, however, Bush negotiated a United States-Iraq Status of Forces Agreement with the Iraqi prime minister, who had to submit it to the Iraqi parliament and Presidency Council for approval. Ironically, the parliament of a failed state in the developing world got a greater say in the status of US forces than did the US Congress, which did not ratify the executive agreement because it was not a treaty that required a two-thirds vote of approval in the US Senate.[65]

For the 2003 invasion of Iraq, Bush, like his father and Bill Clinton, did mobilize the part-time military reserves, but in a reversal of the military's policies, he also began enlarging the active forces and returning key functions such as psychological operations, Special Forces, and civil affairs to them. Thus, this reversal reinstated politicians' ability to more easily involve the US military in unnecessary, costly, and congressionally unapproved armed adventures overseas. Also, having a military intentionally more divorced from the society it is defending has cut down on the popular opposition to such adventures, even when they turn into fiascos. Protests against the ill-fated Iraq War paled in comparison to those during the equally futile Vietnam War.

Using Jimmy Carter's unilateral scrapping of the Mutual Defense Treaty with Taiwan, and the Supreme Court acceptance of it, as a precedent, George W. Bush abrogated the 1972 Anti-Ballistic Missile (ABM) Treaty in 2001. Because the building of missile defenses can scare opponents into thinking that their nuclear deterrents may be undermined, it could cause them to begin building more offensive nuclear weapons, thus potentially starting an arms race. Yet, the Constitution is silent about how to end treaties that are allegedly no longer needed or wanted.

All in all, Bush's ability to fulfill one of his primary policy objectives—increasing the power of the already imperial presidency—was ultimately made possible by the 9/11 tragedy. However, this ambitious goal was there right from his inauguration and was formulated much before those attacks. His agenda likely was emboldened by claiming a majority of the Electoral College tally, even though he lost the popular vote to Al Gore in the 2000 election. Thus, the Electoral College majority may have contributed to Bush's reckless

---

65. Preble, "The Founders, Executive Power, and Military Intervention," 704.

and disastrous "cowboy" invasion of Iraq by making him think voters had given him a "mandate."

In the face of some judicial and congressional pushback, Bush retrenched a little toward the end of his second term to attempt to preserve his vast aggrandizement of presidential power. His Democratic successor, Barack Obama, adopted many of his illegal policies in national security and refused to prosecute Bush administration officials even for clear violations of the law in ordering torture and illegal domestic surveillance. With the exception of torture, which Obama ended, the new president continued broad illegal surveillance, illegal rendition of terror suspects, unconstitutional suspension of habeas corpus by the use of indefinite detention without charge, the unconstitutional use of kangaroo military tribunals instead of civilian courts, and ramped-up targeted assassinations of terror suspects, even US citizens. Obama likely did not prosecute Bush officials, because he did not want officials continuing such policies under his watch to be timid in the face of possible later legal exposure.[66] Also, he may not have wanted any Republican successor to retaliate for his prosecution of Bush officials by prosecuting him or his officials.

Obama did try to close Guantanamo prison, but Republicans in Congress refused, playing on public fears that dangerous terrorism suspects would then need to be transported to the United States. Yet for many years, numerous terrorism suspects already had been successfully held in US prisons. Also, civilian courts have a much higher rate of conviction in terrorism cases than the unconstitutional kangaroo military tribunals at Guantanamo prison, which became a national disgrace worldwide to a free nation.

As far as military interventions overseas, Obama followed Bush's timetable for withdrawing US forces from Iraq, yet unsuccessfully "surged" forces in Afghanistan to attempt to stabilize the country against a Taliban resurgence. In 2011, Obama's ramped-up targeted killing program did eventually eliminate Osama bin Laden, the perpetrator of the 9/11 attacks, but the Afghan War, long ago during the Bush administration converted to a US nation-building quagmire, dragged on. Donald Trump, Obama's successor, is at this writing re-escalating the war there that was lost years ago.

---

66. Posner and Vermeule, *The Executive Unbound*, 48–49.

Obama was unfairly blamed for the resurgence of ISIS in Iraq and Syria after the US withdrawal from Iraq. George W. Bush originally created the precursor to the group, which rose in opposition to his invasion of Iraq and formed in US-run prisons in that country. Unfortunately, when ISIS took over large sections of Iraq and Syria, Obama got sucked back into Iraq and conducted a limited military intervention in the Syrian civil war, using US airpower and local ground forces in each country. The Obama and Trump administrations, Kurdish militias, Iranian-backed militias, and Syrian and Russian forces have freed most Iraqi and Syrian cities from the brutal group's clutches. However, the group is not dead, will probably use guerrilla and terrorist tactics to fight in a hit-and-run manner, and eventually may be resurgent—as the Taliban have been in Afghanistan. Rarely can you extinguish an insurgency by military means alone without the underlying grievance of the extremist rebellion being removed. Obama and Trump, with their limited involvement in the massive Syrian civil war, exacerbated the fighting, but both took in few Syrian refugees compared to Europe. Even after ISIS was eliminated from major cities in Iraq and Syria, Trump unnecessarily kept US forces in Syria—risking combat with Syrian, Iranian, Russian, and even Turkish forces.

Obama had ramped up Bush's war on terror, although he quit calling it by this discredited name. He continued Special Forces and drone and air attacks in Libya, Pakistan, Yemen, Somalia, Niger, and perhaps other unnamed countries. The legal justifications for these US wars, including those in Syria and Iraq, in both administrations were suspect. As noted earlier, the authorizations for the original Iraq War and to go after the perpetrators of 9/11 did not cover these unilateral presidential wars. Trump has further escalated these wars.

Obama, after seeing what chaos the toppling of a dictator could bring in the fractured land of Iraq, let the French convince him to take advantage of the "Arab Spring" revolt against Libya's Muammar Gaddafi to oust him using allied air power and indigenous ground forces—the model that the United States had often used since Clinton employed it in the Balkan Wars of the 1990s. For the Libyan War, Obama did not get congressional approval and flouted the War Powers Resolution by claiming that running an air war was not injecting US forces into an area of hostilities, much as Clinton asserted in the war against Serbia over Kosovo in 1999. Gaddafi was eventually removed, but like post-Saddam Iraq, post-Gaddafi Libya slipped into chaos, anarchy, and became a series of terrorist havens. Also, ousting leaders from a non-nuclear state (Iraq) and a state that agreed to get rid of its nuclear program (Libya) was a bad signal to send to nuclear aspirants, such as North Korea, that they would be at significant risk from US attack or invasion after they gave up their nuclear programs.

Obama did try to improve relations with US adversaries, restoring diplomatic and some economic relations with Cuba and reaching a deal with Iran to suspend its nuclear program for a decade or more in exchange for the removal of some economic sanctions. Attempts by American presidents since 1959 to isolate Cuba had failed; Obama recognized this policy failure, that Cuba was no longer a threat to the United States, and that it was time to turn the page. Although criticized heavily by Republicans, the alternative to the strongly verifiable Iran nuclear deal was a nuclear Iran or likely war with that country. However, for such a major arrangement with a foreign nation, Obama used an executive agreement rather than a constitutionally required treaty. It was a sign of the times.

At this writing Donald Trump—trying to undo all things Obama did, good or bad—has re-tightened economic interactions with Cuba, without totally reversing Obama's attempt to mend relations, and first decertified that Iran was complying with the nuclear deal (a conclusion contrary to almost all other nations and international bodies), and then scrapped it altogether. However, other signatories, including Iran, have remained in the pact, providing some hope that it still can be salvaged.

The illegal expansion of NATO (the alliance was intended to defend Western Europe) eastward during the Clinton and George W. Bush administrations to Russia's border made Russia fear for its security and helped elect a nationalist leader in Russia in 1999: Vladimir Putin. Putin used such Russian security fears and humiliation to become a dictator. When a government friendly to Russia in Ukraine was ousted, Putin, to salvage what was left of an important buffer state in the Russian sphere of influence and to prevent the United States from fulfilling George W. Bush's pledge to allow Ukraine to join NATO, invaded and annexed the Russophilic Ukrainian region of Crimea, housing a strategic naval base, and stirred up Russophilic populations in eastern Ukraine to rebel against the government. Also, Putin has helped the autocratic government of its traditional ally Syria beat back a substantial rebellion in that country; harbored Edward Snowden, who exposed US secrets (but who also exposed US government spying on its own citizens); and interfered in the 2016 elections by the illegal hacking and publishing of Democratic National Committee emails to help elect Donald Trump. The only one of these actions the United States should have really been alarmed about was illegal Russian interference in the US election. Yet Obama imposed only minor diplomatic and economic slaps on the wrist to Russia for this major attack on one of the core aspects of the American republic. Trump, with a weird affinity for Russia and Putin, was exploring removing even Obama's light sanctions before Congress overwhelmingly strengthened them, a rare case of pushback by Congress alarmed by presidential intentions. However, then Trump blatantly and unconstitutionally refused to fully execute Congress's will with no seeming penalty imposed by Congress. Yet in the long run, the United States and Russia will probably need to mend fences to counter a rising China.

Thus, US "security" has become so warped after World War II that the US government, foreign policy elite, and media become alarmed at the slightest "threats" in faraway countries but do not do more to combat severe close-in threats, for example, blatant interference by a foreign power in American elections, the failure of US military air defenses to rapidly respond on 9/11 to hijacked civilian airliners crashing into buildings in major US cities, or destabilization of neighboring Mexico by violence that is a derivative of the US government's failed War on Drugs. Equally important, during the post–World War II period, the Constitution has been shredded by executives of both parties running wild in the foreign policy arena, especially initiating unilateral wars without approval from Congress.

Conclusion

Compared to the text of the Constitution and the debates in the Constitutional Convention generating the document, presidents have aggrandized much power in foreign policy since the Korean War in 1950. Some congressional pushback during the Vietnam and Watergate era temporarily interrupted the arc of expanding executive power. An informal post-Vietnam consensus had emerged that large wars, such as Gulf War I, had to have congressional approval (though a declaration of war was still passé), but smaller military actions could be unilaterally initiated by the executive. For large wars, presidents may have wanted congressional approval for political reasons—to diffuse blame if the war didn't end up going so well. Smaller interventions still seemed somewhat constrained by the timetable for withdrawal by the War Powers Resolution of 1973.

However, the war on terror, beginning in 2001, seems to have retained the former requirement and eliminated the latter. Like his father during Gulf War I, George W. Bush, for the invasion of Iraq (Gulf War II), got congressional approval before launching it. However, the War on Terror—prosecuted by the Bush, Obama, and Trump administrations—seems to allow presidents to choose enemies on their own and continue the small wars indefinitely without any timetable for ending them. The drone or commando wars against the Pakistani Taliban in Pakistan, al Qaeda in the Arabian Peninsula in Yemen, the Shabab in Somalia, and ISIS in Iraq, Syria, Libya, and other nations seem to be endless. Although authorized by the AUMF 2001, the seventeen-year (and counting) war in Afghanistan is going on indefinitely, because Congress is too timid to stop it. Endless wars are especially hard on civil liberties at home.

Restoring the framers' vision that major wars should be declared and even smaller undeclared conflicts, such as the Quasi War against the French in the late 1790s, should be approved of and regulated by Congress might make wars more infrequent. Although this arrangement is not a panacea—Congress was more enthusiastic for combat than the president in the Quasi War, the War of 1812, the Spanish-American War in 1898, and World War I in 1917—at least it's constitutional in a republic.

5

War Empowers Executive Expansion[1]

CONSERVATIVES SHOULD BE leerier of jumping into wars, not only because wars kill and destroy and because the American superpower might become overextended, especially in a time of high national debt and fiscal crisis, but also because war makes the government—that is, the executive branch—expand rapidly at home, even in areas unrelated to national security. (The executive branch now accounts for 99 percent of US government employees.) This chapter shows how domestic government programs and tax regimes seemingly unrelated to war originated during such periods of conflict. The assessment confirms what Randolph Bourne famously stated: "War is the health of the state."[2] War is also the health of executive aggrandizement at home.

Although social scientists tend to neglect war as a major cause of changes in social policy,[3] some noted historians have concluded that war making is the true driver of state making, dwarfing other causes. For example, as early as 1906, German historian Otto Hintze wrote that war was the principal cause of state development, saying that "the form and spirit of the state's organization will not be determined solely by economic and social relations and clashes of interests, but primarily by the necessities of defense and offense, that is, by the

---

1. This chapter is adapted from the author's article, "Warfare State to Welfare State: Conflict Causes Government to Expand at Home," *The Independent Review* 8, no. 2 (Fall 2013). Also, excerpts were published in *The American Conservative* 12, no. 1 (January/February 2013): 28–31.

2. Randolph Bourne, "War Is the Health of the State," 1918, http://www.antiwar.com/bourne.php.

3. Theda Skocpol, *Protecting Soldiers and Mothers: The Political Origins of Social Policy in the United States* (Cambridge, MA: Belknap Press of Harvard University Press, 1992), 39–40.

organization of the army and of warfare."[4] Arthur Schlesinger, Jr., in his book *The Imperial Presidency*, argued that even though war expanded presidential power in the national security arena, conflict also enhanced executive power domestically.

And American history has certainly confirmed James Madison's axiom that warfare is the mother of other sources of government oppression:

> Of all the enemies of public liberty war is, perhaps, the most to be dreaded, because it comprises and develops the germ of every other.
>
> War is the parent of armies; from these proceed debts and taxes; and armies, and debts, and taxes are the known instrument for bringing the many under the domination of the few.[5]

Although these thoughts come from an American founder whom many conservatives revere, conservatives often push back and argue that even if evils stem from warfare, war is nevertheless sometimes necessary.

Two problems arise with this standard rejoinder. First, in American history wars were usually less necessary than the excuses given for them, especially US involvement in brushfire conflicts since World War II.[6] Second, Madison, if anything, understated war's evil consequences to the republic.

Wars Cause Government to Grow, Even Domestically

The Madison quote might lead one to conclude erroneously that war's expenses, which lead to debt and taxes, are the only causes of the erosion of liberty when conflict arises. At minimum, however, Madison was also uneasy with standing armies because they threaten people's liberties. This book goes further and details domestic government programs (that is, the welfare state) that are seemingly unrelated to war efforts at first blush, but originated or expanded in

---

4. Otto Hintze, "Military Organization and the Organization of the State," in *The Historical Essays of Otto Hintze*, edited by Felix Gilbert (Oxford: Oxford University Press, 1975), 183.

5. James Madison, *Letters and Other Writings of James Madison* (Philadelphia: Lippincott, 1865), 491.

6. For a detailed explanation of the thesis that most American wars could have and should have been avoided, see Ivan Eland, "Most Wars in American History Were Unnecessary and Undermined the Republic," *Mediterranean Quarterly* 23, no. 3 (Summer 2012): 4–33.

times of conflict and by means of the new taxes initiated or increased during war to pay for them.

For example, although conservatives routinely criticize Franklin Delano Roosevelt's Depression-era New Deal for ushering in the era of big government, the origins of permanent big government in the United States are really rooted in World War I. Marc Allen Eisner argues that "the New Deal is best understood as part of a larger history, one that dates back at least to U.S. entry into World War I. The models of state–economy relations and administration developed during the war, new patterns of state–group relations, and the experiences of those who were involved in the mobilization process constituted the core elements out of which the New Deal regime was constructed. In essence, this places the war and the 1920s in a more important place than many contemporary histories would allow when seeking to identify the origins of the modern state and to determine what, in reality, was 'new' about the New Deal."[7] Eisner concludes that "one may still assert that [Herbert] Hoover and Roosevelt viewed the calamity of the Great Depression from the perspective of active participants in the war mobilization effort, and each in his own way sought to apply the lessons of war to the events of the depression." He adds that many of Roosevelt's advisers during the Depression were veterans of the wartime agencies and added their prestige to the use of the wartime model to fight the economic downturn.[8]

By what mechanism does war establish an opening for creating or expanding government programs or taxes? War—usually regarded as a significant societal or in some cases existential crisis—creates an opening for the state to take autonomous action that conflicts with dominant interests in the society, which normally have policy locked down during peacetime.[9] In the legal realm, the government can use the war emergency to implement policies that would normally get pushback from people and groups concerned about the usurpation of private-property rights, the expanding role of government in

---

7. Marc A. Eisner, *From Warfare State to Welfare State: World War I, Compensatory State Building, and the Limits of the Modern Order* (University Park: Pennsylvania State University Press, 2000), 299–300.

8. Eisner, *From Warfare State to Welfare State*, 301, 304.

9. Theda Skocpol, *States and Social Revolutions: A Comparative Analysis of France, Russia, and China* (Cambridge, UK: Cambridge University Press, 1979), 31.

society, and the tipping of the constitutional balance of power in the executive's favor at the expense of other governing branches. During wars—especially big conflicts that require mobilization of the entire society, such as World Wars I and II—interest groups see the government doing things it didn't do or wasn't previously allowed to do and realize the possibilities for this trend to continue when the war is over.

After the conflict is done, the newly empowered state bureaucrats and the constituency groups benefiting from wartime expansion lobby to keep at least some of the measures in place—a process termed the "ratchet effect."[10] For example, during World War I the creation of the Food Administration led to the expectation in the farm sector that government regulation could be used to prop up farm incomes. More generally, President Herbert Hoover said in 1931, "We used such emergency powers to win the war; we can use them to fight the depression, the misery and suffering from which are equally great."[11] Finally, the president typically has to "pay off" members of Congress, especially those of the opposition party, to back the war with the commitment that he will support their domestic projects and spending.

Because the potential for tax revenues determines how big the government can get and the number and size of programs that can be supported, let us first examine how major changes in the tax system have accompanied war.

Important Tax Changes Accompany War

In *Federal Taxation in America: A Short History*, tax historian W. Elliot Brownlee concludes: "What would be without precedent . . . is a decisive shift to a new tax regime in the absence of a national crisis or emergency. The moments of sweeping change in tax regimes have come invariably during the nation's great emergencies—the constitutional crisis of the 1780s, the three major wars [the Civil War, World War I, and World War II], and the Great Depression."[12]

---

10. Robert Higgs, *Crisis and Leviathan: Critical Episodes in the Growth of American Government: 25th Anniversary Edition* (Oakland, CA: Independent Institute, 2012 [1987]).

11. Quoted in Eisner, *From Warfare State to Welfare State*, 261.

12. W. Elliot Brownlee, *Federal Taxation in America: A Short History* (Washington, DC: Woodrow Wilson Center Press; Cambridge, UK: Cambridge University Press, 2004), 2.

Greater revenues are always needed to fight a war. When conflict arises, tax systems are often changed or expanded to augment the state's coffers for use in buying added weapons, ammunition, personnel, fuel, and other war materiel. Yet the changes in tax systems usually linger long after the war is over. War overcomes the naturally fragmented nature of American government, giving central authorities more power, which they in turn use to tout the importance of public patriotism and "sacrifice" to justify altering the tax system, further increasing that enduring power. Also, if the tax changes were part of a winning war effort—as they were in all three of the aforementioned major wars—they acquire a legitimacy that endures after the war is over. Thus, after the war ended, with these augmented tax revenues, increased domestic spending could replace war spending.

The Income Tax

The income tax is one of the most intrusive and economically irrational taxes the government can impose. It usurps liberty by necessitating government snooping into the private details of people's lives to ensure tax collection. Commissioner of Internal Revenue Alfred Pleasonton noted in 1871 that the income tax was the tax "most obnoxious to the genius of our people, being inquisitorial in its nature, and dragging into public view an exposition of the most private pecuniary affairs of the citizen."[13]

Unlike sales and excise taxes, which focus on inhibiting consumption, the income tax directly penalizes economically productive work and the just rewards for it—thereby dragging down prosperity. The income tax is unfortunately now the dominant form of federal taxation.

The federal income tax originated during the emergency of the Civil War, although many at that time correctly regarded it as unconstitutional. The Civil War, the nation's first modern war, required huge amounts of additional government revenue to prosecute. Spending by the federal government increased from less than 2 percent of gross national product (GNP) to an average of 15 percent of GNP. The Republican leadership admired how the British Liberals

---

13. Alfred Pleasonton, Income Tax: Letter from the Commissioner of Internal Revenue. House Misc. Doc. 51 (January 23, 1871): 41–43.

had used income taxes to finance the Crimean War instead of imposing higher taxes on property.[14]

The income tax was abolished seven years after the Civil War ended, in 1872. But as with many other government programs and taxes in American history, the income tax began during war, was discontinued, and then was resurrected later. Excise taxes on particular goods and tariffs on imports (which impair trade and unwisely protect American industries from international competition, which makes them stronger)—that is, two consumption taxes— were the primary means of financing the federal government before, during, and after the Civil War. The income tax was subsequently resurrected after imports—and thus tariff revenues—fell during the depression of the 1890s. Grover Cleveland, an otherwise very conservative president, unwisely accepted the income tax in exchange for lower tariff rates in 1894. But then in 1895 the Supreme Court ruled that the new tax was unconstitutional because the US Constitution clearly required any direct tax to be allocated across the states according to population, and taxing people according to their incomes did not meet that requirement.[15]

In both the Civil War and the 1890s, however, the income tax was a levy only on the well-to-do, not the mass tax it would later become. For example, by end of the Civil War only about 10 percent of all Union households were paying this tax, and it accounted for only about 21 percent of federal tax revenues—as opposed to excise taxes, accounting for 50 percent of federal revenues, and tariffs, accounting for 29 percent.[16]

In 1913, the problem of constitutionality was surmounted by the ratification of the Sixteenth Amendment, which specifically allowed the imposition of an income tax. The ratification of this constitutional amendment showed that the federal government could hand out money to get a powerful new mechanism for obtaining even more money. From 1895 to 1909, to get the income tax amendment approved, the federal government bribed—using disproportionate defense and veterans spending—states whose congressional

---

14. Brownlee, *Federal Taxation in America*, 31, 33.
15. Brownlee, *Federal Taxation in America*, 46–47.
16. Brownlee, *Federal Taxation in America*, 35.

delegations were opposed to it.[17] The tax appears to have had roots in the populist and progressive movements. The broad public perception was that tariffs and excise taxes, which then dominated federal taxation, disproportionately taxed the non-wealthy.[18]

However, although the income tax had been resurrected before US entry into World War I in 1917, the war clearly led to its replacing tariffs and excise taxes as the predominant form of federal taxation in America. Before the war, the income tax was anticipated to provide only supplemental revenues. According to Brownlee, "The income tax was a highly tentative experiment until 1916, when America prepared to enter World War I and settled on it as the primary means of raising taxes for the war."[19] The Allied victory in the war increased the income tax's public legitimacy so that it could begin its subsequent domination of federal taxation.

World War I was transformational in bringing about permanent "big government" in the United States, and the war's enhancement of the income tax's role in taxation made that possible. During wars, trade and thus tariff revenues are disrupted, requiring greater internal taxes. The income tax showed once again during this world war and during the ensuing peace that it had great capacity for generating the huge revenues needed for government expansion. After the war, the ballooning of revenues allowed the vast expansion of federal domestic programs during the Republican Hoover administration, Franklin Roosevelt's Democratic New Deal in the 1930s, and beyond.

But it took another war, World War II, to turn the income tax from a burden on only the well-to-do into a mass tax on almost all earners of income. Experts built on their experiences with the income tax in World War I to insert the tentacles of this intrusive and pernicious levy into all economic classes. The government used war propaganda to stanch public resistance to converting

---

17. Bennett D. Baack and Edward J. Ray, "Special Interests and the Adoption of the Income Tax in the United States," *Journal of Economic History* 45 (September 1985); and Charlotte Twight. "Evolution of Federal Income Tax Withholding: The Machinery of Institutional Change," *Cato Journal* 14, no. 3 (1995): 359–96.

18. J. D. Buenker, "The Ratification of the Federal Income Tax Amendment," *Cato Journal* 1, no. 1 (1981).

19. Brownlee, *Federal Taxation in America*, 2.

the income tax from a "class tax" to a "mass tax."[20] From 1939 to 1945, the number of people paying the income tax rose from 3.9 million to 42.6 million (roughly 60 percent of the labor force), and income tax revenues ballooned from $2.2 billion to $35.1 billion. The federal government could now take in massive revenues from taxing middle-class salaries and wages. Roosevelt and the New Dealers believed that a mass-based income tax was the best way to guarantee a permanent stream of revenues to fund federal programs of "social justice."[21]

They were right. In 1940, before America's entry into World War II, the federal income tax accounted for only 16 percent of government tax revenues. By 1950, it had spectacularly grown to 51 percent of government tax revenues. The war had made a mass federal income tax possible, and the glorious victory over the Axis powers gave this tax the legitimacy to continue to the present day. The World War II tax regime was advertised as temporary, but it unfortunately became permanent.[22]

As Brownlee explains the situation, "In the realm of tax policy, the World War II emergency institutionalized a new tax regime. It had three elements: (1) a progressive but mass-based personal income tax for general revenues; (2) a flat-rate tax on corporate income, also for general revenues; and (3) a regressive payroll tax for social insurance [Social Security]."[23]

During the postwar period until the late 1970s, the broad base of the mass income tax, combined with economic growth and inflation that pushed people into ever higher tax brackets, allowed the federal government to swim in swollen revenues, which were used to enlarge domestic and foreign programs while cutting excise and corporate levies. The augmented domestic programs funded by this means included health care (for example, Medicare), education, welfare, urban development, and federal aid to state and local governments.[24]

---

20. C. C. Jones, "Class Tax to Mass Tax: The Role of Propaganda in the Expansion of the Income Tax During World War II," *Buffalo Law Review* 37, no. 3 (1989).

21. Brownlee, *Federal Taxation in America*, 112.

22. Jim Powell, *FDR's Folly: How Roosevelt and His New Deal Prolonged the Great Depression* (New York: Three Rivers Press, 2003).

23. Brownlee, *Federal Taxation in America*, 121.

24. Brownlee, *Federal Taxation in America*, 117, 128.

In 2001, George W. Bush was able to secure reductions in the income tax. He then wanted to accelerate these cuts, but Democratic Senate majority leader Tom Daschle wanted to roll back the 2001 cuts. To secure the support of Democrats for the new war on terrorism and the invasion of Afghanistan after the attacks on September 11, 2001, Bush had to compromise and agree to a package of Keynesian demand-side measures (read: new federal spending) and neoconservative supply-side features that did not include an acceleration of the 2001 cuts.[25]

Progressive Taxation

During wartime, "sacrifice" needs to be perceived as "fair." In political terms, that merely means allocating the tax burden so that a majority of the population refrains from opposing the war. That goal usually means introducing progressive taxation, which draws most of the revenues from the smaller wealthier classes rather than from the larger middle and lower classes.[26] Progressive income taxation was first introduced not out of concern with equity or fairness, but because it enhanced revenues.[27] In other words, greater taxes could be milked from those best able to pay them.

In 1798, the Federalists, always searching for ways to enhance the power of the federal government, used the Quasi War with France as an excuse to exercise the power of direct taxation on people (before this point, federal taxes had usually fallen on goods, such as tariffs on imports and excise taxes on the consumption of certain items). To aid in funding naval expansion during the conflict, the Federalists imposed a direct tax on property, including land, houses, and slaves; but to increase political support for the levy, they taxed more expensive houses at a higher rate. In 1802, President Thomas Jefferson and Congress abolished these direct taxes, but they were brought back during and after the War of 1812.

During the Civil War, the federal government experimented with a new income tax that was progressive—that is, it targeted only upper-income groups.

25. Brownlee, *Federal Taxation in America*, 231.
26. Eisner, *From Warfare State to Welfare State*.
27. Tom Huntington, "Death and Taxes," *Civil War Times* 43 (February 2005).

Progressive income taxation, however, was introduced in a big way only during the two world wars. For example, during World War I, the wealthiest 1 percent of families had to pay 80 percent of the personal income tax, and only 15 percent of families had to pay the tax at all. During World War II, when the income tax went from being a class tax to a mass tax, tax rates rose most dramatically for the wealthy minority so that the less well-off majority would support the war.

In 1942, President Franklin Roosevelt issued a shocking executive order that nobody in the country could have a net salary—that is, after taxes—of more than $25,000 per year.[28] That salary cap ($350,000 in 2011 dollars), implemented in an executive order under the wartime Amendment to the Emergency Price Control Act of 1942, was later overturned by Congress. FDR lost that battle but eventually won the war (on the rich). During World War II, the income tax for the wealthiest hit an astronomical marginal rate of 94 percent.[29]

With such confiscatory taxes, people tried to reduce their tax obligations. During the 1950s, after the emergency was over and broad public support was no longer needed, income tax rates for minority wealthy interests were lowered from those stratospheric wartime levels but remained higher than they were before the war.[30] This phenomenon is common when war occurs and demonstrates the ratchet effect that conflict has on taxes (and federal spending).

Double Taxation

To get broad support for a war, sometimes it is necessary to tax a rich minority not once, but twice. During World War I, the Revenue Act of 1916 intentionally began taxing dividends issued by corporations and then taxing them again as income received by individual stockholders. The act consciously used both corporate and personal income taxes to tax the well-to-do. The law did this by

---

28. Jim Powell cites President Franklin D. Roosevelt's Executive Order Providing for the Stabilizing of the National Economy, October 3, 1942, http://www.ibiblio.org/pha/policy/1942/421003a.html. Jim Powell, *FDR's Folly: How Roosevelt and His New Deal Prolonged the Great Depression* (New York: Three Rivers Press, 2003), 245–46.

29. National Taxpayers Union, "History of Federal Individual Income Bottom and Top Bracket Rates" (Alexandria, VA: National Taxpayers Union, 2013), http://www.ntu.org/tax-basics/history-of-federal-individual-i.html.

30. Brownlee, *Federal Taxation in America*.

eliminating the personal income tax exemption for dividends. Yet such layered taxation has endured to the present and continues to drag productivity gains in the American economy.

Tax Withholding

In 1943, during World War II, the government figured out how to dramatically increase the efficiency of its income tax enforcement effort and lower people's resistance to heavy taxation. The crisis afforded government officials the power to impose mandatory withholding from paychecks of income taxes eventually due, which triumphed over public opposition to such a policy from 1914 to 1942.

Instead of continuing to rely on taxpayers to send in their entire income tax payments after the close of the tax year, the government coercively began requiring employers to confiscate money out of employees' paychecks periodically during the tax year. The new withholding system foisted the cost of collection on businesses, emphasized the supposed convenience and ease of payment to taxpayers, and euphemistically called the process "collection at the source." As Charlotte Twight notes, the government learned what car salesman had known for a long time: people will be willing to pay more if they focus on smaller installment payments rather than on a larger lump sum owed.[31] With the withholding system, not only would the government be more assured of getting the money and getting it earlier, people would be less likely to miss money they never saw in their paychecks. This trick allowed the government to conceal how much people really paid in taxes.

Limited withholding was first used for income taxes during the Civil War, which were withheld from the paychecks of government employees, and briefly during the lead up to World War I, when the income tax was first reestablished after the Sixteenth Amendment made it constitutionally kosher.[32] As with respect to other government taxes and programs, war set a precedent for withholding, then the policy disappeared and was reestablished permanently

---

31. Twight, "Evolution of Federal Income Tax Withholding."

32. Brownlee, *Federal Taxation in America*, 112–13; and Huntington, "Death and Taxes," 22–25.

later—in this case, withholding payroll taxes from workers' wages beginning in 1937 to fund the new Social Security system.

Income tax withholding was resumed during World War II. To overcome longstanding public opposition to income tax withholding, the government used the propaganda of patriotic sacrifice for the war effort and the argument that what amounted to a tax increase would absorb citizens' spending power, thus helping to constrain usual wartime inflation.[33]

Tax Expenditures (a.k.a. Tax Loopholes)

The first federal income tax brought the first income tax loophole. The income tax is especially prone to such unfairness. And, unsurprisingly, the first tax loophole the government handed out benefited itself. During the Civil War, the government sold bonds to finance the war. In order to boost sales, the interest from such bonds was taxed only at a rate of 1.5 percent; regular income was taxed at 3 percent.[34]

Accompanying the very progressive tax system created to win the support of the masses for World War I came the rising influence of the tax-writing committees in Congress.[35] Handing out goodies in the form of arcane exemptions, deductions, and other loopholes in the income tax code gave the tax committees enhanced power. After the war was over, many well-to-do people chafed under the heavy tax burden imposed by the conflict. Both to relieve the pressure on the progressive tax system and to preserve it, these committees discovered during the 1920s that they could covertly subsidize certain privileged groups by creating tax loopholes (preferential treatment) for them. The complexity of the tax system increased even more dramatically during and after World War II, as measured by the number of pages in the tax code.

The Estate Tax and More

Taxing a person's estate after his or her death originated from the effort to garner more revenue for the Spanish-American War (1898). After funding

---

33. Twight, "Evolution of Federal Income Tax Withholding."
34. Huntington, "Death and Taxes."
35. Brownlee, *Federal Taxation in America*, 75–76.

the war against the Spanish, the counterinsurgency war against the Filipinos whom the United States had "liberated" from the Spanish, and the suppression of the Chinese Boxer Rebellion against the Western colonial powers carving up China, the tax was repealed in 1902. But it was resurrected during World War I to fight a much larger and more expensive war.

Also to pay for the war, a federal excise tax on long-distance telephone calls was imposed. However, the tax lingered for more than a century until it was repealed in 2006.

Gas Taxes

In October 1990, after Saddam Hussein invaded Kuwait, President George H. W. Bush and Congress raised the tax on gasoline and increased the progressiveness of the income tax by expanding the Earned Income Tax Credit for the poor and raising the marginal income tax rates on the wealthy. In the former case, Bush said that the gas tax increase "does have the virtue not only of contributing to deficit reduction, but also, over time, of decreasing America's dependence on foreign oil, an objective whose importance has been made increasingly evident in the face of the Iraqi invasion of Kuwait."[36] As for the latter two, in the time-honored tradition of making the tax system more progressive during a conflict to broaden public support for the war effort, Bush was bribing opposition Democrats and the majority non-wealthy faction in America to support the likely upcoming war with Iraq.

The Internal Revenue Service

The roots of what would become the Internal Revenue Service (IRS) were planted during the Civil War. The massive added revenues required to fight the war meant having a large, dedicated organization to collect them. In 1862, the Republicans created the Office of the Commissioner of Internal Revenue, which headed Treasury's new Bureau of Internal Revenue. By the time the war ended in 1865, the bureaucracy had grown to 4,000 employees.

---

36. George H. W. Bush, "Remarks Announcing a Federal Budget Agreement," 1990, Public Papers of George H. W. Bush. Presidential Library, http://bushlibrary.tamu.edu /papers/1990/90093002.html.

During World War I, the Bureau of Internal Revenue was greatly strengthened. The bureau's employees almost quadrupled, from 4,000 in 1913 to almost 16,000 by 1920.[37] The advent of income tax withholding during World War II also had the unintended outcome of vastly expanding the successor Internal Revenue Service. The administration of withholding taxes from the wages of 30 million people required hiring about 11,000 more IRS employees and drastically increasing the budget for the agency. Of course, costs also increased to private employers, who had to collect the taxes from workers' paychecks.[38]

Government Programs Originating During War

Governments don't like to give back money to taxpayers. Taxes increased during wars are usually just used to expand government programs after the conflicts are over. The civilian programs, seemingly unrelated to war, which arose or were expanded because of conflict, are many and varied and have spent many taxpayer dollars.

Relief for the Poor and Public Works

During World War I, the War Finance Corporation (WFC) acted as a forerunner for all later federal efforts at relief and public works. The New Deal's chief relief agencies, including the Federal Emergency Relief Administration (FERA) and the Public Works Administration (PWA), were originally part of Herbert Hoover's Reconstruction Finance Corporation (RFC)—which was a resurrection of the WFC. Setting a precedent, Hoover's RFC lent money to states to give to the poor. During FDR's administration, the federal government, through the FERA, PWA, and other agencies, gave aid directly to the poor.

During the war and even after it, the WFC distributed welfare in the form of loans to bankers, industries, commodity producers, and exporters. During the Depression, the government's list of welfare recipients merely expanded.[39] The WFC was also the forerunner of the post–World War II Export–Import Bank, which still provides loans to subsidize exports.

---

37. Huntington, "Death and Taxes."

38. Powell, *FDR's Folly*, 247.

39. Eisner, *From Warfare State to Welfare State*.

Social Security

First Precedent for Social Security: Revolutionary War Pensions

Today's Social Security retirement pensions, created by the Social Security Act of 1935, have their roots in pensions for fighters in the Revolutionary and Civil wars. Because bureaucracies and constituencies arise as advocates, pensions, like other entitlement programs, expand their benefits and beneficiaries over time.

In 1776, the Continental Congress passed "invalid pension" legislation providing half-pay during disability or for life to Continental army soldiers and sailors who lost a limb or otherwise were made unable to earn a living by the war. Later amendments broadened coverage to any disabled Continental veterans who applied within six months of the enactment date, June 11, 1788. An 1805 law further broadened coverage to those wounded in the revolution who had since the conflict become disabled so that they couldn't do manual labor. This change allowed the linking of later disabilities to war injuries. An 1817 law similarly expanded naval pensions to widows and orphans of those who died after the Revolutionary War from diseases or injuries received in the war. In 1824, Congress had to revoke the naval provision because costs went out of control. The 1805 and 1817 laws, however, set a precedent for later Civil War pensions, which were abused and came at an exorbitant cost to taxpayers.[40]

Although George Washington originally resisted the creation of service pensions for Continental army officers—pensions given to poor soldiers merely for their service rather than for a disability caused by the war—even when he was losing officers during the harsh winter at Valley Forge in 1777, he eventually began lobbying the Continental Congress to expand them once they had been enacted in 1778. Washington's initial resistance to the idea of service pensions stemmed from the reality that many Americans opposed a standing army and perceived a responsibility of a citizen to the state (called republican virtue).

In 1778, as a tool to recruit and retain troops, Congress created a service pension of half-pay for seven years for officers staying in the Continental army

---

40. Laura S. Jensen, "The Early American Origins of Entitlements," *Studies in American Political Development* 10 (Fall 1996).

for the duration of the war. In 1779, Washington began pressuring Congress to extend officers' half-pay for the rest of their lives and enact pensions for soldiers' widows and orphans. In 1780, Congress enacted both of Washington's requests. The former set a significant precedent for the government provision of open-ended selective pension benefits. The latter was a recruitment tool because many able-bodied breadwinners were reluctant to sign up for military service when their possible death could leave their families financially destitute. These measures helped keep the Continental army together until the end of the war but did not quell the threat of a coup in 1783 in Newburgh, New York, by that army against the government over back pay and pensions. Laura S. Jensen argues that the near coup at Newburgh, which Washington's prestige helped stamp out, demonstrated that pension legislation for Revolutionary War officers and their survivors was key to the nationalist leadership's empowering of the central government in the nascent nation.[41] In March 1783, after the Newburgh incident, Congress rushed to pass even more generous pension legislation: instead of half-pay for life, Continental officers would receive five years of full pay or securities earning 6 percent per year.

The War of 1812 instilled a sense of nationalism in the country and overwhelmed thirty-five years of American resistance to selective, exclusionary government benefits and forty years of congressional balking at rewarding military service with lifetime pensions. In 1817, President James Monroe, a Continental Revolutionary War officer himself, proposed service pensions—half-pay for life—not only for all those officers who were poor, but for enlisted soldiers, too. Yet at the time there was much objection to the concept that the federal government would discriminate between "deserving" and "undeserving" citizens—that is, excluding some citizens to hand out selective entitlements. To some, exclusionary pensions seemed to violate the Constitution's need to "promote the general Welfare" and to give too much discretionary power to the national government.

Despite these objections, in 1818 Congress created pensions for those in the Continental army or navy who served to the end of the Revolutionary War or at least nine months during the war and were poor. The original pensions for disabled Continentals and these new pensions only for service were the first

---

41. Jensen, "The Early American Origins of Entitlements."

categorical, national entitlements in the nation's history. These entitlements set the precedent for subsequent veterans' programs and for doling out preferential, exclusionary benefits to special groups to solve the nation's socioeconomic problems.

Although Monroe maintained in 1818 that few Revolutionary War veterans were still alive at this time, the government was overwhelmed with demands for pensions under the new law. The program was supposed to be short and cheap but, like most government efforts, turned out to be long and expensive. As this first entitlement—and all that followed—demonstrated, the nature of entitlements is that once given they can balloon out of control and become almost impossible to take away from recipients. The first entitlements also demonstrated a standard phenomenon: expanding benefits over time. One of the reasons for this vast expansion, in addition to the lobbying by the potent "entitled" pressure group of Revolutionary War veterans, was that veterans not covered under the 1818 law pushed for inclusion.[42] Another reason for the widening of benefits was the creation of a central administrative bureaucracy under a system of government that was supposed to be decentralized. As has happened with many subsequent federal programs, the bureaucracy also pushed for program expansion to augment its own functions, power, and funding. Members of Congress, mirroring modern practice, used the program to get reelected by bringing home additional benefits as pork.

Jensen summarizes the historical legacy of Revolutionary War pensions:

> State actors of the 1780s understood that land grants and pension enactments could simultaneously secure the services of military leaders, direct their energies toward the nationalist purposes of the new American state, and strengthen the central government by justifying congressional revenue measures and rationalizing Federal administration. The implementation and extension of veterans' pensions and other selective entitlements during the first part of the nineteenth century led to increased fiscal and administrative capacity at the center as presidents and members of Congress acquired a powerful means of appealing directly to a growing electorate, creating a new nexus between the national government and individual citizens. . . .

---

42. Jensen, "The Early American Origins of Entitlements."

... [T]he highly discretionary, early pension legislation stood as a policy precedent awaiting the nationalistic fervor and treasury surplus of the post–War 1812 years. The enactment of the categorical 1818 pension act that finally implemented a program of benefits for certain Revolutionary veterans "in need of assistance" was a defining moment in the development of the American welfare state. . . .

It was this policy legacy that helped pave the way for the national government's creation of the highly categorical, non-universal, "programmatic rights" of the post–New Deal era and the concomitant rise of an expanded, national policy-driven, administrative state. . . .

Where once a national community of regular, relatively equal citizens might have evolved, the American polity had begun to be divided into multiple, overlapping, legally circumscribed categories of "special" clients and claimants.[43]

Second Precedent for Social Security: Civil War Pensions

Ever since colonial times, to encourage enlistment of male breadwinners, all levels of government, including the federal government, had paid widows and orphans who had lost a soldier in war. And in 1862, as early Union defeats on the battlefield tempered patriotic enlistment in the North, the federal government for the same reason increased the level of compensation for such dependents and widened the range of family members covered by the payments, including widows, orphans, and elderly parents and siblings of those killed in battle. This compensation had the humanitarian byproduct of helping such victims of war, but nonetheless created, over time, the monster of modern entitlement programs that have much less relation to war and that are busting the federal budget today.

During the post–Civil War period, the vast pension system created by the war was later used to deal with the societal issues of the elderly and widows. This social program served a major fraction of the population. From 1776 to 1861, the federal government had paid 143,644 pension claims; from 1861 to 1890, it paid out more than five times that number in Civil War pensions. By 1889, US pension spending alone was greater than the entire federal budget

---

43. Jensen, "The Early American Origins of Entitlements," 402–03.

before the Civil War. By 1893, a whopping 40 percent of the federal budget was allocated for disabled troops, widows, orphans, and the elderly. The patronage-oriented politics of the Republican Party—the winning party of the Civil War, which maintained dominance of American politics in the last half of the 1800s and the early decades of the 1900s—had led to the huge expansion of pension benefits to win votes. High tariffs and their revenues paid for those benefits.[44]

In 1879, the Arrears Act allowed veterans who hadn't realized they were disabled until the government offered $1,000 or more for finding aches and disabilities to flood the Bureau of Pensions with such claims. In 1890, twenty-five years after the Civil War ended, pensions expanded to include any soldier who had served ninety days or more during the war and was unable to do manual labor—whether he was injured during the conflict or not or even whether he had seen combat or not. Thus, the cause of the veteran's disability did not have to be the war and could just be old age. Similarly, widows of soldiers serving in the Civil War for ninety days or more received pensions regardless of whether their husbands had died in the war.

During and just after the war, mothers and fathers who had been dependent on dead veterans for their livelihood were added as pension recipients, as long as the veteran had died of a war-related illness or injury, in whole or in part. So in 1873 and 1890, long after the war was over, Congress expanded federal responsibility for care of the elderly. In 1890, the requirement to prove dependency on the deceased veteran was removed, thus providing pensions to elderly mothers and fathers as long their son's death resulted from war service.[45] Thus, Civil War pensions had evolved from payments for combat wounds and death to a munificent system of old-age and disability benefits.[46]

The expanded program was not merely a military pension program. As Megan McClintock concludes, "Civil War pensions were not simply a military benefits program, however, but also a social welfare system that contained assumptions about familial relationships. Only those pension claimants whose domestic arrangements met with approval received federal moneys. In the

44. Megan J. McClintock, "Civil War Pensions and the Reconstruction of Union Families," *Journal of American History* 83 (September 1996): 456–80.

45. McClintock, "Civil War Pensions and the Reconstruction of Union Families."

46. Theda Skocpol, "America's First Social Security System: The Expansion of Benefits for Civil War Veterans," *Political Science Quarterly* 108, no. 1 (1993).

case of mothers and fathers, the ideal of filial devotion encouraged the federal government to become a provider of poor relief for the elderly in the late nineteenth century."[47]

McClintock provides a good summary of the Civil War mobilization's dramatic—but now neglected—effect on widening the federal government's social welfare role:

> Before the Civil War, the federal government had assumed only limited responsibility for military dependents and virtually none for the civilian poor and disabled. Pre–Civil War military benefits were piecemeal and limited to veterans, widows, and orphans; moreover, the federal government abstained from social welfare spending for the civilian poor, and local charity was stigmatized and parsimonious. The nation's first "modern" war transformed the landscape of relief, forging new ties between the federal government and families, and between public and private economies, as the government sought to increase the number of men willing to leave their families in the 1860s and to prepare future citizen soldiers for patriotic sacrifice.[48]

According to Theda Skocpol, the Civil War pension system degraded into what became America's first massive, federally funded old-age and disability welfare system:

> By the time the elected politicians—especially Republicans—had finished liberalizing eligibility for Civil War pensions, over a third of all the elderly men living in the North, along with quite a few elderly men in other parts of the country and many widows and dependents across the nation, were receiving quarterly payments from the United States Pension Bureau. In terms of the large share of the federal budget spent, the hefty proportion of citizens covered, and the relative generosity of the disability and old-age benefits offered, the United States had become a precocious social spending state. Its post–Civil War system of social provision in many respects exceeded what early programs

---

47. McClintock, "Civil War Pensions and the Reconstruction of Union Families," 466.
48. McClintock, "Civil War Pensions and the Reconstruction of Union Families," 479–80.

of "workman's insurance" were giving old people or superannuated industrial wage earners in fledgling Western welfare states around the world.[49]

Skocpol argues that public revulsion in America toward the expansion, excesses, and corruption of the Civil War pension system from the 1870s to 1910 may have stalled the onset of the American welfare state—which was then taking hold in other Western countries—until the New Deal in the 1930s. Americans may have been repelled by Civil War pensions because—in a classic case of high taxes leading to surplus government revenues leading to excess spending—Republicans supported lavish pensions to groups in their political constituency (Union veterans) to justify continued high tariff walls (which generated high tax revenues) to protect northern industries, which were among the most influential supporters in the Republicans' political coalition. The interests of such industrialists coincided with those of pension-recipient lobbies and the bureaucratic empire of the Bureau of Pensions to widen the pension program greatly over time. Moreover, the expansion of Civil War benefits came even as claims from direct battle casualties had gone down. So although the Grand Army of the Republic, a powerful lobbying organization of Civil War veterans, promoted the nation's hallowed obligation to protect Union veterans who had saved it, many people who derived pensions from the Civil War didn't suffer from war wounds or poverty. By 1910, forty-five years after the end of the war, about 28 percent of American men sixty-five years of age and older were receiving federal benefits.[50] This fact likely led to the erosion of public confidence in the system.

In a pattern seen throughout US history, government expansion during warfare is initially attenuated, and more rarely reversed, after the war is over—yet can come roaring back at a future date. So although permanent general old-age pensions and social insurance were delayed, pensions for widowed mothers at the state level—a direct descendant of war widows' pensions—were

---

49. Theda Skocpol, *Protecting Soldiers and Mothers: The Political Origins of Social Policy in the United States* (Cambridge, MA: Belknap Press of Harvard University Press), 1992, 1–2.

50. Skocpol, "America's First Social Security System," 85.

enacted during the period from 1900 to 1930, and Social Security and other welfare-state programs grew out of control after that.

In short, Civil War pensions were America's first system of federal social security for the disabled and elderly. And they were a precedent for other even broader and more expensive federal programs to come.

Beyond Taxes and Pensions

The ratchet effect of war on the growth of government has penetrated our lives much beyond new taxes levied for war and sustained after that and beyond the payment of pensions.

Federal Involvement in Regulating Marriage

Concomitant with the government's involvement in marriage to monitor the moral conduct of widows to enforce Civil War pension rights and demonstrating that war means growth in government even in areas that seem remotely connected to conflict, the government began to regulate marriage itself. During the nineteenth century, marital relations were fluid and laissez-faire. Moral "reformers," however, argued that the private practice of marriage caused instability in the family and society. So common-law marriage came under attack from those who saw a "public interest in matrimony." Government registration of marriages and formal ceremonies were thought to be the answer.[51]

Expansion of Medicaid to Cover Preventive Care for Children

By September 30, 1963, things were not looking good in the Vietnam War. Communist guerillas had won several major military victories. John F. Kennedy sharply increased the number of US "advisers" in Vietnam. This situation was the backdrop for Kennedy's establishing the Task Force on Manpower Conservation to investigate why in 1962 an incredible 50 percent of draftees were bounced from qualifying for induction into the armed forces because they failed their medical or mental aptitude exams. The task force issued its

---

51. McClintock, "Civil War Pensions and the Reconstruction of Union Families."

report on January 1, 1964, early in Lyndon Johnson's administration. The report, *One Third of a Nation: A Report on Young Men Found Unqualified for Military Service*, found that the majority of young men rejected for the draft had failed as a result of mental, physical, and developmental conditions, many of which could have been diagnosed and treated in childhood and adolescence. The young adults rejected usually came from poor families. The report supported Lyndon Johnson's notion that improving the health and wellness of the nation's impoverished required closing income, social, and health gaps. Most of the report's recommendations were directed toward programs to help poor potential recruits barred from military induction. Yet it also suggested improvements in screening, diagnosis, and treatment of medical maladies in younger children and adolescents, especially such programs in schools.

Thus, the report significantly affected the passage of comprehensive and precedent-setting legislation that expanded Medicaid for poor children in the general population to include early and periodic preventive screening and diagnosis. Sara Rosenbaum and her colleagues conclude that "evidence of the poor health status of young military recruits played a powerful role in this set of policy reforms" and that "the national security study" laid "the foundation of [the] Medicaid child health policy."[52] In sum, the report had a big role in the expansion of Medicaid for children passed in 1967.

Public Housing and Rent Control

Up until World War I, the United States had no history of government-provided housing. The war created severe housing shortages because it sucked capital, workers, and raw materials from the housing industry and increased demand for housing near war-related facilities. Thus, rents exploded. In response, the Ordinance Department started building living space for workers in the armament industry. The government's Emergency Fleet Corporation began building dwellings for shipyard workers. The Labor Department created the US Housing Corporation to build housing for workers supplying the war.

52. Sara Rosenbaum, Richard Mauery, Peter Shin, and Julia Hidalgo, *National Security and U.S. Child Health Policy: The Origins and Continuing Role of Medicaid and EPSDT*, Policy brief (Washington, DC: School of Public Health and Health Services, George Washington University, 2005), 2, 11.

After the war, these housing projects were sold to the private sector.[53] After this wartime experience, however, the government now had a precedent to interfere in and compete with the private housing market.

Rents also exploded during World War II for the same reasons. Because of fears of a wartime housing shortage, New York City imposed rent controls in 1943 that are still in place today.[54]

Federal Involvement in Daycare

During World War II, men went to the front, and women substituted for them in workplaces, so something had to be done with the kids while mom was riveting aircraft. In response, federal involvement in daycare became a "national security" item. The federal government subsidized a nationwide program of child-care centers.[55]

Grants-in-Aid to States

During World War I, the federal government first gave grants-in-aid to states to use for transportation, agricultural extension programs, and other purposes. Grants-in-aid are revenues derived from federal taxes given to states. The rise of the income tax during the war gave the federal government better sources of revenue than the states—thus facilitating such grants.

Measures to Combat Unemployment

World War I began the federal government's first foray into providing people with jobs, which the public had previously not thought was a major federal responsibility. Because the federal government had by this time deeply pen-

---

53. Ronald Schaffer, *America in the Great War: The Rise of the War Welfare State* (Oxford: Oxford University Press, 1991).

54. Christopher Preble, "The Founders, Executive Power, and Military Intervention," *Pace Law Review* 30, no. 2 (Winter 2010): 702.

55. Emilie Stolzfus, "Child Care: The Federal Role During World War II," Report for Congress (Washington, DC: Congressional Research Service, n.d.), http://congressional research.com/RS20615/document.php?study=child care the federal role during world war ii.

etrated the nation's economy, federal responsibility for maintaining employment in the economy eventually became widely accepted, including by the Wilson administration. For example, during the war the United States Employment Service, a federal labor-exchange network, was created to help people find the right job. The office would set a precedent for the later entry of the federal government into helping people find jobs during peacetime. Its postwar funding was reduced, but labor unions and bureaucrats in the Department of Labor kept the office alive to fund state government employment services.[56]

During the postwar recession, a flurry of reconstruction bills, including federal spending on public works, were submitted in Congress. One public-works bill, put forth by the Department of Labor, foreshadowed the Emergency Relief and Construction Act of the Hoover administration during the first years of the Great Depression.

An unnerving war-induced but delayed depression from 1921 to 1922 caused the normally laissez-faire Harding administration to convene the landmark President's Conference on Unemployment in the fall of 1921. Udo Sautter concludes that in holding the conference, the federal government for the first time formally acknowledged, at least in principle, some responsibility for the lot of the unemployed.[57] He notes that this acknowledgment was natural in the wake of the federally run war. The conference was a critical event because it carried the idea of a federal role in combating unemployment into times of prosperity. Then–commerce secretary Herbert Hoover played a prominent role in the conference, and his later administration was the first to adopt significant policies establishing the federal government's responsibility for getting people jobs during peacetime.

In the wake of the conference, a highway bill contained a small sum of money for public works, but it was the first time that the federal government used public works to increase employment during a peacetime economic emergency.[58] It would not be the last.

---

56. Udo Sautter, "Preparing the Welfare State: American Unemployment Reform in the Early Twentieth Century," *Journal of the Canadian Historical Association* 1, no. 1 (1990): 247–50.

57. Sautter, "Preparing the Welfare State."

58. Sautter, "Preparing the Welfare State," 250.

Price Controls

World War I, unlike even the Civil War, created the precedent of deep government penetration of the economy and use of it to prosecute a war. During World War II, a similar but even more intrusive model applied to an even bigger economy. As part of those war efforts, the government controlled some prices more directly. During the first war, the government set some wages, thus establishing a precedent for the later federal minimum wage.

In the summer of 1917, Congress passed the Lever Food and Fuel Control Act, which was one of the most draconian grants of governmental authority in US history. The war blocked normal international trade in food, and the US government had to feed not only its own military, but also its overseas allies. Thus, food shortages arose at home. The Lever Act gave President Woodrow Wilson the power to control food output, distribution, and prices and to regulate any product used in food production, including fuel. In one of the most egregious examples of price controls, the government arbitrarily set the price of coal so high that even inefficient coal producers remained viable. All this regulation of food and fuel was designed to expand output while restricting domestic civilian consumption.[59] In other words, the government increased the price of food to already hungry people to facilitate the war effort.

Although the retail prices of scarce essentials, such as food and fuel, were directly controlled during World War I, most retail prices were indirectly controlled through "commodity controls." Those controls rationed—and many times denied—coal, raw materials, freight car rail transportation, capital, and credit to industries deemed "nonessential" to the war effort. During the war, most of the direct price controls were applied at the producer or wholesale level. Nonetheless, although all prices were not directly controlled during the war, a bad precedent was set for more ambitious attempts at price regulation in the future.

Thus, during World War II, inflation created by the expansion of the money supply and bank credit resulted in direct government control of many retail prices. Such drastic, comprehensive regulation of prices led to a deterioration

---

59. Schaffer, *America in the Great War*.

in the quality of the goods sold and the rise of a significant subterranean black-market economy.[60]

And during the second global conflict, reflecting the precedent set in World War I, the US government controlled much more than prices. Burton Folsom and Anita Folsom describe how FDR's influential War Production Board (WPB) operated during that conflict:

> And powerful it was: The War Production Board halted all construction projects that were not essential to the war effort, and it decreed what was essential. It directed the conversion of civilian industries to meet wartime needs, allocated scarce materials, and decided what services to the public would be curtailed. It rationed heating oil, gasoline, metals, rubber, paper, and plastic. The WPB's clothing section even regulated the amount of fabric that retailers could use per garment, avoiding wasteful styles such as long, full skirts for women. Clothing would be more formfitting, and skirts would be shorter.[61]

Price controls during the much smaller Vietnam War followed the precedent set by such controls in the two larger world wars. In 1971, to attempt to stanch inflation caused by the government's guns-and-butter policy (referring to spending on the Vietnam War and simultaneous heavy domestic spending) and excessive money-supply growth designed to artificially pump up the economy before the 1972 election, President Richard Nixon, who had previously been a rabid opponent of price controls, now imposed them.[62] As usual, the controls did not deal with the principal underlying causes of the disease of inflation—excessive government spending and growth in the money supply—but instead focused on

---

60. Benjamin M. Anderson, *Economics and the Public Welfare: Financial and Economic History of the United States, 1914–1946* (Princeton, NJ: Van Nostrand, 1949); and Burton Folsom and Anita Folsom, *FDR Goes to War: How Expanded Executive Power, Spiraling National Debt, and Restricted Civil Liberties Shaped Wartime America* (New York: Simon & Schuster, 2011).

61. Folsom, *FDR Goes to War*, 119.

62. John H. Wood, *A History of Macroeconomic Policy in the United States* (London: Routledge, 2009), 169–71; and Michael Lind, *Land of Promise: An Economic History of the United States* (New York: Harper Collins, 2012), 380–81.

the symptom of rising prices. When the economy-wide controls were eventually removed, pent-up inflation surged.

Government Distortion of the Health Care Market

As a result of government controls on wages and salaries during World War II, businesses started providing health insurance to their employees in a widespread manner as a recruiting incentive during the labor shortages caused by war production and those very controls. From this origin, although it is still an inefficient way to provide health insurance for society, people have come to expect their employer to pay at least part of the bill for such coverage.[63] In turn, the government gives businesses a tax break for doing so, but there isn't a free lunch: the government also takes the opportunity to regulate the practice. For example, it more recently mandated that all organizations providing health insurance for their employees—including Catholic schools, hospitals, and universities—cover contraceptives free of charge. An uproar resulted, but it was over the First Amendment right to freely exercise religion (by not providing benefits that raised religious objections) rather than over whether government should tell private organizations and insurers what to cover in private insurance policies.

All of this government interference has the effect of distorting the markets for health insurance and thus health care, thus contributing to their soaring costs.

Nationalization of Industries

The standard textbook definition of socialism is government takeover of the means of production—hence, the term war socialism. During World War I, the government—desiring a seamless rail web throughout the country to transport raw materials, manufactured goods such as weapons and ammunition, and personnel for the war effort—nationalized nearly three thousand rail

---

63. Thomas C. Buchmueller and Alan C. Monheit, "Employer-Sponsored Health Insurance and the Promise of Health Insurance Reform," NBER Working Paper 14839 (Cambridge, MA: National Bureau of Economic Research, 2009).

and related companies. President Woodrow Wilson created the Railroad Administration and named William G. McAdoo, the secretary of the Treasury, as its head. The administration could ignore competition, antitrust laws, money owed to creditors, and even shipping orders from other government agencies.

During the war, the private railroad companies lost profit opportunities and experienced severely depreciated capital. But as with most government regulation, even war socialism eventually provided at least some benefits to the industry. Private railroad managers dominated the war administration and steamrolled it into policies they had wanted before the war. The managers were now effectively exempt from antitrust law and from state regulatory commissions. The shipping and telegraph companies were also nationalized.[64] The latter had dire implications for free speech and communication during wartime.

Alternatively, during war the government sometimes threatens to take over industries unless they play ball with official policy. For example, during World War I the government threatened to take over steel companies if their owners balked at charging government-"recommended" prices. Following this precedent, during the Korean War President Harry Truman tried to take over steel companies to end strikes but was thwarted by the US Supreme Court.

In a time of economic crisis, Republican George W. Bush and Democrat Barack Obama followed wartime precedent, effectively nationalizing the AIG insurance company and the Chrysler and General Motors auto companies, respectively.

"Associationalism" and Industry Self-Regulation

"Associationalism" gained great impetus during World War I. In order to increase war production, this concept involved the government creating cartels in industry and letting the industries self-regulate. A proponent of associationalism, Herbert Hoover probably never would have become commerce secretary or president had it not been for World War I. During the Great Depression, Herbert Hoover's associationalism in the late 1920s was patterned after this

---

64. Schaffer, *America in the Great War*.

war experience, as was much of FDR's New Deal. Although the US Supreme Court rejected the New Deal's National Industrial Recovery Act and the Agricultural Adjustment Act of 1933, the model survived in the form of regulations in the following industries: agriculture, trucking, commercial air travel, public utilities, communications, investment banking, and the stock market. Although such regulatory initiatives always had an excuse—either protecting consumers or lessening the uncertainty of economic fluctuations—the reality was that the regulations, enforced to the benefit of large corporations, blocked the entry of competitors, artificially inflated prices for consumers, and led to technological sluggishness in the industries. Government agencies essentially became cartel overseers.[65]

Government Involvement in Labor Relations

During peacetime, government and business often have a common interest in nipping labor unrest in the bud, sometimes using coercion or the threat thereof. During wartime, however, organized labor is in a better bargaining position due to the very urgency of the war. To thwart this potential, during both world wars, new government agencies were created to negotiate labor disputes, manage working conditions and wages, and reassign labor to war industries. During World War I, in exchange for formal government approval of the right to organize and collectively bargain—implemented by the National War Labor Board (NWLB)—labor leaders asked workers to curtail strikes. After the war, the government temporarily reduced its role in managing labor relations, but then the Great Depression reinvigorated the wartime precedent of heavy government involvement. New Deal legislation facilitated the organization of unions, required businesses to bargain collectively with them, and, based on the wartime National War Labor Board, deepened government involvement in the collective-bargaining process through the creation of the coercive National Labor Relations Board.[66]

---

65. Eisner, *From Warfare State to Welfare State*.
66. Eisner, *From Warfare State to Welfare State*.

Rich Tradition of Inflationary Money Printing During Wartime

Governments are rarely honest about the high costs of armed conflict.[67] In order to avoid raising taxes too much, they resort to borrowing money—which pushes off the pain of additional taxes until later—or, even worse, to printing money. Printing money leads to too much money chasing too few consumer goods, the production of which have been cut back to allow the manufacture of war materiel. The result is inflation—a general increase in prices throughout the economy. High inflation distorts investment decisions in the economy, which can have dire effects on growth in economic output and thus prosperity. Yet even though printing money is the worst way to fund a war, it is also less politically costly for the government elite because it camouflages the high cost of war. As a result, in US history starting with the American Revolution the government has printed money to pay for a significant portion of the expenses to fight most of its wars.

To finance the American Revolution against Britain, the Continental Congress increased the money supply almost nineteen-fold, and the states issued their own debt.[68] By the termination of hostilities, citizens had lost trust in paper money, which resulted in the slogan "not worth a continental." All of this worthless money caused a period of severe inflation.[69] Many of the nation's founders wanted the states to default on their debt, but Secretary of the Treasury Alexander Hamilton, both believing that such defaults would discourage foreign investors from putting money into the US economy and desiring to increase the power of the new federal government, proposed the creation of a national bank. The Bank of the United States, created in 1791 and modeled on the Bank of England, was, as an agent of the US Treasury, to assume state debts.

---

67. Much of the information in this section came from research assistance provided by Justin Merrill.

68. Murray N. Rothbard, *A History of Money and Banking in the United States: The Colonial Era to World War II* (Auburn, AL: Ludwig von Mises Institute, 2002).

69. Eric Newman, *The Early Paper Money of America*, 3rd ed. (Iola, WI: Krause, 1990).

Although the national bank charter was not renewed after twenty years of operation, the precedent for a national bank was later revisited and eventually became in the early years of the twentieth century the disaster known as the Federal Reserve. So war led to high inflation and set a precedent for unconstitutional central banking in the United States.

During the War of 1812, in the first bailout of banks in US history, the government allowed them to suspend their obligation to redeem their notes in specie (gold). This policy encouraged banks to expand issuance of notes, thus increasing the money supply and devaluing paper money. The ballooning bank-insolvency problem caused the government to resurrect a national bank in 1816 to buy up the devalued debt from banks. It didn't work; massive customer runs on the banks led to a collapse of the banking system in the Panic of 1817.[70] Again, inflation and a precedent for unconstitutional central banking came out of war, but this time a precedent was also set for the government's bailing out of banks.

Following the wartime precedent, during the peacetime panic of 1857, the government again allowed banks to suspend their obligation to redeem their notes in gold. Some banks also spurned this obligation in late 1860, when Abraham Lincoln's election led to an economic panic.[71]

During the Civil War, both the Union and Confederacy issued paper money to pay for war expenses. So-called greenbacks, issued in the North, were not redeemable in gold. In December 1861, the first year of the conflict, Lincoln also suspended banks' obligation to redeem their notes in gold. By early 1862, the Northern public had lost so much faith in banks and paper money that Congress had to pass legal-tender laws. This unorthodox method of public finance said that both paper money and metal coins were legal tender and had the same face value for economic transactions. The unredeemable greenbacks and legal-tender laws allowed banks to expand the money supply, which was needed because the government was flummoxed in its attempts to finance the war via borrowing from the public—that is, its bond auctions had failed to raise enough funds.

---

70. John H. Wood, *A History of Macroeconomic Policy in the United States* (London: Routledge, 2009), 95–99.

71. Russell McClintock, *Lincoln and the Decision for War: Northern Response to Secession* (Chapel Hill: University of North Carolina Press, 2008).

During World War I, inflation averaged almost 20 percent per year. Contributing to this problem was the government's expansion of the money supply by buying the US Treasury's debt, by lowering the requirement for private banks reserves and thus increasing their lending, and by creating the WFC. The WFC was a publicly owned bank that gave credit to corporations involved in the war effort. As noted earlier, the organization later became a model for the peacetime RFC under the Hoover administration and FDR's New Deal.[72]

During World War II, even with government wage-and-price controls in effect, the Consumer Price Index went up 18 percent.[73] Two-thirds of the money used to finance war spending was either borrowed from the public via war bonds or printed via the Federal Reserve's monetization of the debt (the money supply increased at an annualized rate of 25.5 percent during the war).

The Vietnam War (as usual) caused the inflation rate to rise and effectively destroyed the global monetary system created under Bretton Woods. Democrat Lyndon Johnson's and Republican Richard Nixon's guns-and-butter policies created doubts in countries holding US dollar reserves about whether the United States was printing more money than it could back with gold. The Federal Reserve purchased (monetized) about 23 percent of the US government's added debt during the war years (from 1965 to 1973). These nervous countries began trading their dollars for gold at the then fixed rate. This run on US gold necessitated Nixon's termination of convertibility of US dollars into gold—on which the world's financial system (the Bretton Woods framework) was then based. Thus, from that time forward, the sound commodity-based money-exchange standard was destroyed and replaced with an international floating fiat dollar-exchange standard.

In the decade before the start of heavy US involvement in the Vietnam War (1955–65), prices increased only 17 percent; in the decade after entry into the war (1965–75), prices increased 71 percent. This high inflation did not let up until the early 1980s, when Paul Volcker, chairman of the Federal Reserve, slammed on the monetary brakes, causing a steep recession but ultimately

---

72. Benjamin M. Anderson, Jr., *Effects of the War on Money, Credit, and Banking in France and the United States* (Oxford: Oxford University Press, 1919), http://publicdebt.treas.gov/history.

73. Wood, *A History of Macroeconomic Policy in the United States*, 171.

helping create low inflation and prosperity during the Reagan administration and thereafter.

Bailouts of Banks

George W. Bush's bailout of banks during the Great Recession was nothing new. The first federal bank bailout had occurred during the War of 1812, when the financial stress induced by that war had caused the federal government to allow banks to suspend their obligation to redeem their notes in gold. This bad precedent led to government bailouts of financial institutions thereafter—even if they have behaved irresponsibly—because government financial authorities believe that banks are the vital circulatory system for the economy and that large banks are "too big to fail."

During that war, as in most conflicts, the government expanded the money supply—doubling it to help fund war expenses—and allowed banks to suspend payments of their notes in gold. After the war, the government collapsed the money bubble to try to thwart war-induced inflation—a common occurrence during wars because consumption is restricted in favor of war production, thus leading too much money to chase too few goods. This action caused the collapse of the banking system.[74]

In 1913, just prior to World War I, the Federal Reserve System was created—a descendent of the Bank of the United States. The Fed's profligate expansion of the money supply during the war and again during the 1920s helped bring about an artificial economic bubble that fueled excessive speculation in the stock market, leading eventually to the stock market crash, the bursting of the economic bubble in 1929, and the onset of the Great Depression.[75]

Just after taking office in 1933, during the worst of the Great Depression, FDR followed the precedent set in the wartime-related emergency in 1817, closing the banks for a few days to halt a run on them by depositors wanting their cash. In effect, his closure suspended all required payments by banks to the public, thus acting as disguised welfare to bankers. Later presidents, in-

---

74. Wood, *A History of Macroeconomic Policy in the United States*, 88–90.
75. Wood, *A History of Macroeconomic Policy in the United States*, 96–102.

cluding George W. Bush and Barak Obama, have enacted wider bank bailouts based on this precedent.

More General Bailouts of Wall Street

In 1914, after World War I erupted in Europe but before the United States was involved, William Gibbs McAdoo, Secretary of the Treasury, shut down the New York Stock Exchange for four months. This US government action ostensibly prevented foreigners involved in the conflict from having access to US securities, thus impairing their war-fighting ability. In reality, the action bailed out the American stock market. The likely rush of foreigners cashing in their stocks for money to use in the war would have made the US market plunge.

Such government intervention set a bad precedent for future bailouts of Wall Street and stock market closures. For example, the government also closed the stock market in 1933 during the Great Depression and for almost a week after the September 11, 2001, attacks.

Intrusive Government Collection of Economic Data

As noted earlier, during World War I, for the first time in American history, the government deeply penetrated the economy and mobilized it for war. To succeed in this Herculean socialist task, federal authorities first began collecting nationwide and sector wide economic data. Of course, such extensive data collection required businesses to turn over much information—and their privacy—to the government. After the war ended, officials wanted to keep the information from commercial interests flowing in. All the new government bureaucrats, empowered to do an expanded set of tasks, wanted augmented data collection to carry out these tasks. More extensive data in turn led to a further expansion of government activities.

The Commerce Department researched the multitude of goods produced and decided that it should standardize them. Based on the data the department was now collecting, the Federal Reserve sought to manage the business cycle in the economy. Its intervention in the economy has been especially pernicious to the nation over the years. The Department of Agriculture began forecasting harvests and thus prices, which led to the bureaucracy's attempt to interfere with farmers' choice of crops.[76] All of these dubious government activities would have been impossible in the prewar years, when much less data were collected by the government.

Regulation of Food and Alcohol

The on-ramp to the ill-conceived Eighteenth Amendment—prohibiting the manufacture, sale, transportation, import, or export of alcoholic beverages—grew shorter during World War I. The Selective Service Act of 1917, which began drafting young men for military service, created dry areas around military bases and prohibited people from giving or selling drinks to military personnel in public or private places. In August 1917, a part of the aforementioned Lever Food and Fuel Control Act banned the use of food for distilling booze. In early December 1917, President Woodrow Wilson limited the brewing of beer to that containing 2.75 percent alcohol or less and curtailed dramatically the amount of grain brewers could use.[77] All of this was done ostensibly to save food for the war effort but was mainly a moral pronouncement on the evils of drinking. On December 22, 1917, Congress passed the Eighteenth Amendment, which was ratified over the course of two years; prohibition began in January 1920.

As Ronald Schaffer notes, "The United States government responded favorably to the political strength of the prohibitionists because of the personal sympathy certain government officials had for their cause and also because prohibition was a way of managing the nation at war; it held promise for diverting food supplies to war production, increasing the output of war workers, and building a fighting force that could be sent into battle physically and morally strong and soberly efficient."[78]

The prohibition of alcohol was a widely violated policy disaster. Many people wanted to drink, no matter what the government ordered. The rise

---

76. Eisner, *From Warfare State to Welfare State.*
77. Schaffer, *America in the Great War,* 98.
78. Schaffer, *America in the Great War,* 98.

of organized crime in America—as it took over the dangerous production, sale, and transportation of a governmentally banned substance during this period—only helped fuel the expansion of federal law enforcement agencies.

Yet the ignominious results of failed prohibition nevertheless have strangely inspired the current massive, failed war on drugs—a war that similarly enhances dangerous organized crime elements that earn huge profits on products made much more expensive by their illegality.

War on Prostitution

During World War I, defenders of "morality" also attacked prostitution. And they concentrated their cleansing on the US Army. The army had always had the philosophy that prostitution was an outlet for the troops and during the guerilla war in the Philippines ran the biggest licensed house of ill repute in the world. When the army greatly enlarged for World War I, however, the moralists could no longer put up with regulated prostitution. To keep the troops away from prostitutes, the army declared Seattle and Birmingham off limits and sent the marines to patrol the streets of Philadelphia.

As in the more recent campaign against cigarettes, the government used movies, pamphlets, and grotesque and scary photos of the medical effects of venereal disease. The amazing effect of this effort was that by the close of 1917 every red light district in every American city had been shut down.

But the government didn't stop its eradication campaign with prostitution; it began to guard against troops having sex with flappers and other "unsavory women" who would "destroy their fighting power." Thus, the War Department established the Committee on the Protection of Girls. The committee dispatched "purifiers" to military bases to follow soldiers and their women to secluded spots and to browbeat communities to close burlesque shows that would tempt young troops and their lady friends to have intercourse.

And the violations of rights just kept getting worse. Federal and local governments forced women in areas surrounding military bases to undergo mandatory physical exams and carried out vice raids that swept up working-class, unemployed, and unescorted women, who were denied bail while they were tested and treated for venereal disease. From 1918 to 1920, new federal prisons were set up to house eighteen thousand women busted on prostitution charges.[79]

Thus, during World War I the federal government became heavily involved in defending morals and eliminating vice.

Daylight Savings Time

Does the government even have to control and manipulate the time? Apparently it does during wartime (and thereafter).

In the 1880s, the American railroads had standardized time based on four time zones (before that, each town or city was on its own time), and most large towns and cities had rapidly adopted the standard voluntarily. World War I, however, resulted in Congress making railroad time mandatory everywhere.[80] Also, to save energy during World War I, the government invented daylight savings time for part of the year.[81] During the war, the duration of daylight savings time was only six months. In 1973, 1986, and 2007, ostensibly to save even more energy, the government extended it further, so that it now lasts eight months. It still seems odd, though, that the government wants to save daylight during the period of the year when the days are longest.

Conclusion

War frequently leads to large increases in taxes, regulation, and government spending, both for the military and for ostensibly unrelated domestic programs. Conservatives should not ignore that war is probably the most prominent cause of the massive welfare state that has been erected in the United States. Although other wars—such as the Civil War and even the American Revolution—played their part in ballooning government, World War I instituted permanent big government in the United States. The government's deep penetration of the economy in order to prosecute the war set bad prec-

---

79. Schaffer, *America in the Great War*, 99–103.

80. Seymour Morris, *American History Revised: 200 Startling Facts That Never Made It into the Textbooks* (New York: Broadway Books, 2010).

81. Schaffer, *America in the Great War*, 35.

edents for excessive public spending, taxes, and regulation that are roundly and wrongly believed to have originated during the Great Depression—first in the Hoover administration and then in Roosevelt's New Deal. The template for public programs and agencies during the Depression came from intrusive government management during World War I, and many of the people who managed such wartime efforts were brought back during the economic downturn. The model used for the even deeper penetration of the civilian economy during World War II came from that of World War I. And the expansion of non-military parts of the federal government was faster during World War II than it was even in the New Deal during the Great Depression.

Many conservatives today might argue that despite the ballooning of government, war is sometimes necessary for US security. However, most of the nation's big wars were unneeded, downright foolish, or counterproductive.[82] Traditional conservatives recognized in the past that war is the primary cause of big government in human history, so they promoted peace. Since the rise of William F. Buckley and the neoconservatives in the mid-1950s, however, the Right has forgotten that the best way to limit government is to have peace. That important lesson needs to be relearned.

---

82. See Ivan Eland, "Most Wars in American History Were Unnecessary and Undermined the Republic," *Mediterranean Quarterly* 23 (Summer 2012).

6

Reclaiming Congressional Authority

THE EXPANSION OF executive power over the nation's history —especially since the dawn of the long Cold War and seemingly perpetual war on terror—has been less caused by presidential usurpation and more a result of congressional abdication. The Congress is the first branch of government in the Constitution, granted a litany of enumerated powers in Article I, and thus has the most potential power of the three federal branches of government; that power needs to be restored. Thus, as political scientist Andrew Rudalevige notes, the presidency is not inherently imperial, it's "contingently imperial."[1] For most of the late 1700s, 1800s, and early 1900s, the era of congressionally dominant government, the United States was involved in fewer major wars and grew its economy into the largest in the world. Yet, despite the likelihood of better policy, if Congressional authority becomes resurgent vis-à-vis executive power, the main purpose of the framers' system of checks and balances was to prevent the tyranny of any one branch of government— which the rogue presidency now presents to the republic.

At this point in time, restoring congressional power in foreign policy— especially that of the critical war power—may not be as hopeless as it seems. The post–Vietnam and Watergate internal "reforms" of the Congresses in the 1970s—which decentralized power by taking decision-making authority away from congressional committees and transferring it to the more numerous subcommittees—made Congress even less governable and more chaotic than it had been previously, thus inadvertently allowed even more cession of power to the executive. Such internal reforms also tended to undermine the

---

1. Rudalevige, *The New Imperial Presidency*, 15.

attempted reassertion of legislative authority against executive power that was occurring at the same time—for example, the War Powers Resolution of 1973, the Congressional Budget and Impoundment Control Acts of 1974, and the Case-Zablocki Act of 1972, which annually required the president to provide a list of new executive agreements with foreign nations. Most of the internal reforms, however, occurred in the then-Democratic majority's caucus rules on the assignment of members to committees and the selection of committee and subcommittee chairs. As a reaction to such internal "reforms" by his own party, Democratic Speaker Jim Wright began to assert more authority in 1987 and 1988.

The "reforms" began to further erode when Republicans took over Congress in 1995, and some authority to committees was restored at the expense of the subcommittees. Although committee chairs were term limited and their staffs cut, they also got more say over the designation of subcommittee chairs and members and control over subcommittee staffs. Yet generally, the Republican majority continued the Democratic trend of weakening the committees, especially with term-limited chairs, and strengthening the party leadership.[2] For example, in 1995, newly elected Speaker Newt Gingrich got more authority to designate committee chairs and assign majority party members to committees.[3]

In short, in the House, to rein in the plethora of subcommittees and to deal with extreme partisan polarization, which arose in the late 1980s and 1990s and continues to the present, the House leadership began to accrue more power—in times of both Democratic and Republican control. The committees have never returned to their original luster—one reason among many being the abbreviated congressional workweek. Recorded votes are held only from Tuesday night to Thursday, which leads to much less time for committee meetings and oversight hearings of the executive branch. The reality of strong leadership and weakened committees and subcommittees is unlikely to change in the near future, perhaps offering the possibility of a resurgence of Congress vis-à-vis the executive.

---

2. Barbara Sinclair, *Unorthodox Lawmaking: New Legislative Processes in the U.S. Congress* (Thousand Oaks, CA: Sage Publications, Inc., 2017), 163, 165.

3. Eric Schickler, *Disjointed Pluralism: Institutional Innovation and the Development of the U.S. Congress* (Princeton and Oxford: Princeton University Press, 2001), 272–73.

Yet despite a decades-old trend of leadership strength, even the House speaker, who has more control of his chamber than does the Senate majority leader, cannot become too authoritarian, because he has to be reelected by the majority party caucus. Even the powerful Speaker Newt Gingrich resigned because his zealous pursuit of impeachment against Bill Clinton led to a Republican election disaster in 1998, and Speaker John Boehner had to resign in 2015 when he lost the confidence of the conservative Freedom Caucus in the Republican majority.

Nonetheless, at this point in time, the congressional leadership is very powerful and has many powers at its disposal: The leadership in each chamber can refer bills to multiple committees (especially in the House, which dilutes the power of any one committee), completely bypass all committees all together to drive legislation, tinker with committee-reported bills before they go to the floor to raise the chances of passage, combine legislation into omnibus bills to pass unpopular provisions, use the budget process to change policy, and use summits between the party leadership in each house or between the congressional leadership and White House to reach policy compromises. In the House, the leadership, through control of the Rules Committee, often imposes restrictive rules limiting debate and amendments. Data shows that the use of these legislative techniques makes it more likely that legislation will pass in both chambers.[4] Therefore, this increased leadership effectiveness, at the expense of the committees, at least has created the potential for congressional pushback on an imperial presidency.

In the Senate, the majority and minority leaders have also accrued more power; however, rank-and-file members' increased use of the filibuster (a delaying tactic) and rules allowing non-germane amendments to unrelated bills pose challenges to that chamber's leadership. The Senate majority leader can block the latter on certain occasions by filling the amendment tree with his amendments.[5]

Because congressional leadership is now powerful, it could more easily lead, if so inclined, the chambers to push back on executive power, especially in the crucial areas of war, treaties, and budget. In addition, given some of the

---

4. Sinclair, *Unorthodox Lawmaking*, 261–63.
5. Sinclair, *Unorthodox Lawmaking*, 5, 256–59.

excesses of the Trump presidency to date, no matter how it ends, there may be some impetus after it is over to restore congressional power—as there was after executive aggrandizement during major wars and Vietnam/Watergate. However, as a result of the stark political polarization in the country (one of the factors, in the first place, that has bedeviled the legislative chambers and has thus required strong leadership to make them function in any manner), the willingness of congressional or chamber majority leadership to push back against excessive executive action may very well depend on whether they share the same party affiliation as the president.

If congressional leaders wanted to challenge a president on the war power— to restore the constitutional tradition of the executive asking Congress for a declaration of war *before* committing US forces—they probably would first need to terminate the more recent unconstitutional custom of presidents committing troops without congressional approval. To break this bad presidential habit, after the president has committed US forces to a conflict, no matter how small, without authorization by Congress, the legislature would need to invoke the War Powers Resolution—using a majority vote in both chambers, to dictate the withdrawal of US forces from the action. Congress, also by majority vote in both chambers, would also need to cut off funding for the military action. The congressional leadership could use some of the aforementioned powerful tools to speed such legislative action: Bypassing committees to expedite the repudiation of the executive military adventure and the use of budgetary actions (a funding cutoff) to end resources for the prosecution of the war. (Better yet would be congressional disapproval and funding cutoffs of provocative executive troop deployments overseas before they could trigger hostilities.)

Problems would still remain with the political will to rebuff such executive actions on such a perceived critical issue. The president would likely pull out all the stops to continue his or her war—painting opposition to the war as unpatriotic (even though the anti-militaristic founders would gasp at this rendition of "patriotism") and portraying a funding cutoff as pulling the rug out from under heroic US forces while they are under fire. The busy American public has a limited knowledge of how the founders' system of a congressional check against unilateral executive war has severely eroded over time and is largely ignorant of the founders' preferred foreign policy of staying out of most foreign wars. Thus, the president can use his high-tech communication bully pulpit provided by a willing national media, always reluctant to be seen as "unpatriotic" in time of war, to score pro-war propaganda points. Also, members of Congress get nervous when they need to vote for any kind of war, because their institutional loyalty to a powerful Congress exercising its constitutional war power comes in a poor second to surviving the next election. If they vote against what becomes a US military triumph, it can be used to vote them out of office—as Democrats who voted against the George H.W. Bush's First Gulf War found out. If they vote for what becomes a debacle, that can be held against them too in the political process—one of the reasons Hillary Clinton lost to Barack Obama in the 2008 Democratic primaries and caucuses was her vote for George W. Bush's Second Gulf War (the invasion of Iraq), which became an endless and costly quagmire. That's why members of Congress quietly prefer that the president unconstitutionally engage in military action without getting congressional approval. For example, congressional resolutions approving the war against al Qaeda (2001) and the invasion of Iraq (2002) are grossly out of date for fighting continuing wars on terrorists in unapproved places such as Pakistan, Somalia, Yemen, Syria, Libya, Niger, and Iraq (again). However, Congress has ignored pleas from some of its members to pass a comprehensive authorization for a war on terror in all these places. Obviously, too many political risks exist for those members.

Thus, even if congressional leaders, who have more of an incentive to maintain their institutional loyalty to a powerful Congress than do their rank-and-file members, wanted to push back on any one of these wars or at least demand that Congress pass an authorization, they might think twice, because their caucus of members ultimately elects them to their high positions. Keeping leadership positions requires protecting your members against defeat at the polls. Yet members' incentives can change if the president begins losing a war or it drags out into a quagmire, in either case losing public support—as Vietnam and the Second Iraq War eventually did. Of course, better late than never, but it's still too tardy.

Genuine congressional internal reforms are needed to strengthen congressional leaders even further, so that they have the incentives and wherewithal to make the tough decisions to lead the House and Senate as institutions to oppose unilateral unconstitutional presidential war and other usurpations of power by the executive. Some proposals for internal congressional reforms follow. After those proposed changes, proposals are made for congressional pushback against executive aggrandizement in the treaty, intelligence, budget, and other realms. Finally, proposals will be made to diminish presidential incentives to overstep the executive office's limited powers enumerated in the Constitution.

Power in Congress Needs to Be Further Centralized

As was established in an earlier chapter, the post–Vietnam/Watergate web of new laws to constrain the president in various policy areas was largely ineffective or reversed because of a lack of legislative will to make them work. In fact, many times such laws formally legitimated what had theretofore been informal executive action. Any "restraining" laws are merely parchment barriers if the incentives of members of Congress continue to differ from those of institutional competition with the executive, resulting in Congress's continued abdication of its constitutional responsibilities. Therefore, incentives within Congress to guard its constitutional powers need to be improved.

Centralization of power in Congress makes the two houses more effective in challenging executive power, but there have been periodic swings back to decentralization as more members want a significant role in committees and subcommittees to help them get reelected. For example, Republicans centralized control in the House in the early to mid-1890s, but this action undermined the power and interests of individual members. Disgruntlement with centralization led to the election of a figurehead speaker in 1899. Then the decentralized House began to play second fiddle to the Senate. The cycle then continued with the election of the assertive speaker Joseph Cannon. However, the conservative Cannon's overbearing manner led progressive Republicans and Democrats to revolt against him at the end of the first decade of the twentieth century. In contrast, to this centralization-decentralization cycle in the House, from 1890 to 1910, centralization of the Senate failed because the seniority system was used to select committee chairs (precluding selection by

Senate leadership) and because unlimited debate, which had been done away with in the House because of its larger size, remained in the Senate.[6]

In the 1920s, magnifying the loosening of party discipline was dispersion of power in the Congress from the speaker of the House and the majority leader of the Senate to the increasingly powerful congressional committees and the expanding number of subcommittees. As a reaction, in 1925, Republican Nicholas Longworth resurrected the power of the speakership for the benefit of the leadership of both parties.

In response to executive aggrandizement during the FDR and Truman administrations, leading to angst about congressional institutional viability on the part of both liberals and conservatives, the number of congressional investigations increased in the 1940s, and Congress formed the Joint Committee on Atomic Energy. These reforms even challenged presidential control of the executive branch.[7] Also, the Legislative Reorganization Act of 1946 cut the number of committees but enhanced the remaining ones by increasing staffs and giving them oversight powers, which strengthened Congress as a whole and the bipartisan conservative coalition. However, the number of subcommittees continued to expand, and the seniority system for committee and subcommittee leadership became entrenched. In 1950, when Congress allowed Harry Truman, for the first time in American history, to get away without asking for a declaration of war for a major conflict, the power in a decentralized Congress was with committee chairman and not the party leaders of the chambers. This arrangement continued through most of the 1950s. Yet in the 1960s and 1970s, the rise of television and the flooding of the nation's capital with interest groups needing champions to obtain government pork provided opportunities for rank-and-file members of Congress to become policy entrepreneurs who sought reelection through more individual influence. (Thus, the rise of television advantaged the executive, because it is easier for the national media to focus on a single person, and disadvantaged Congress, because each member could operate more independently of party and congressional leadership by snaring more local and national media

---

6. Schickler, *Disjointed Pluralism*, 17, 252.
7. Schickler, *Disjointed Pluralism*, 24, 250–51, 257.

coverage than ever before.) In the Senate, decentralization moved to outright individualism, as senators filibustered more often and offered more amendments on the floor rather than in committee.[8]

The Legislative Reorganization Act of 1970—which pitted liberals, junior members, and minority party members against conservative Democratic committee chairs—sought to democratize House committee processes; institute sunshine rules to open committee proceedings to the public through broadcast of hearings and through making public committee votes and transcripts; and enhance the power of the minority by its hiring staff and calling of witnesses. House floor proceedings were also opened by replacing secret votes in the committee of the whole (where most of the amendments are offered on the floor) with recorded votes. However, the Act did not alter the seniority system.[9] More open processes gave individual members more power by allowing them to grandstand before the cameras.

Additional decentralization of Congress, during the Watergate era in the 1970s, by creating more subcommittees, had the effect of weakening committee chairs and diffusing power further within the institution to subcommittee chairs. Committee chairs no longer selected subcommittee chairs; this selection was now in the hands of majority committee members. Thus, with such fragmentation, more members could do their own thing rather than stick up for constitutional congressional prerogatives relative to the executive and his massive bureaucracies.[10] During this period, the seniority system was undermined by the election of committee chairpersons through secret ballot by the party caucus, and subcommittees became semiautonomous from their parent committees—setting their own budgets, appointing their own staff, creating their own agendas, and meeting and taking action when they wanted.[11] In other words, in economic jargon, given the way the ever-more-decentralized Congress was set up and operated, defending legislative prerogatives was a

---

8. Sinclair, *Unorthodox Lawmaking*, 137–39.

9. Donald R. Wolfensberger, *A Brief History of Congressional Reform Efforts*, Bipartisan Policy Center, February 22, 2013, 1–3.

10. Crenson and Ginsberg, *Presidential Power: Unchecked and Unbalanced*, 289–90; and Sinclair, *Unorthodox Lawmaking*, 139–41.

11. Wolfensberger, *A Brief History of Congressional Reform Efforts*, 3.

collective good, which was underproduced.[12] However, in the House, the speaker's power was increased somewhat, getting the power to choose majority members on the Rules Committee, a greater say in the assignment of members to other committees, and new sway over the referral of bills to committees. Reducing the power of the committees by decentralization to the subcommittees reduced the power of the majority party to pass legislation. The chaos caused by the huge numbers of floor amendments offered by individual members began to cause pressure to recentralize power in the leadership. In the House, the leadership began to use restrictive rules to limit amendments. Also, leaders began informally negotiating post-committee changes to bills to increase their chances of a passage on the floor.[13]

Whereas the House had failed to cut the number of its committees in the 1970s, the Senate laudably cut seven committees.[14] In the Senate, in 1975, a rule change—requiring only 60 percent of all senators to end a filibuster instead of the two-thirds of senators present and voting—made it harder to block legislation. Nevertheless, overall, the Senate has been less successful in giving its leadership the power to overcome the individuality that still reigns in the chamber. In fact, individual senators now use the filibuster so frequently that most major legislation—even vital appropriation bills to fund parts of the federal government—requires sixty votes instead of fifty-one. Getting the sixty votes to end debate on almost every issue before the Senate is very time consuming. Also, because a two-thirds vote is needed to end debate on altering the Senate rules, they are very difficult to change. (Some argue that only a majority vote is needed at the beginning of a new legislative session, but this gambit usually leads to extreme partisan rancor.)

In sum, the Democratic Party reforms of the 1970s replaced committee dominance in Congress with sprawling and unmanageable subcommittee ascendancy. According to political scientist Eric Schickler, the plethora of committees and subcommittees may have impeded passage of Jimmy Carter's program in the late 1970s and Bill Clinton's in 1993 and 1994.[15] As a result,

---

12. Posner and Vermeule, *The Executive Unbound*, 27.
13. Sinclair, *Unorthodox Lawmaking*, 139–41.
14. Wolfensberger, *A Brief History of Congressional Reform Efforts*, 4.
15. Schickler, *Disjointed Pluralism*, 271–73.

this chaotic Democratic scheme was later replaced by governance by party leadership in each house in consultation with their membership caucus. Although greater openness had been the original goal of congressional "reforms," the backlash against the unwieldy outcome was secret party and committee leadership negotiations with the party and committee leadership of the other chamber—to the point of even, in some cases, nixing conference committees to reconcile bills from the two chambers.[16] As noted earlier, other changes increased the leadership's control over the two chambers: leadership can refer legislation to more than one committee, can bypass committees altogether for important legislation, can informally work out post-committee changes to increase passage of a bill on the floor, can wrap up more than one piece of legislation into a huge omnibus bill, can conduct congressional leadership-White House or intra-congressional leadership summits to reach policy compromises, and can bring bills to the floor under restrictive rules limiting debate or amendments (House only).

Congress needs to be recentralized even more to become a more effective counterweight to the president—as it was for much of the nineteenth century. Indirectly, members' reelection partially depends on Congress remaining a powerful and prestigious institution, although congressional leaders certainly have a greater interest in guarding institutional influence than do rank-and-file members. The Constitution allows each chamber of Congress to make its own rules, and that is the mechanism by which further recentralization can occur.

Many subcommittees need to be eliminated and even more power restored to the leaders of the both the Senate and the House of Representatives and committee chairs. In addition, the number of committees needs to be reduced: currently, the House has twenty, the much smaller Senate has twenty-one, and there are four joint committees. All these changes would also help improve party discipline. Any significant reduction of the executive branch through budget sequestration (see below) might also facilitate cuts in the number of congressional committees and subcommittees required to conduct effective oversight over executive agencies.

In addition to reducing the number of committees and subcommittees, the seniority system in both chambers needs to be replaced by the leadership

---

16. Wolfensberger, *A Brief History of Congressional Reform Efforts*, 10.

assigning members to all committees and designating committee chairpersons. This should dramatically increase the power of House and Senate leadership. Remaining subcommittees need to be brought under the tight control of each committee chair. Further centralization of power in both chambers offers a greater assertion of congressional power vis-à-vis the executive, including in foreign policy.

After periods of executive dominance or abuse (for example, in the Vietnam/Watergate era), Congress has often tried to push back on the executive. Eric Schickler best summed up this phenomenon:

> Studies of presidential-congressional relations agree that major wars and economic crises tend to empower the president. . . . By that criterion, the years following World War I, the Great Depression, World War II, the Korean War, and the Vietnam War should be marked by congressional reassertion. These periods coincide quite closely with efforts to strengthen congressional capacity and power. Indeed, *all* of these changes that primarily served this interest occurred during or shortly after World War I, World War II, or Vietnam.

After World War I:	Recentralizing Appropriations, 1920–1922
	Senate Committee Consolidation, 1920
After World War II:	Investigation explosion, 1940s
	Legislative Reorganization of 1946
After Vietnam:	Budget Act of 1974
	Multiple referrals, 1974
	Stevenson committee reforms, 1977

> This evidence shows that interest in congressional capacity and power depends on (perceived) presidential aggrandizement. This interest also became more salient as the twentieth century unfolded.[17]

Thus, after the Trump presidency, no matter how it ends, an impetus may exist to centralize congressional power to push back in reaction to presidential aggrandizement.

---

17. Schickler, *Disjointed Pluralism*, 257.

Fix the Congressional Budget Process

More effective recentralization needs to occur on congressional authority over the budget as well. During the nineteenth century, Congress's money power was diminished by the splintering of the money committees in both houses and the annual appropriations bill into several pieces of legislation. Under the strain of massive Civil War financing, the money committees in both chambers—the Finance Committee in the Senate and the Ways and Means Committee in the House—were stripped of their authority over federal appropriations but retained their authority over taxes. Responsibility for appropriations in both chambers was parceled out to other committees, including new Appropriations Committees. Then, after the Civil War, the Appropriations Committees fragmented. Thus, by decentralizing congressional authority over money bills, the Civil War diminished Congress's money power.[18]

Beginning in 1921, with Congress allowing the creation of a unified executive budget for the first time, a flood of budget-making power flowed from the legislature to the executive. To counter the new executive budget, the Senate recentralized appropriations in 1922, but the reform was compromised by the other committees that lost jurisdiction getting *ex officio* members on the Appropriations Committee.[19] Thus, each year, Congress, lacking a centralized mechanism for making budget decisions, merely made incremental changes to the president's budget proposal. However, when Richard Nixon declared that congressional appropriations were only a ceiling and began to unconstitutionally impound (refuse to spend) appropriated funds, the Congress passed the Congressional Budget and Impoundment Control Act of 1974 to push back against Nixon's non-execution of spending laws. Even more important, the budget statute tried to create a more centralized congressional budget process by adding budget committees in both chambers to generate a yearly congressional budget resolution, which was supposed to constrain appropriations committees and subcommittees in their funding of federal programs. The budget process created by the 1974 law has been used to make significant policy changes; one factor encouraging the use of this vehicle for such changes is that the law effectively prevents budget resolutions and associated measures

---

18. Fisher, *Presidential Spending Power*, 19–21.
19. Schickler, *Disjointed Pluralism*, 252.

from being filibustered, thereby requiring only fifty-one votes to pass in the Senate instead of sixty.

However, in the forty-four years of its existence, the process has functioned normally in only four budget years. Now the process has completely broken down and needs an overhaul. Often, either budget resolutions or appropriation bills are not passed, leading to temporary continuing resolutions, and ultimately to omnibus bills containing multiple appropriations bills. The huge omnibus bills usually encourage horse trading among vested interests that adds to the federal government's spending addiction. Occasionally, however, omnibus bills allow unpopular fiscal measures (unpassable standing alone) to be included in such bills and passed by telling members of Congress that the party's reputation is on the line. The percentage of omnibus legislation as a percentage of major congressional legislation has been increasing in recent decades.[20]

The proposed strengthening of the leadership in both chambers should increase the chances of passing an annual congressional budget resolution, just as the strengthening to date has been effective in passing other legislation. The budget is so important—including to US defense and foreign policy—that the Budget Committees in both chambers should be brought under the tight control of the chambers' leadership. Also, the recentralization of the appropriation process is needed in both houses of Congress. All of the powerful subcommittees on the Appropriations Committees in both houses should be reined in under the central authority of the chairs of the full committees.

Procedural techniques during the George H.W. Bush and Clinton administrations helped clean up Ronald Reagan's fiscal mess—massive budget deficits generated by cutting taxes but increasing government spending. George W. Bush adopted the same irresponsible policies, prompting other procedural techniques to be used during the Obama administration to reduce huge deficits. Apparently, not learning anything from the Reagan and George W. Bush fiscal debacles, Donald Trump has recently also promulgated significant tax cuts and substantial spending increases, even though existing budget deficits were already high, and the economy was already performing fairly well. So procedural tactics will again be needed to cut budgetary red ink.

---

20. Sinclair, *Unorthodox Lawmaking*, 158–60.

To cut deficits during the George H.W. Bush and Clinton administrations, Congress adopted PAYGO (pay-as-you-go) rules, which required any tax cuts or spending increases in entitlement programs to be offset with either revenue hikes or spending reductions of the same magnitude. In 2011, during the Obama administration, Obama proposed that if he and Congress could not reach a budget deal that reduced the deficit by $1.2 trillion, automatic across-the-board-cuts (called sequestration) to both defense and non-defense discretionary spending would be made to reach that total of deficit shrinkage. Although the tenure of the law was limited (2013–2021), most entitlement spending was unfortunately exempted, and Congress and the president in some years raised the spending caps, the Act was reducing the deficit until Trump came into office and blew a hole in the deficit with tax cuts and spending increases allowed by raising both the defense and non-defense spending caps.

At a time when Trump's fiscal policies will likely add $14 trillion over ten years to an existing $2 trillion national debt, the large baby-boom generation will be retiring, thus further increasing government spending; significant across-the-board spending cuts will therefore be needed that include popular entitlement programs. In a dismal fiscal climate such as this, further automatic across-the-board sequestration cuts can be justified as fair, because everyone needs to sacrifice to get budget deficits and the accumulating debt under control.

Eliminate the Seniority System in Congress

Chamber leadership positions, committee chairs, subcommittee chairs, and order of seating on committees and subcommittees are usually heavily influenced by a member of Congress's seniority—that is, time served in the legislative chamber. Before the revolt against Speaker Joe Cannon in 1910, seniority was only one of several factors, including party loyalty, used by leadership in handing out these plum assignments. After 1910, seniority became the dominant factor considered, thereby weakening the congressional leadership's power to enforce party discipline.

Things have gotten so democratic in the Congress that, in 1998, Republicans ousted Republican House Speaker Newt Gingrich for election losses.

In 2003, the Senate Republican caucus ousted Republican Senate Minority Leader Trent Lott. In 2015, unable to control the conservative Republican caucus in the House, Republican Speaker John Boehner had to resign his post.

To help improve party discipline in Congress and thus the power of the leadership in each congressional chamber to control votes, the designation of committee chairs, remaining subcommittee chairs, and membership and rank on specific committees and subcommittees should be based on party loyalty and competence—as assessed by party leadership. This congressional reform would increase the party discipline and unity needed to push back against executive power, including in foreign policy.

Further Recentralization of Congress by Ending the Senate's Non-Germaneness Rule

In recent decades, the leaders of the Senate have gained in power. However, in the Senate, individual members garner more power relative to members of the House by taking advantage of loose rules in the upper chamber. In any given era, the relaxed milieu in the Senate has made leaders weaker and the individual members stronger than in the House.

The lax rules in the Senate allow senators to try to add an unlimited number of amendments to any bill, even those unrelated to the substance of the main measure under consideration. Thus, they may be able to slip through provisions that would not otherwise be passed, because other senators ardently want to enact the main bill. The Senate can be more effective without the uncertainty, and sometimes abuse, that the non-germaneness rule generates, and the Senate majority leader can thus better control his chamber as a counterweight to aggrandizement of executive power.

The Filibuster in the Senate Should Be Retained

Despite the desirability of further centralizing power in the leadership in both chambers to increase the chances of Congress guarding its institutional powers vis-à-vis executive encroachment, the Senate filibuster should be retained as a safety valve. Although the filibuster can be used by the minority or even dissenting majority members to stymie progress on legislation—unless sixty members of the one hundred in the Senate vote to invoke cloture and resume action on proposed legislation—the tactic acts as a brake on bad legislation.

In these partisan times, if the recentralized legislative chambers and the president are of different parties, Congress may be more likely to act as a brake on questionable executive actions—for example, declining to authorize a presidentially desired war. In contrast, if the recentralized congressional chambers are of the same party as the executive, they may enable such presidential military adventures. The filibuster is a safety valve by which such bad policy has a better chance of being rejected. Also, in domestic policy, the filibuster can block or slow down legislation, thus being a force for limiting government. With the further recentralization of congressional power suggested in this volume—by eliminating some subcommittees and committees, further strengthening the leadership of both chambers, and by strengthening the Budget Committees and bringing them under the tight control of that leadership—the plethora of committees and subcommittees that impeded the Carter administration program in the late 1970s and the Clinton program in 1993 and 1994 will have been neutralized. Thus, the last chance to halt legislation is the Senate filibuster, which should be retained.

Many people think that the filibuster was created or desired by the nation's founders, but that is hardly the case. Although early in the history of both houses of Congress, unlimited debate was a tradition, it is not enshrined in the Constitution. However, that document allows each chamber of Congress to make its own rules. The House became so large that its rules were amended to eliminate unlimited debate. Unlimited debate continued in the Senate until 1917—probably not coincidentally the first year of US participation in World War I—when President Woodrow Wilson urged that the Senate change its rules to limit debate by a two-thirds vote to invoke cloture. The necessary threshold was lowered in 1975 to sixty votes out of one hundred. The use of the filibuster has exploded in recent years, and President Donald Trump demanded that the Senate lower the threshold to cut off debate to a majority vote. Even many in the Senate Republican majority slow-rolled the president on his entreaty, because they know they could again someday be in the minority, and also they at least purport to advocate limited government. Retaining the filibuster provides a barrier to bad laws, especially domestically.

Voter Participation and Congressional Party Discipline Within Congress Need to Be Increased

As a reaction to the presidential excesses of Andrew Jackson in the early 1800s, Congress reasserted its powers for the rest of the nineteenth century—except during Lincoln's dictator-like presidency during the Civil War. The reasons for this peacetime congressional resurgence should be looked to in the present day to bolster sagging congressional power against a now-imperial president.

As a reaction to Jackson's powerful presidency, a new Whig Party was formed (not to be confused with the small-government Whig Party in Britain) that stood for little else except to be anti-Jackson. The increased party competition caused voter participation to soar to 80 to 90 percent. Such public mobilization and political activism strengthened the people's houses of Congress vis-à-vis the executive. In addition, party discipline increased in Congress, making a congressional majority much stronger in pushing back against the president and defending the legislature's institutional powers in the Constitution. Powerful congressional leaders arose, and the speaker of the House was treated as more powerful than the president. This period ended in 1910, with an uprising by the rank and file in the House of Representatives against the powerful speaker Joseph Cannon. For example, President Taft tried to institute a unified executive budget, but Cannon stopped him. However, the more power-diffused congresses after 1920 allowed the president to abscond with some of Congress's power of the purse.[21] In 1921, Congress relented and gave President Harding a permanent unified executive budget.

More recently, because candidates could begin to get nominated on their own without being as dependent on their party structure, party discipline in Congress eroded. Without party discipline, members of Congress became more concerned with their own reelection rather than standing up for congressional constitutional powers vis-à-vis the executive branch. For example, instead of conducting the traditional rigorous oversight of executive bureaucracies, members of Congress now are beholden to those same administrative agencies to provide solutions to their constituents' problems with the massive and sclerotic federal government; constituency service is a must for members to be reelected in the days of more independence from political party apparatuses.

---

21. Crenson and Ginsberg, *Presidential Power*, 288–89.

Also, American voter participation rates have fallen to some of the lowest in the industrialized world. Only roughly half of eligible voters cast their ballots in presidential elections, and the percentage is about half of even that meager showing in congressional bi-elections.[22] Much of this has occurred because voters no longer think they can influence the massive and distant federal government and believe that their vote doesn't count as much in heavy gerrymandered congressional districts. (The author proposes solutions to these problems later in the chapter.) The drop-in participation has hurt congressional power vis-à-vis the executive.

From the beginning of the party system, each party's congressional caucus chose its presidential nominee for the election. By 1832, the nomination process moved to national political conventions in which faithful party members, often controlled by the elites of party factions, filtered the nomination choice. Often conventions became deadlocked among party factions and chose compromise candidates that had only weak independent political constituencies. During the 19th century, in was thought unseemly to campaign openly among the mass of voters.

Then candidates began to become independent of their party establishments. At the presidential level, this trend began in 1896, when candidates won their parties' nomination by campaigning against their party apparatus. William McKinley, the first modern president, ran a campaign controlled by his own people rather than party leaders. As president, he took advantage of a new national media market—with the development of national wire services and huge newspaper organizations, such as Hearst and Pulitzer—cultivating press coverage by taking frequent media-friendly speaking tours around the country. He thus spoke directly to the national electorate and diverted media attention from the multitudes in Congress to the more easily covered single executive. Teddy Roosevelt and Woodrow Wilson saw the success of this practice and followed suit.[23] In 1916, Wilson was the first incumbent president to travel the country campaigning for reelection.

Nowadays, all presidential candidates run fairly independently of the party apparatus in caucuses and primaries, using their own free and paid

---

22. Crenson and Ginsberg, *Presidential Power*, 359.
23. Crenson and Ginsberg, *Presidential Power*, 283–87.

media, thereby developing independent constituencies and usually rendering party conventions merely meaningless window dressing. This process has contributed to the rise of a plebiscitary presidency, which gets its powerful legitimacy from mass popular appeal—something that the framers of the Constitution sought to avoid with checks and balances.

Candidates now have access to huge amounts of media to get elected without the filtering function of the party's congressional leaders or other party elites. Also, selection of presidential candidates by party bosses, or even party stalwarts at conventions, has been replaced by wider party caucus votes or direct primary elections by party-affiliated voters (by 1976, primaries dominated the presidential nomination process). Appealing to larger populations of voters costs greater amounts of money. However, candidates saw that they could finance and run, through their own campaign organizations, their own campaigns and get nominated without subservience to the party apparatus.

In short, enhanced democracy—begun in Andrew Jackson's time, further increased during the Progressive Era, and exploding in recent decades—may be a bad thing, because it has made both congressional and presidential candidates more independent of their party organizations. This development has helped augment executive power, while diminishing that of Congress and the states.

Although the move to democracy is very likely irreversible in an age of worldwide instant communication, Gene Healy, an optimist, mentions several traits of our modern-day political system that do push back against the aggrandizement of executive power—declining political trust among the public, a desire for divided government, and the use of the legal system to push back against executive power to replace current congressional timidity. The declining public trust began after Vietnam and Watergate. He also cites a study by William G. Howell and Jon C. Pevehouse showing that presidents are less likely to resort to war when the opposition party picks up seats in Congress, thus making a case for voters adopting divided government.[24] Finally, if interest groups don't like executive overreach, they now rely less on lobbying a neutered Congress and more on suing the executive in the ascendant federal

---

24. Healy, *The Cult of the Presidency*, 269, 290.

court system. Regrettably, however, the federal judiciary still rules favorably for the federal executive branch in an overwhelming proportion of cases.

Voter participation might be increased by reducing the size of the federal government, thereby making it less intimidating and more accessible to the average voter, and eliminating the gerrymandering of congressional districts (more on these solutions later in the chapter). Party discipline in Congress can be increased by further centralization of power in the congressional leadership.

Such Changes in Congress's Operations Might Alter Congress's Timidity Toward Executive Overreach

The executive branch, unlike Congress and the Supreme Court, is at least theoretically organized hierarchically with the president as the boss—a theoretical unity that gives the chief executive advantages in "decision, activity, secrecy, and dispatch" over the many in Congress,[25] who face the intrinsic challenges of collective decision-making. Also, the mammoth executive branch, which accounts for 99 percent of government personnel, has much more information than the other two much smaller branches of government. Thus, the president can often formulate decisions in relative secrecy and then act quickly through executive orders domestically or executive agreements with foreign nations—forcing a fait accompli in which the legislative branch or the courts face undoing what already has been done.

The previously proposed changes in how Congress operates—further consolidating authority in the leaders of the two legislative chambers and thus going back to the future in recreating the more unified actions of congresses in the nineteenth century—might make Congress more willing and able to defend its constitutional prerogatives and push back against executive aggrandizement. With such further internal centralization, Congress may therefore be more willing to brandish its ultimate weapon—funding cutoffs or threats of them—against unconstitutional presidential activities, including unilateral executive wars.

---

25. Alexander Hamilton, *Federalist* No. 70, 471–80, March 15, 1788, www.press-pubs .uchicago.edu.

Once such internal congressional reforms are made to strengthen the incentives and wherewithal of legislative leaders to push back against the imperial presidency, a plan of key legislative measures to be taken needs to be created. Some suggestions follow.

Congress Should Be More Aggressive in Obtaining Information from the Executive Branch

Presidential usurpation of power has been based on withholding information from the other branches of government and the public through the bogus doctrine of executive privilege and through excessive classification of government documents as confidential, secret, top secret, or code word (intelligence) designation.

Ever since George Washington, presidents have improperly withheld information from Congress, using either their alleged "inherent" authority as commander in chief (brandishing the "vesting clause" argument, which was debunked in Chapter 2) or their purported but bogus status as the "sole organ" of US foreign policy. Dwight Eisenhower later justified such withholding of information as "executive privilege," when he tried to shield the internal deliberations of the entire executive branch from Congress. In *United States vs Nixon*, when ruling on whether Richard Nixon had to turn over White House tapes to the Watergate special prosecutor, the Supreme Court ruled that executive privilege could not be used to shield information from a criminal investigation; yet in that case, the Supreme Court unfortunately invited further executive abuse by recognizing that the fallacious doctrine of executive privilege existed. The court was deferential to presidential withholding of information in the national security field and of internal executive branch deliberations. During Watergate, the term received a bad reputation, indicating possible presidential stonewalling, so post–Watergate presidents have often withheld information from Congress without using the term—instead using "internal deliberations" or many other variants of it. Congress should be more aggressive in demanding all such material from the executive. Congressional will can overcome executive privilege, as was seen with the creation of the 9/11 commission to investigate those attacks and the Bush administration's response to them.

Executive privilege or similar words that would justify the president withholding information from Congress, the Constitution's first branch of government, are not found in that document. In contrast, the Constitution gives the Congress the power to make rules for the government and regulation of the land and naval forces, and Congress needs information from the executive for oversight to make sure the president is properly implementing and enforcing congressionally passed laws.

The same could be said for the classification of information. Again, specious "inherent" authority of the commander in chief, whether stated or not, has been used to justify almost sole executive dominance over classifying and protecting public information, starting with Woodrow Wilson's executive order establishing a three-tier information classification system during World War I. Usually added to this justification is the clause that says the executive must take care that the laws are faithfully executed. Mostly, classification guidelines have been done by executive order, with skimpy statutory basis. Curiously, the exception might be the Freedom of Information Act (FOIA) of 1966, which was actually passed by Congress to limit the executive's ability to conceal information from the public, but in the national security area actually cemented executive dominance by finally recognizing the president's ability to classify information by executive order.[26] Although the FOIA Amendments of 1974 authorized the courts to overrule executive branch decisions about classification, they have showed continued deference to executive rulings.

In *The Imperial Presidency*, Arthur Schlesinger cogently maintained that the modern executive has used such secrecy to hide nefarious objectives and errors and enhance its dominance.[27] For example, the secretive Nixon sold his executive order modifying how information was classified as a step toward openness, but it was really an attempt to tighten enforcement to stop leaks surrounding the war in Southeast Asia.

Because the entire government system for classifying national security information is based on skimpy legal quicksand, Congress should put the entire system on a statutory footing. It has tried before and has failed repeatedly. When Congress eventually does so, it should order a massive classification

---

26. Mayer, *With the Stroke of a Pen*, 142–44, 146, 155–56.
27. Schlesinger, *The Imperial Presidency*, 345.

review in the executive branch, with the presumption being to declassify much information that should not be classified or to reduce the level of much over-classified information. In a republic, information withheld from the public should be kept to a minimum. In addition, if the United States would adopt a more restrained foreign policy and not try to police the world using armed force, perhaps much less information would need to be kept from the public.

Congress Should Repeal the Confusing War Powers Resolution and Enforce the Constitution

Legal scholars David Gray Adler and Louis Fisher have characterized the War Powers Resolution as being "ill-conceived and badly compromised from the start, replete with tortured ambiguity and self-contradiction." They concluded that it was "time to say good-bye" to the resolution.[28]

The War Powers Resolution was supposed to give Congress a heads-up when the president was going to use US forces in a military action and then allow the Congress to limit the duration of the intervention. Since the passage of the resolution, presidents have intervened militarily many times without prior congressional notification or authorization. For example, Reagan's troop deployment to Lebanon in 1983; his invasion of Grenada in the same year; his sending US Navy ships to participate in a tanker war in the Persian Gulf in 1987–1988; his multiple instances of air combat against Libya in the 1980s; George H.W. Bush's invasion of Panama in 1989; his and Bill Clinton's deployment of US "peacekeeping" troops into Somalia in 1992 and 1993; Bill Clinton's strikes on Iraq during the "no-fly zone" era in the 1990s; his threatened invasion and troop deployment to Haiti in 1994; his air strikes on Bosnia in 1995; his cruise missile strikes on Sudan and Afghanistan in 1998; and his air war in Kosovo in 1999, which violated the War Powers Resolution's provision that any military action must end within ninety days without authorization of both houses of Congress. The House refused to agree with a Senate-passed authorization for the air campaign.

Also, after the 9/11 attacks, George W. Bush, Barack Obama, and Donald Trump have used drones, manned aircraft, and cruise missiles in the war on

---

28. Rudalevige, *The New Imperial Presidency*, 192–93.

terror to attack Pakistan, Syria, Yemen, Somalia, Libya, and Niger without congressional authorization. Barack Obama ran an extended air attack on Libya to overthrow Libyan leader Muammar Gaddafi in 2011. Only once, shortly after the War Powers Resolution was passed, did a president follow the notification provisions of the act, but in rescuing the crew of the US ship *Mayaquez* from Cambodia in 1975, Gerald Ford notified Congress only after the operation was over. All presidents have disputed the constitutionality of the resolution and have often refused formal compliance with its requirements.

Despite presidents conducting all of these post–War Powers Resolution military actions without prior congressional authorization and despite Harry Truman's failing to get a declaration for a major war (the Korean War) for the first time in American history, an informal norm subsequently has crystalized that presidents will get some form of congressional approval for major wars (Vietnam, the Gulf War, the post–9/11 war against the Taliban and al Qaeda, and the invasion of Iraq). However, executives often make the dubious claim they don't need such approval because their inherent power as commander in chief allows them to take the nation to war without prior congressional sanction. However, as politicians in a democracy, most presidents realize that they need congressional and public support for large wars involving many ground troops, much expense, and potentially lots of body bags or other snafus. However, this informal arrangement is not good enough.

Even small unilateral presidential interventions can unintentionally turn into large ones (for example, Eisenhower and JFK's congressionally unapproved minor war in Vietnam led to LBJ and Nixon's enormous quagmire there) or can have severe unintended consequences (for example, Obama's unauthorized use of force to overthrow Libyan dictator Gaddafi led to chaos, civil war, and the rise of the ISIS terror group there without that strong leader to hold the country together). Or they can have both effects simultaneously: Ike's and Kennedy's secret congressionally unauthorized scheme to overthrow Castro by planning and supporting the Bay of Pigs invasion of Cuba came very close to eventually leading to global thermonuclear war between the United States and the Soviet Union in the Cuban Missile Crisis of 1962.

Thus, Congress should say good-bye to the complicated and unclear War Powers Resolution and instead enforce the original constitutional framework for the war power—Congress must declare war, but an exception is made for unilateral presidential war in an emergency if the homeland is attacked. Congress should even insist on its prior approval for lesser offensive uses of military force, as the framers demanded by giving Congress the power to authorize letters of marque and reprisal for small-scale excursions of state-sponsored pirates against an adversary's ships. Congress should make it clear, by legislation, that prior legislative approval is needed for all deployments of US forces overseas and that "war" is a term that encompasses all intensities of offensive military action. The intrinsically secure geographical position of the United States across huge oceans from the world's zones of conflict, bordering weak and friendly neighbors, and with the most potent nuclear arsenal on the planet should make this "back to the future" solution work well.

However, Congress as an institution will need to summon up the courage to enforce the framers' original conception of the war power. Since the beginning of the Cold War, this vigor has been difficult for members of Congress to summon. They often punt the tough decisions on war by delegating them to an eager executive. Then-congressman Ron Paul said it best: "Congress would rather give up its most important authorized power to the President and the UN than risk losing an election if the war goes badly."[29] But if the structural and institutional remedies proposed in this chapter—to help realign Congress' members' incentives with the legislative body's institutional interests—are adopted, maybe the congressional spine can be stiffened where the war power is concerned.

Repeal the AUMF for the War on Terror Because Presidents Have Abused It

From now on, Congress, in the spirit of the Constitution's implied direction that the Congress approve and regulate even limited presidential military actions—such as the undeclared Quasi-War with France in 1798 and the required issuance of letters of marque and reprisal—Congress should repeal the AUMF for the war against the main al Qaeda group passed in 2001 and

---

29. Ron Paul, "Congress Abdicates War Powers," *New American* (November 4, 2002), 5.

henceforth require all military actions against specific terrorist threats to be individually approved. No more lumping wars in Pakistan, Yemen, Somalia, Libya, and Niger under the 2001 resolution, which really covered only the perpetrators of 9/11 and their Afghan Taliban hosts.

The Only Valid Agreements with Foreign Governments Are Congressionally Ratified Treaties

Presidents' executive agreements with other nations have gotten out of hand. Very few treaties, requiring the constitutionally mandated two-thirds vote of approval in the Senate, are put forward for ratification anymore. Since the 1920s, executive agreements have outnumbered treaties.

Yet the numerous executive agreements between the president and foreign nations are nowhere to be found in the Constitution. Some executive agreements are submitted to Congress, but get only a majority vote in each house of Congress. Other such agreements are not submitted to Congress at all. Still others have been reached secretly, without the knowledge of Congress or the American public. This practice is scandalous in a republic. In World War I, the British people were surprised to learn that the British government had established a much deeper alliance with France than had been made public. That alliance dragged them into a cataclysmic and deadly war that the country should better have stayed out of. Yet no debate was had on this alliance, because the British public did not know about it. The same disaster could happen in the United States if all arrangements with foreign nations are not made public or at least do not have the approval of two-thirds of the people's representatives in the Senate.

The Case-Zablocki Act of 1972 required the president to give Congress every year a list of new international agreements. Presidents have never fully complied with this law, unilaterally exempting national security directives and other national security arrangements with foreign nations. In a republic such security arrangements, above all, should get at least some public scrutiny. Thus, in the late 1980s, Congress tried to get from the executive branch a list of National Security Directives but failed. However, if only congressionally ratified treaties become acceptable, this law would no longer be needed going forward.

Requirement to Explicate Legal Justification for New Laws and Executive Orders

For each bill coming to the floor of either chamber, Congress requires the Congressional Budget Office to estimate the cost. Similarly, Congress should require sponsors of each bill to justify any new proposed statute by citing a provision of the Constitution that allows it. Remember, the Constitution, made even more explicit by the Tenth Amendment, is a document that restricts powers of the federal government to those enumerated in the document. Given the fact that much of what the current federal government does is likely unconstitutional (by the framer's original text), this provision just might shame some lawmakers into having second thoughts about introducing legislation that they have trouble justifying by some section of the Constitution.

Similarly, then-congressman Ron Paul introduced a bill in 1999 that required the executive branch to justify any new executive order by citing a relevant passage from the Constitution or existing statute that allowed it. Also, the bill would have permitted any legislator to challenge suspect executive orders in court.[30] A similar bill should be reintroduced and enacted.

Congress Should Establish a Statutory Charter for the Intelligence Community

Most agencies in the intelligence community have no statutory authorization and have been created by executive action—the National Security Agency, Defense Intelligence Agency, National Reconnaissance Office, and National Geospatial-Intelligence Agency. In fact, the only one of the "big five" national intelligence agencies that has been enshrined in law is the Central Intelligence Agency in the National Security Act of 1947.

Similar to four of the big five, the Federal Bureau of Investigation, which performs counterintelligence against foreign spies and domestic federal law enforcement (a function not mentioned in the Constitution) was created in 1908 by the Department of Justice when the use of Secret Service (created by statute during the Civil War to investigate "frauds upon the revenue") agents for criminal investigations ran into Congress' statutory limits.

---

30. H.R. 2655, 106th Congress.

With no overarching statutory charter enumerating the intelligence community's functions, no general legal framework exists on how most intelligence agencies should go about their business. Every post–World War II president has just used executive orders to reorganize the intelligence community and define its permissible activities.

Proponents of executive power argue, as the Supreme Court did in *Chicago and Southern Airlines v. Waterman Steamship Corp.*, that the president has "inherent" authority to conduct foreign policy and that intelligence gathering and covert action are logical extensions of that power.[31] The argument that "inherent" presidential powers are somehow contained in a Constitution of strictly enumerated powers has always been a stretch and was debunked in chapter 1. In fact, contrary to the inventions of politicians (Alexander Hamilton) and the Supreme Court, the document gives Congress (the First Branch) more power than the executive, even in foreign policy and defense. Intelligence itself is not specifically mentioned in the Constitution and can only be governed by the executive as commander in chief—the original narrow meaning of which was commander of armed forces in battle—in the area of tactical battlefield intelligence performed by the military services. Even then, the Constitution gives Congress the power to regulate the land and naval forces. Only commanding these tactical intelligence forces in battle fell to the commander in chief—much as the document gives the president the role of implementing and enforcing domestic laws at home.

Yet despite such advantage in constitutional powers, Congress historically has let the executive generally run wild in intelligence, even more so than in other policy areas. Having attempted to conduct congressional oversight over the intelligence community for a time, the author experienced first-hand the "I don't want to know" attitude of the vast majority of members of Congress. Thus, the executive has been able to shield intelligence practices and covert action even from the congressional intelligence committees and congressional leadership without them asking many questions. The shocking "hear no evil, see no evil" attitude of Congress was exemplified by Sen. Barry Goldwater, then-chairman of the Senate Intelligence Committee, "I don't even like to have an intelligence oversight committee. I don't think it's any of our business."

---

31. Mayer, *With the Stroke of a Pen*, 161–65.

Congress has largely accepted presidential intelligence policy, organization, and funding requests, even though its members can't really tell what is being spent on what items in the black accounts.[32]

Because no statutory charter exists for the intelligence community that specifies its responsibilities, organizational structure, and permissible activities, presidents have abused the role of these agencies through illegal, unconstitutional, or questionable practices, such as domestic warrantless spying on Americans (most recently used by George W. Bush after 9/11 and continuing to the present), even disruption of domestic groups (for example, anti-Vietnam War and civil rights groups during the 1960s and 1970s), assassination attempts on foreign leaders (for example, Fidel Castro in Cuba), and the destabilization of foreign democratic governments during peacetime (for example, overthrowing the democratically elected leader of Iran in 1953 and reinstating the Shah). All of these actions should be prohibited by an intelligence community charter, which should require a pruning of the seventeen duplicative intelligence agencies and restriction of the remaining organizations to only legal and constitutional intelligence collection on foreign targets.

Historically presidential maneuvering using executive orders has purposefully preempted rigorous and effective congressional oversight, legislative restraints, and the passage of a statutory charter for the intelligence community. That state of affairs has to change. In the 1970s, intelligence abuses uncovered by Congress led to the creation of intelligence committees in both houses of Congress and the Hughes-Ryan Amendment of 1974 and the Intelligence Oversight Act of 1980, which only required the timely reporting of covert actions to Congress, rather than the legislative body being able to give prior approval or disapproval or being able to control such operations. The post–Iran-Contra tightening of the reporting requirements did not materially change such executive dominance of covert operations.[33] A new intelligence community charter would establish congressional primacy in intelligence activities and appropriately control them in a republic, including the prohibition of covert action during peacetime.

---

32. Quoted in Rudalevige, *The New Imperial Presidency*, 201, 205.
33. Mayer, *With the Stroke of a Pen*, 174, 176.

Outlaw the Covert Destabilization
of Other Governments During Peacetime

The Office of Strategic Services, established by FDR during World War II, unfortunately had fused the vital intelligence-collection function with the covert-action (subversion of other countries) function but had kept the agency under the control of the Joint Chiefs of Staff during wartime. Congress, in the National Security Act of 1947 that created the CIA, kept the two functions in the new agency during peacetime. The act did not explicitly direct the CIA to conduct covert subversion of other countries, but instead vaguely authorized the agency "to perform such other functions and duties related to intelligence affecting the national security as the National Security Council may from time to time direct." The aforementioned Hughes-Ryan Amendment of 1974 did finally inadvertently legally acknowledge that covert operations existed and that the president was implicitly permitted to authorize them. The CIA has defined covert action as "any clandestine operation or activity designed to influence foreign governments, organizations, persons or events in support of United States foreign policy," which clearly goes way beyond the mere collection of intelligence[34] (which is supposed to be separated from policy so that intelligence does not become biased).

Almost from the start, the CIA placed more emphasis on the more glamorous covert operations rather than the more mundane intelligence collection. However, to comport with the original war power in the Constitution, covert action undertaken by the president before a declaration of war would be constitutional only to defend against an attack on the United States. A statutory charter for the intelligence community, mentioned in the previous section, should contain an explicit prohibition on offensive covert action during peacetime.

Unfortunately, profligate offensive covert subversion of other countries by presidents during peacetime, with little congressional or public oversight, has become a real problem. Unilateral presidential national security directives have secretly authorized covert actions by the CIA to undermine foreign governments without congressional approval or (in some cases) even legislative awareness.

---

34. Quoted in Mayer, *With the Stroke of a Pen*, 168–69, 174.

Using the CIA or the military clandestinely, without the knowledge of Congress or the public, amounts to running secret wars, which in a republic should be regarded as dangerous. Congress cannot fulfill its important function on deciding whether the nation should go to war if the executive has already taken the United States to war, albeit on a small scale, without its knowledge or approval. Unanticipated escalation and unintended consequences can occur from such congressionally unsanctioned mini-wars—for example, as noted earlier, the CIA's secret Bay of Pigs invasion of Cuba not only failed but led inadvertently to the Cuban Missile Crisis.

During peacetime, gathering intelligence on foreign nations is vital, but meddling in their internal affairs has not been very successful in the post–World War II era. For example, in his book *Legacy of Ashes*, Tim Wiener, a former *New York Times* reporter, details the CIA's long history of misadventures.[35] For example, the CIA's greatest "success"—assisting the militant Mujahideen fighters to drive the Soviets out Afghanistan—inadvertently resulted in one of America's greatest tragedies—the creation of al Qaeda and the deadly blowback terror attacks on 9/11, which constituted the deadliest attack on the US mainland since the War of 1812. These covert actions hardly improve the nation's security, and in this instance catastrophically undermined it. Covert actions during a declared war are a different matter and may be needed to help defeat the enemy. Thus, Congress should outlaw covert actions to destabilize other countries during peacetime.

Congress Should Require That Intelligence and Other Secret Funding Be Made Public

In *Federalist* No. 58, James Madison asserted that the power of the purse

> may, in fact, be regarded as the most complete and effectual weapon with which any constitution can arm the immediate representatives of the people, for obtaining a redress of every grievance, and for carrying into effect every just and salutary measure.[36]

---

35. Tim Wiener, *Legacy of Ashes: The History of the CIA* (New York: Doubleday, 2007).
36. James Madison, *Federalist* No. 58.

The US Constitution's Statement and Accounting Clause seems to back up Madison's view and provide the Congress a weapon to use that power: transparency of finances. The clause states, "a regular Statement and Account of Receipts and Expenditures of *all* [author's emphasis] public Money shall be published from time to time."[37]

The classification of the overall budget for US intelligence and other secret buckets of funding deny the public and their representatives in Congress the ability to monitor what the executive branch is doing in areas that might lead to war. Then-CIA director William Colby and his predecessor James Schlesinger once testified before Congress that publication of the aggregate figure for the intelligence budget would not harm the nation's security. Colby even offered that the American Constitution might require making public more budget information than the intelligence committee might be comfortable with. However, Schlesinger did allude to the likely real reason why the intelligence agencies, including the CIA, have absurdly fought against the publication of the total intelligence spending figure—and in certain years have lost that battle. He admitted that he feared the ill-informed Congress and public might be invited to make percentage cuts in that budget.[38] This justification is a misuse of secrecy and, in a republic, shouldn't fly. As much budget data on US intelligence as possible should be made public.

End All Warrantless Spying on Americans, as the Constitution Requires

The US intelligence community is still spying on Americans' communications with foreigners suspected of terrorism and espionage without warrants, under provisions of the USA PATRIOT Act, and it also is still requiring maintenance of metadata (data on the sender, recipient, date, and length of the communication) on all Americans' electronic communications with other Americans. All of this violates the Fourth Amendment to the Constitution, which requires a judicially approved warrant (as a check on the executive branch), based on "probable cause" that a crime has been committed. Nothing

---

37. US Constitution, Article 1, Section 9.
38. Fisher, *Presidential Spending Power*, 221–23.

in the text of the Fourth Amendment provides for exemptions to requirements for warrants in national security cases.

In the former case—surveillance of Americans communicating with suspected foreign spies or terrorists—the existing secret Foreign Intelligence and Surveillance Act (FISA) court needs to make things constitutional by approving such surveillance warrants. In the latter case, this blatantly unconstitutional database should be expunged, because the government has no "probable cause" to believe all Americans are terrorists or foreign spies.

Congress Should Take Back Budgetary Power That Has Moved to the Executive Branch

Although attempts had been made before to consolidate the executive budget under the White House's authority, the nation's involvement in World War I made it a reality in 1921 during the Harding administration. Previously, in general, individual executive branch agencies negotiated their annual budget with congressional committees in charge of their programs—for example, the Department of Agriculture would negotiate with the Agriculture Committees of both houses of Congress—with the congressional committees maintaining the upper hand. Over time, the commitment to spend federal dollars has moved from Congress to the executive branch in the budget execution phase—in which the president or his executive agencies can impound, transfer, or reprogram billions of dollars, or they can covertly use funds unbeknownst to Congress or the American people. In other words, a major function of Congress in the Constitution—the government can do hardly anything without funding—has been unconstitutionally delegated from that legislative body to the executive branch. Thus, directions given by congressional appropriators can be countermanded by the administration in the budget execution phase.[39]

The most important function of Congress every year is to approve a budget, yet it nearly always struggles to do so. Either the legislature doesn't approve a congressional budget resolution or all of the thirteen required appropriations bills to fund federal agencies, resulting in a continuing resolution maintaining

---

39. Fisher, *Presidential Spending Power,* 3–7.

funding at the prior year's levels until a massive omnibus funding bill for the current year is often belatedly adopted. Such must-pass omnibus bills increase spending because of log rolling among vested interests and allow the executive too much leverage over how federal money is spent, because presidential vetoes could shut down the government. For example, Clinton won budget battles with congressional Republicans in 1995 and 1996 by vetoing spending bills, shutting down the government, and blaming it on them.

In 2002, Dan Crippen, the outgoing director of the Congressional Budget Office, declared that "the Congressional budget process is dead. . . . Without this kind of process . . . the Congress is going to be dominated by any President." He added that unless the Congress had the will to pass and enforce a budget resolution, it would be very difficult to send any appropriation bill to the president that he didn't want, given the importance of executive veto threat in the absence of any viable alternative congressional budget. Thus, "the President's budget is the only game in town [and] the President's veto is the only power in town when it comes to budgetary decisions." He concluded that Congress needed "again to grab back some of that budgetary power," but until it did, "the Congress has given up, I think, a large measure of what it had grabbed back from President Nixon."[40]

The broken budget process aggravates the tendency of Congress to only nibble around the edges of the massive presidential budget proposal. A new congressional budget process must be created that will allow Congress the discipline to effectively push back against excessive executive power in the budget arena. The House and Senate Budget Committees should be strengthened, become the most important committees in Congress and be controlled by the leadership in both houses. The tax committees (Senate Finance Committee and House Ways and Means Committee) and the House and Senate Appropriations Committees would merely implement the Budget Committees' mandatory budget resolution containing revenues and spending targets. In other words, budgeting in the Congress should be centralized to compete with the Office of Management and Budget-led budgeting in the executive branch.

---

40. Rudalevige, *The New Imperial Presidency*, 154–55.

Also, Congress should no longer allow the executive branch to impound, transfer, or reprogram funding appropriated by Congress without specific congressional approval. In addition, overall budgets for intelligence agencies should be made public and the congressional Government Accountability Office should audit all executive branch covert spending.

Congress Should Wield the Budget Power When the Executive Abuses Signing Statements

Richard Nixon, when he signed some laws, abused signing statements by declaring that the executive branch would not enforce selected provisions. However, Ronald Reagan accelerated this form of constitutional abuse. Like presidential impoundments of congressionally appropriated funds for programs, signing statements are similar to an unconstitutional line item veto disguised in constitutional rhetoric. In the 1990s, the Supreme Court ruled as unconstitutional the executive line item veto—that is, the president vetoing only certain items in a congressionally passed bill. Also, if a president selectively enforces the law in any manner, he is violating his constitutional duty to "take Care that the Laws be faithfully executed." Thus, Congress should use its funding power to penalize presidents who abuse these signing statements in this manner. The monetary penalty would not even need to be in the strict policy realm in which the signing statement was abused, but Congress should make clear that any penalty is in response to the executive's use of the signing statement to pervert his or her duty to faithfully enforce the laws. The aim would be to deter such future unconstitutional executive behavior.

Congress Should Estimate and Pay the Total Costs of Any War

Congress has required that every bill that comes onto the floors of its chambers has a cost estimate from the non-partisan Congressional Budget Office (CBO). If Congress begins to require the executive to get legislative approval for any offensive military action, no matter the scale, the budget side of CBO should therefore estimate the cost of that military action in dollars. Yet CBO also has a policy side, which should be required to estimate US military and civilian casualties for any offensive US military action. Such accurate estimates of cost—in blood and treasure—might make some members of Congress, or even the president, blanch before the armed intervention is approved and executed. Instead, if presidents estimate the costs of military action at all, they grossly low-ball it—as the George W. Bush administration did for the invasion of Iraq. A more credible estimate from CBO would rectify this problem.

James Madison declared that "each generation should be made to bear the burden of its own wars, instead of carrying them on at the expence of other generations."[41] Therefore, Congress should require that all money spent on wars be subject to PAYGO ("pay as you go") requirements, which require cutting other spending or raising taxes to pay for new federal activities. Presidents could no longer put even sizable wars on a credit card, as George W. Bush did with the Iraq War, ballooning budget deficits and national debt—thus dumping the huge bill of principal and interest on future generations. With a whopping $21 trillion national debt, the United States can no longer afford such irresponsible credit card spending, even for war.

Even better, wars should not be funded by supplemental appropriations. That is what the Department of the Defense's budget should be for. If wars were instead funded out of the department's base budget, even the military would have an incentive to avoid unnecessary wars, because money would be burned that could buy new high-technology weaponry and sensors and pay military personnel.

Congress Should Transfer More Military Assets to the Reserves and National Guard and Increase Training for Those Forces

As a check on unneeded and costly wars, such as the Vietnam and second Iraq wars, some have called for return of the military draft. Yet the government coercing people to fight for freedom is not a good policy. Although it is true

---

41. James Madison, "Universal Peace," *National Gazette*, February 2, 1792, in Gaillard Hunt, ed., *The Writings of James Madison 1790–1802: Comprising His Public Papers and His Private Correspondence, Including His Numerous Letters and Documents Now for the First Time Printed*, Vol. 6 (1906), 90.

that the draft increased opposition to the questionable Vietnam War, other less coercive methods may be substituted for this draconian remedy.

After the Vietnam War, the generals tried to restrain the politicians from any more stupid wars by putting more key military support assets—such as engineers, medical personnel, and civil affairs specialists—in the reserves, so politicians would need to show the war was important enough to mobilize part-time soldiers from a broad swath of American society. During the Vietnam War, Lyndon Johnson and Richard Nixon had been reluctant to mobilize the reserves. During the Iraq War, Bush's secretary of defense, Donald Rumsfeld undid much of this effort by transferring such functions back to the active forces. To attempt to avoid unnecessary wars in the future, this tack should be tried again by drastically reducing the active forces (not done last time) and putting heavier combat forces and their support into the Guard and reserves. Thus, the active forces would be called on to fight only smaller military actions. If a bigger threat arose, the heavier forces in the Guard and reserves could be mobilized. Although this would save much money overall and be a barrier to Vietnam- and Iraq-style military misadventures, some of the savings would need to be put to keeping Guard and reserve readiness at a high level.

Congress Should Legislate a Second Person to Co-sign a Nuclear Launch

Jeet Heer, writing in the *New Republic*, has proposed this useful suggestion to prevent an unstable or excessively aggressive president from launching an unnecessary nuclear strike against a rival nation. However, Heer advocates designating the speaker of the House of Representatives as that person, because that would restore congressional input in war making, as required in the Constitution.[42]

Heer's general suggestion is a good one, but his selection for the ideal person to be a co-signer on any nuclear strike may raise objections to violating "the separation of powers" in the Constitution. Also, his proposal deprives

---

42. Jeet Heer, "Don't Just Impeach Trump. End the Imperial Presidency," *New Republic*, August 12, 2017, https://newrepublic.com/article/144297/dont-just-impeach-trump-end-imperial-presidency.

the entire Congress of a decision to launch an offensive nuclear war. As noted earlier, the advent of nuclear weapons during the Cold War did not make the founders' conception of the war power obsolete. Without congressional approval, the president, and any second person designated in the executive branch to co-sign a nuclear strike, would be confined to authorizing a defensive or preemptive (striking on imminent threat of being attacked) nuclear strike. In contrast, any unlikely, non-time-sensitive offensive nuclear strike against a foreign power—most likely to prevent an aspiring nuclear power from developing atomic weapons in deep underground bunkers or against a nuclear power without the delivery systems to get its atomic warheads to the United States, such as perhaps North Korea—should be first approved by Congress. That solves the issue of congressional involvement by sticking to the Constitution rather than perverting it in order to save it. Thus, Congress should legislate that either the vice president or secretary of defense should be the co-signer, not the speaker of the House.

Even if this proposal is not adopted, the top military brass should advise military personnel that their oath is to the Constitution, not to the president. If any president should give an illegal order—for example, to launch an offensive, non-preemptive nuclear strike without congressional approval—military officers have a constitutional responsibility to disobey the order.

Congress Should Require the President to Liberally Allow Media Access to the Battlefield

Opposition to George W. Bush's dishonest and disastrous Iraq War was muted for two main reasons: 1) media access to the battlefield was restricted and 2) no military draft existed.

During the Vietnam War, the media had practically free rein on the battlefield to cover what it wanted. Because the media brought home to the American public the carnage caused by a questionable war, domestic opposition eventually help end the war. To prevent this outcome from recurring, presidential administrations have restricted access of the media in subsequent American wars. The first military ground war after Vietnam was Reagan's invasion of Grenada in 1983. The Reagan administration learned its lesson from Vietnam and kept the press far away from the fighting. Even so, evidence of some administration bungling trickled out. Subsequent presidents have continued these restrictive practices.

Unfortunately, the limited media access has impeded congressional and public oversight of any administration lying or incompetence during conflicts. Some might say that extensive media coverage will undermine the war effort in any future dustup, but if the conflict can be justified as vital to US security and the presidential administration is competent in its conduct, the war effort should withstand, and may even benefit, from fuller media coverage.

Congress Should Cut the DoD's Budget If the Department Cannot Pass an Audit

An argument can be made that the Department of Defense (DoD) is the worst-run agency in the federal government. DoD's accounting system has been broken for a long time, and it is the only department that consistently has been unable to pass an audit in decades. DoD cannot account for trillions of dollars in spending, yet politicians, pounding their chests and yelling "support the troops" and "national security is in danger," continue slathering the department with about $700 billion per year. Congress should instead cut DoD's budget until its accounting system is healthy enough to track where the taxpayers' money is going. Given DoD's legendary fraud, waste, and abuse, how do we even know the money is supporting the troops?

Congress Should Restore the Posse Comitatus Act to Its Former Luster

The Posse Comitatus Act wisely limits the role of the US armed forces in law enforcement. Exceptions to the Act were passed for the drug war in the 1980s and for natural disasters after Hurricane Katrina in 2005. According to a cogent analysis by Gene Healy, those loopholes should be rescinded.[43]

---

43. Healy, *The Cult of the Presidency*, 275.

Gerrymandering of Congressional Districts Needs to End

Both parties have practiced gerrymandering—the drawing of congressional districts for partisan advantage—since the dawn of the republic. The practice essentially lets politicians choose their voters rather than vice versa, thus significantly reducing the number of competitive congressional districts. Incumbents in tailored districts are much stronger and thus their reelection does not depend as much on the party apparatus or elites—making party discipline even more lax and Congress a weaker institution vis-à-vis the executive. Gerrymandering has recently increased with the advent of new technology to more fully exploit demographic data from the Bureau of the Census.

Ending gerrymandering will not remove hyper-ideological partisanship—from which the executive benefits greatly—but removing the practice would help attenuate it somewhat. If competition is better than monopoly for consumers in economics, the same is true for politics. More competitive congressional districts would mean that competition would be greater in general elections rather than in merely primary elections.

The president benefits from hyper-partisanship either by being the head of a strong party that controls Congress or by being encouraged to engage in unconstitutional or illegal executive maneuvering when the opposition party controls Congress. In the first case, the system of checks and balances enshrined in the Constitution did not foresee the rise of parties, which sometimes tend to reduce competition between branches. In the second case, the resulting legislative gridlock usually causes the imperial president to abandon legislative solutions to govern using unconstitutional executive orders, executive agreements, national security memoranda, and proclamations.

The courts have traditionally stayed out of gerrymandering cases, because every conceivable redistricting plan would likely advantage one party or the other. Yet technology also may be changing that situation. Political scientists have now come up with mathematical algorithms that optimize the representatives/votes ratio. State courts should mandate its use in drawing the boundaries of congressional districts. Federal courts traditionally have tried to stay out of state elections (a prominent exception was *Bush v. Gore* in the 2000 election, when the Supreme Court decided the election) and should continue this general practice.

An even better—and more radical—solution would be to eliminate all congressional districts in states. The Constitution does not require such geographical divisions; Congress should change the late-1960s law requiring them.[44] In contrast to changes in the Electoral College (the next proposal), eliminating congressional districts could dramatically change the political system. If, for example, a state such as Iowa has four members of Congress in the House, one statewide election could be held and the top four vote-getting candidates, regardless of party, would be elected to Congress. Alternatively, parties could put up slates of candidates and either the top vote-getting party would get all the congressional seats on a winner-take-all basis or the seats would be assigned to parties on the basis of proportional representation. The latter preferred scenario—where membership of the state's congressional delegation is allocated roughly on each party's percentage of the vote—could open the way for increased competition in the political system through the creation of a multiparty system.

All of the preceding are measures that Congress could take to bolster its constitutional role and counter the imperial presidency. However, the legislature is not the only branch of government to have rolled over in the face of executive aggrandizement. Over time, the judiciary has blessed Congress' unconstitutional delegation of its powers and the executive's usurpation of the same. Measures the judiciary could take to strengthen its role are as follows:

The Courts Should Enforce the Non-Delegation Doctrine Among Government Branches

Until World War II put the last nail in the coffin of the Non-Delegation Doctrine, it was considered unconstitutional for one branch (usually Congress) to delegate its constitutional authority to another branch (usually the executive branch). Thus, during the postwar era, Congress delegated many of its powers to the president, especially in foreign policy. The Supreme Court should put its foot down and once again enforce this doctrine. How one gets an unelected body to enforce a basic principle needed to have a written Constitution that

---

44. Michael Tomasky, "Who Needs Congressional Districts?" *New York Times*, February 21, 2018, A23.

specifically enumerates the powers of the legislative, executive, and judicial branches of the federal government is uncertain.

However, sometimes the president issues executive orders without any statutory underpinning, solely on the basis of the "inherent power" of the president. The courts could rightfully strike such orders down, but often even this modest action is too tall a task, and they instead defer to the executive. If the courts became even more ambitious, they could rule unconstitutional general and vague laws passed by Congress that allow the executive branch in enforcement to run wild filling in the missing guidance.

The analysis has thus far centered on strengthening Congress and the courts vis-à-vis the executive branch, yet some structural changes in the executive branch could reduce the power of the branch and the presidency in particular.

Cut Executive Power by Reducing the Size of Government Drastically

The executive branch has two intrinsic advantages over the Congress. First, the president can act more quickly and secretively than Congress because he or she is at least theoretically a unified decision-maker, while Congress' collective-action problem renders it slower and more transparent than the executive. Alexander Hamilton noted in *Pacificus* that because the executive can act first he can shape the playing field on which later congressional decisions will be based: "The executive, in the exercise of its constitutional powers, may establish an antecedent state of things, which ought to weigh in the legislative decision."[45]

Second, the executive can act rapidly because he manages executive agencies that have, since the dawn of the republic, been much larger than the congressional and judicial branches. The executive branch is the only branch of the three that has the personnel and physical assets to carry out its decisions and those of the other two branches. In the twentieth century, the US

---

45. Alexander Hamilton, *Pacificus*, no. 1.

Congress is not the only legislative body in the world that has declined in the face of a rising executive and an expanding administration state.[46]

With the dramatic growth of government, Congress has delegated ever more power to executive agencies by passing vague statutes and letting the bureaucracies fill in the details. As the primary interest of members of Congress (getting reelected) began to deviate from that of their institution (pushing back against executive encroachment on Congress' constitutional powers), the members found that if they delegated greater rulemaking to the executive agencies, they could take credit for the general policies (for example, "making the environment cleaner"), while blaming specific problems with regulation, including overregulation, on the bureaucracies.

Therefore, one important way to cut executive power vis-à-vis the Congress and the judiciary is to significantly reduce the size of government—of which the executive branch accounts for 99 percent of the personnel employed. Many ways have been tried to cut back executive agencies, but they just keep growing, much like antibiotic-resistant bacteria. The only thing that has at least reduced budget growth is a decision rule—that is, across-the-board budget cuts, otherwise known as "sequestration," with every budget item receiving the same percentage reduction. A mild version is currently the law of the land, but it exempts entitlement programs, which are by far the fastest growing sector of the executive branch. Also, both parties keep trying, and occasionally succeed, in undoing this spending straitjacket. Any future sequestration must make more severe cuts and include defense, non-defense discretionary, and entitlement programs. Such draconian measures could be sold by a simple pitch: "With more than $22 trillion in public debt, everyone needs to sacrifice." The policy will not be popular, but will be perceived as fair. The normal way of doing things leads to "log rolling," which essentially says, "I'll vote to save your program, if you vote to save mine." That's why across-the-board cuts of the same percentage are perceived as most fair and also pragmatically reflect and respect the strength of various political forces that result in existing relative spending levels in the budget.

---

46. Schickler, *Disjointed Pluralism*, 7.

Eliminate the Electoral College

Executive aggrandizement and the diminishing power of Congress and the states in the eroding American system of checks and balances has led to a "plebiscitary presidency" in which the primary constraint on the hugely powerful president is satisfying public opinion to win the next election, either personally or by a successor within the ruling party. In 1959, *National Review's* James Burnham, a conservative cold warrior, predicted that the diminution of the power of Congress risked a "plebiscitary despotism for the United States in place of constitutional government, and thus the end of political liberty."[47]

But wouldn't eliminating the Electoral College, by eliminating another intermediary between the president and the people, make this problem worse? Not really, because early in the country's history, the Electoral College ceased to function as the framers of the Constitution had envisioned, and the country has become more democratic over time—likely irreversibly so. The framers never feared an imperial presidency because they anticipated that a chief executive indirectly elected by either the House of Representatives or the Electoral College would lack the power of a president chosen directly by the people. In fact, the country was so geographically large, and communication and transportation were so rudimentary that the framers didn't think any candidate from one part of the country would get a majority of electoral votes, thus throwing most elections into the House of Representatives (with each state having one vote). Therefore, the framers envisioned that in most elections, the compromise Electoral College, by functioning as a nominating mechanism, would winnow the top vote getters, and the House would choose the president from among them.[48]

As James Madison, in *Federalist* No. 39, explained the framers' general conception of how the system to elect the president would work:

The executive power will be derived from a very compound source. The immediate election [step one] of the President is to be made by the

---

47. James Burnham, *Congress and the American Tradition* (Chicago: Henry Regnery Co., 1959), 352.

48. Gary and Carolyn Adler, *The Evolution and Destruction of the Original Electoral College*, 3rd ed. (Advance Freedom, LLC: Cokevill, WY, 2013), 21–22.

States in their political characters. The votes allotted to them are in a compound ratio, which considers them partly as distinct and equal societies, partly as unequal members of the same society [a state's electoral votes = number of seats in the Senate + number of seats in the House]. The eventual election [step two], again, is to be made by that branch of the legislature which consists of the national representatives; but in this particular act they are to be thrown into the form of individual delegations, from so many distinct and coequal bodies politic [the ultimate selection of the president would be done by the House with each delegate having one vote].[49]

When the Constitution was written, most delegates to the Constitutional Convention seemed to agree with George Mason, who predicted that nineteen times in twenty the election would end up in the House.[50] However, transportation and communication improved and, in most elections throughout American history, a candidate, whether he got a plurality of the popular vote or not, managed to get a majority of votes in the Electoral College. So far, only two elections in almost 230 years of American history have gone to the House—and those were long ago in 1800 and 1824. Thus, instead of being a body that nominated candidates for the presidency, as the founders had envisioned, the Electoral College has, in the vast majority of elections, decided the contest.

Furthermore, according to Alexander Hamilton in *Federalist* No. 68, "A small number of persons, selected by their fellow citizens from the general mass, will be most likely to possess the information and discernment requisite to so complicated an investigation."[51] State legislatures were supposed to choose how to select their electors, but by 1832, fairly early in American history, all states but one had decided to choose their electors by popular vote—completely nullifying the concept that the state legislators would hire experts to select the national president.

---

49. James Madison, *Federalist* No. 39.

50. James A. Michener, *Presidential Lottery: The Reckless Gamble in Our Electoral System* (New York: The Dial Press, 2016), 23.

51. Alexander Hamilton, *Federalist* No. 68, March 12, 1788.

Electors were supposed to be experts that could better select the best nominees for president than the unwashed masses; but the country quickly became more democratic after the ratification of the Constitution, thus relegating the Electoral College rapidly to the category of faux federalism.

Now political hacks, selected in party conventions or by party committees, have replaced these experts and are ironically now severely penalized either within the party, or in some states by law, if they substitute their judgment for the party's choice. Even some conservatives, who want to keep the Electoral College, want to reform it to eliminate the dreaded "unfaithful" elector, although historically their fear never has been much of a problem.[52]

Around the same time in the early 1800s, property restrictions on voting went by the wayside and, by Andrew Jackson's election in the late 1820s, the electorate had dramatically expanded in the United States to all white men. That is, the country had become more democratic, casting into doubt the republican principle of the people's state representatives hiring experts to nominate presidential candidates.[53]

The Electoral College seldom nominated candidates for president, because early in the country's history, candidates did get a majority in the college. Instead, congressional caucuses first nominated a party's candidates for president, then this moved to party political conventions, and is now really done in party caucuses and primary elections as the country became even more democratic.

With all of these changes, today the Electoral College merely distorts the popular vote. The state legislatures do not select wise men, who know better than a semiliterate public who the best candidates are—true to the republican principle of selecting the best people to represent the masses. Now the political parties select the electors, usually political hacks chosen for their loyalty to the party, and those who are seated in the Electoral College are from the party whose candidate won a plurality of the vote in each state. In all but two states—Maine and Nebraska—the candidate who won that popular vote plurality wins all the electors for the state (the number of votes the state

---

52. Tara Ross, *Enlightened Democracy: The Case for the Electoral College* (Dallas, TX: Colonial Press, L.P., 2012), 109–20.

53. Rudalevige, *The New Imperial Presidency*, 33–34.

has in the US Senate plus its number of representatives in the US House of Representatives), thus distorting the popular vote.

In the vast majority of elections, the Electoral College, because of its mostly winner-take-all, state-by-state vote tally, inflates the margin of victory of the winner compared to that of the popular vote. Such results can easily convince the winner that he or she has a bigger mandate to govern than the reality provides, thus leading to rash acts, such as going to war. For example, one of the major factors leading to the Civil War, the biggest calamity in American history, was Abraham Lincoln's huge Electoral College majority of almost 60 percent, while earning less than 40 percent of the popular vote in a four-candidate field. This big Electoral College win made Lincoln resist compromise with the seceding South, thus triggering the most cataclysmic war in American history. He famously asked rhetorically why Southerners should get to undo by secession what the Republican Party had won in the election. Thus, many US elections have failed to result in a popular vote majority, but very few have failed to achieve an Electoral College majority—so the "exaggerated mandate" problem, which has fueled grandiose presidential acts, is very real and fairly common. In another example, in 1912, although Woodrow Wilson polled only 41.8 percent of the popular vote in a three-way race with Theodore Roosevelt and President William Howard Taft, his garnering of 81.9 percent of the electoral vote motivated him to attempt to enact an ambitious agenda, which significantly expanded the federal government and executive power.[54] Upon re-election in 1916, Wilson's grand ambitions migrated overseas, as he helped ruin the entire twentieth century by tipping World War I to the allies, thus helping eventually to cause World War II and the Cold War.

In other elections, using the current Electoral College system, a "wrong-winner" scenario can result in which the Electoral College winner does not even get a plurality of the popular vote. In the modern United States—with its more democratic nature than at the founding, which is not going back to the original republican bent any time soon—a "wrong-winner" president

---

54. George F. Will, "Foreword," in Tara Ross, *Enlightened Democracy: The Case for the Electoral College* (Dallas, TX: Colonial Press, L. P., 2012), ix.

should face legitimacy problems in governing. Yet swaggering presidents like George W. Bush and Donald J. Trump focus on the Electoral College win as a mandate, brushing their loss of the popular vote under the carpet. George W. Bush took advantage of his Electoral College majority, even though he had lost the popular vote in the 2000 election, to push an ambitious agenda, including the invasion of Iraq to carry out his vendetta against Saddam Hussein, who had nothing to do with the 9/11 terrorist attacks. He also boldly took the congressional authorization for the use of military force (AUMF) from its narrow focus against the 9/11 attackers (al Qaeda) and those who harbored them (the Afghan Taliban) and expanded into a worldwide war on terrorism in many countries. After the "stolen" 1876 election, a dispute over who won the Electoral College led Rutherford B. Hayes to agree to end Reconstruction in the South in exchange for winning the presidency. The only two elections in which the decision has ended up in the House—1800 and 1824—were disasters of backroom deal making, recrimination, and sometimes perceived illegitimacy.[55]

Undoubtedly, the framers wanted constraints on majority rule and enshrined many of them in the US Constitution, but they didn't really want minority rule—they had had that with the British king. The wrong-winner scenario enshrines minority rule.

Although the four times in American history that a wrong winner situation has arisen—twice in the nineteenth century and twice already in the twenty-first century—Republicans have won the electoral vote but lost the popular vote. However, Republicans should not be so smug about their dominance of the Electoral College. Most experts believe that if the popular vote from Alabama had been allocated correctly in the 1960 election, Democrat JFK would have lost the popular vote but won the Electoral College. Right now, the history books questionably show him winning both tallies. Furthermore, in 2004, with a change of tens of thousands of votes in Ohio, Democrat John Kerry would have spoiled George W. Bush's reelection by winning the Electoral College, even though Bush had won the popular vote. (Even in 2000, when George W. Bush won the Electoral College and Al Gore won the popular vote, the Gore campaign, when looking at the close electoral map prior to the

---

55. Michener, *Presidential Lottery*, 19–23.

election, was ready for the opposite election outcome.) Tara Ross, a conservative proponent of the Electoral College, concluded, "the Electoral College does not serve one political party to the exclusion of the other. In 2000, it 'benefited' Republicans, but it just as easily could have reversed course in favor of the Democrats in 2004."[56]

With the country fairly evenly divided politically and the electoral map always in flux (for example, the American electoral map in the early twenty-first century is exactly the opposite of what it was in the early twentieth century), the Republicans, in the future, could just as easily fall victim to the "wrong winner" outcome that has fallen to their benefit so far in the twenty-first century. For example, Texas shifted from voting Democratic to voting Republican in the 1980s and 1990s, but with a growing Hispanic population, could switch back to the Democratic column in the not-too-distant future. Finally, Republicans commonly believe the Electoral College proportionally favors the least-populated states, in which they have the electoral advantage, but the winner-take-all mechanism to determine the electoral vote, which most states use because it maximizes their clout in any election,[57] favors the most-populous states, in which the Democrats have the advantage. In fact, experts say the winner-take-all advantage of the large states is greater than the "plus two" electoral votes that the small states get.[58]

Thus, the Electoral College has really never been a useful constraint on presidential power and even has been very counterproductive in that regard. Thus, it should be eliminated, and efforts concentrated on restoring the diminished power of other institutions in the constitutional system of checks and balances—such as Congress, the courts, and the states.

The Electoral College was originally instituted by the nations' founders at the Constitutional Convention as a compromise between direct election of the president by voters and election of the chief executive by Congress. The founders were deathly scared of "mob rule" that direct democracy might

---

56. Ross, *Enlightened Democracy*, 8.

57. Mark Weston, *The Runner-Up Presidency: The Elections That Defied America's Popular Will and How Democracy Remains in Danger* (Guilford, CT: Rowman & Littlefield, 2016), 125.

58. Robert W. Bennett, *Taming the Electoral College* (Stanford, CA: Stanford University Press, 2006), 161–62.

bring, so they created an Electoral College of experts to choose the president. The founders thought that in a large country with limited transportation and communication, the semiliterate voters would not be informed enough to make intelligent decisions at election time.

Yet as noted, the Electoral College does not now work the way the founders had intended. As with slaves being counted as three-fifths of a person for representation in the House of Representatives in the original Constitution (but whites got to control the slaves' votes), one purpose of the Electoral College also was to give slave states extra representation to protect slavery as an institution. Also, ironically in view of the 2016 election results, electors were supposed to prevent public opinion from being swept up by demagogues, and the electors meeting around the nation in state capitals were supposed to guard against foreign meddling in US elections.

The Electoral College system can violate the common-sense principle that the person who wins the most votes should win the election. That is the principle that elections at all other levels in the United States follow. There is no Electoral College for any other offices in the American election system. Furthermore, the Electoral College violates the principle of "one person one vote"—for example, a voter in Wyoming, the least-populous state, has more than three-and-a-half times the voting power of a voter in California, the most-populous state.[59] Also, states get the same number of electoral votes in the election, no matter whether only one of their voters shows up at the polls or whether 100 percent of elgibile voters vote; there are significant differences in turnout between states, and this issue would not arise if elections were decided by popular vote.[60] In the Electoral College, states with low voter turnout are inadvertently rewarded, because their voters have more influence than states with higher voter participation.[61] Finally, the Electoral College is more susceptible to fraud or recounts than is the popular vote. Anyone wanting to tamper with the vote can easily discern the few large swing states in which the election will be decided. It seems the Russian meddlers had an inkling of which states were key to the election in 2016. It is much easier to

---

59. George C. Edwards III, *Why the Electoral College Is Bad for America* (New Haven, CT: Yale University Press, 2011), 46.

60. Bennett, *Taming the Electoral College*, 163.

61. Edwards, *Why the Electoral College Is Bad*, 47–48.

meddle in one or more of these states and change a few thousand votes than it is to illegally change millions of popular votes from all over the country. Also, if the Electoral College had not remained for the 2000 election, a contentious recount would not have been needed, because the popular vote nationwide is seldom as close as it can be in an important swing state, such as Florida.

Although some argue that eliminating the Electoral College would undermine America's two-party system (Americans simultaneously love their maximum-choice free market economic system at the same time they adore a restricted-choice political system), quite the opposite is the case. First, the main thing holding the two-party system together is America's "first-past-the-post" winner system in geographically defined electoral areas, not the Electoral College. (In a first-past-the-post system, unlike the proportional representation systems in, say, Europe, a party does not get a percentage of seats roughly comparable to the number of votes it gets. In America, the party gets nothing if it doesn't get a plurality of the votes, causing factions to coalesce into two major parties.) In fact, the Electoral College encourages third-party candidates to get into the presidential race to win as many states—and electoral votes—as possible and then try to bargain with the two major party candidates if neither gets a majority in the Electoral College. This situation almost happened in 1968, when George Wallace, a third-party segregationist candidate, won some states in the South. Fortunately, one of the major party candidates got enough Electoral Votes to win a majority and take away Wallace's bargaining power.

American history shows that the Electoral College either can lead popular vote winners to a bigger margin than they achieved in the popular vote (eighteen elections have had majority electoral vote winners that did not win a majority of the popular vote) or to lose the election to a candidate that didn't even win a plurality in the popular vote. Either outcome can lead politicians to assume they have a bigger electoral mandate than they received. Exaggerated perceptions of mandates can lead politicians to war and other grandiose executive actions and expansions of government.

Thus, if the Electoral College were abolished, it would eliminate politicians perceiving that they had a bigger mandate than they earned. This humbling could result in fewer needless wars. Because the few states that get disproportionate influence in the Electoral College system—big swing states—would not be likely to ratify a constitutional amendment abolishing the Electoral College, its termination could be done twenty years hence from the ratification of the amendment. The electoral map changes all the time, so this might encourage more states to ratify the amendment, given the long period of implementation.

Getting two-thirds majorities in both houses of Congress or two-thirds of state legislatures to call a Constitutional Convention to pass a constitutional amendment to abolish the Electoral College and three-fourths of state legislatures or ratification conventions to ratify it is a high bar. Therefore, some innovators have proposed a "National Popular Vote" agreement among states. States joining the pact promise to allocate all their electoral votes to the winner of the nationwide popular vote. If enough states joining the agreement have a majority (270) of all electoral votes (538), which puts the pact in force, the Electoral College vote is effectively nullified and the popular vote winner becomes president.[62] Some analysts have argued, however, that any such agreement among states would violate the Constitution's prohibition on interstate compacts—although recent Supreme Court rulings have allowed similar pacts. In short, it's not as good as a constitutional amendment, but it is a whole lot easier to bring to fruition.

Congress as a Proper Check Against the Rogue Executive

As this book and the prior recommendations indicate, this author doesn't believe that we are stuck with the current plebiscitary presidency—an all-powerful executive constrained only by periodic elections and public opinion. James Madison's system of checks and balances, enshrined in the Constitution, can be revitalized if the aforementioned measures are taken to restore Congress's standing and if the federal courts abandon their fear of pushing back on executive aggrandizement in the national security and foreign policy arenas. If Congress and the courts are an important check on unilateral executive expansion in domestic affairs, they are an even-more-important check on what is now a dangerous and rogue executive in foreign policy. The president

---

62. Weston, *The Runner-Up Presidency*, 130–31.

now unilaterally starts wars, kills people overseas (including Americans) without legal due process, reaches unratified executive agreements with foreign nations, and is dominant even in Congress's area of primary responsibility—funding federal activities.

Congress is still the most powerful branch constitutionally. Thus, the presidency is only contingently imperial until the sleeping congressional leviathan reawakens. Rejuvenating Madison's system of checks and balances would not only generate better policy but achieve what the system was originally designed to do—avoid tyranny. Tyranny is now knocking at the door, given a rogue presidency developed over the last three-quarters of a century and a current incumbent who seems intent on exploiting every power it has aggrandized. Congress must reawaken for the survival of the republic.

CONCLUSION
Restoring the Founders'
Vision of the Republic

MOST OF THE foregoing proposals attempt to change the incentives for members of Congress to fight for the legislative body's ample constitutional prerogatives vis-à-vis an aggrandizing imperial president. Also, the suggestions explore certain important measures of congressional pushback once such internal legislative incentives are altered. However, one of the most important proposals in this volume is the elimination of the Electoral College. If this came to fruition, some friends of republicanism might be concerned with the erosion of federalism. Yet federalism was all but drained out of the Electoral College in the early 1800s, when state legislatures quit picking the electors and instead turned the task over to whatever party won the popular vote in each state. Now the Electoral College merely distorts the popular vote nationwide and erodes the legitimacy of US elections by deviating from the "one-person-one-vote" principle. So, keeping this antiquated institution does not retain much federalism. The main drawback of the status quo is that when presidential candidates who don't win a majority, or even a plurality, of the popular vote wrack up a sizable Electoral College majority—many American elections end up in one of those two categories—it can make them have exaggerated thoughts of an electoral "mandate." The Civil War was most clearly caused by Lincoln experiencing this nirvana, even though he garnered only 39 percent of the popular vote nationwide. Visions of a mandate may have also been a factor in the swaggering George W. Bush's invasion of Iraq for no good reason in 2003, even though he didn't win the popular vote.

In general, however, the Constitution's enumeration of many more powers for the Congress than the executive, even in defense and foreign policy, indicates that the nation's founders wanted the legislative body to dominate the US government. It is high time for Congress to reassert this power, and the presidency of Donald Trump may provide a necessity and an opportunity to do so. In the late 1700s and 1800s, the United States had a congressionally dominated federal government—a time of relative peace, prosperity, and liberty. We must now restore this vision that the founders so presciently designed into the Constitution. Hopefully, the proposals in this volume, if implemented, will take us toward that end. The presidency is only contingently imperial.

Selected Bibliography

Abraham Lincoln, Message to Congress, July 4, 1861.

Adler, David Gray. "Court, Constitution, and Foreign Affairs." In *The Constitution and the Conduct of American Foreign Policy* edited by David G. Adler and Larry N. George. Lawrence, Kansas: University Press of Kansas, 1996.

Adler, Gary, and Carolyn Adler. *The Evolution and Destruction of the Original Electoral College*, 3rd ed. Salt Lake City, UT: Advance Freedom, LLC, 2013.

Alexander Hamilton, "Letters of Pacificus No. 1" (June 29, 1793) reprinted in Henry Cabot Lodge, ed., *The Works of Alexander Hamilton*. New York: G.P. Putnam's Sons, 1904.

Alexander Hamilton, *Federalist* No. 70, 471–80, March 15, 1788, www.press-pubs .uchicago.edu.

Anderson, Benjamin M., Jr. *Effects of the War on Money, Credit, and Banking in France and the United States*. Oxford: Oxford University Press, 1919. http:// publicdebt.treas.gov/history.

———. *Economics and the Public Welfare: Financial and Economic History of the United States, 1914–1946*. Princeton, NJ: Van Nostrand, 1949.

Annals of Congress, 9th Congress, 1st Session (December 1805), 19.

Antonin Scalia's dissenting opinion in *Hamdi v. Rumsfeld*, 542, US 507, 554–55 (2004).

Baack, Bennett D., and Edward John Ray. "Special Interests and the Adoption of the Income Tax in the United States." *Journal of Economic History* 45 (September 1985).

Barron, David J. *Waging War: The Clash Between Presidents and Congress 1776 to ISIS*. New York: Simon and Schuster, 2016.

Bennett, Robert W. *Taming the Electoral College*. Stanford, CA: Stanford University Press, 2006.

Bestor, Arthur. "Separation of Powers in the Domain of Foreign Affairs: The Intent of the Constitution Historically Examined." *Seton Hall Law Review* 5 (1974).

Botts, John Minor. *The Great Rebellion: Its Secret History, Rise, Progress, and Disastrous Failure.* Charleston, SC: Nabu Press, 2010.

Bourne, Randolph. "War Is the Health of the State." 1918. http://www.antiwar .com/bourne.php.

Bradley, Curtis A., and Martin S. Flaherty. "Executive Power Essentialism and Foreign Affairs." *Michigan Law Review* 102 (February 2004).

Brownlee, W. Elliot. *Federal Taxation in America: A Short History.* Washington, DC: Woodrow Wilson Center Press; Cambridge, UK: Cambridge University Press, 2004.

Buchmueller, Thomas C., and Alan C. Monheit. "Employer-Sponsored Health Insurance and the Promise of Health Insurance Reform." NBER Working Paper 14839. Cambridge, MA: National Bureau of Economic Research, 2009.

Buenker, J. D. "The Ratification of the Federal Income Tax Amendment." *Cato Journal* 1, no. 1 (1981).

Bueno de Mesquita, Bruce Bueno, and Alastair Smith. *Spoils of War: Greed, Power, and the Conflicts That Made Our Greatest Presidents.* New York: Public Affairs, 2016.

Burnham, James. *Congress and the American Tradition.* Chicago: Henry Regnery Co., 1959.

Bush, George H. W. "Remarks Announcing a Federal Budget Agreement." Public Papers of George H. W. Bush. Presidential Library. http://bushlibrary.tamu .edu/papers/1990/90093002.html.

Byrne, Malcom. *Iran-Contra: Reagan's Scandal and the Unchecked Abuse of Presidential Power.* Lawrence: University Press of Kansas, 2014.

Canes-Wrone, Brandice, William G. Howell, and David E. Lewis. "Toward a Broader Understanding of Presidential Power: A Reevaluation of the Two Presidencies Thesis." *Journal of Politics* 70, no. 1 (January 2008).

Crenson, Matthew, and Benjamin Ginsberg. *Presidential Power: Unchecked and Unbalanced.* New York: W. W. Norton & Company, 2007.

Edwards, George C. III. *Why the Electoral College Is Bad for America.* New Haven: Yale University Press, 2011.

Eisenhower, Dwight D. Farewell Radio and Television Address, January 17, 1961.

Eisner, Marc Allen. *From Warfare State to Welfare State: World War I, Compensatory State Building, and the Limits of the Modern Order.* University Park: Pennsylvania State University Press, 2000.

Eland, Ivan. *No War for Oil: U.S. Dependency and the Middle East.* Oakland, CA: Independent Institute, 2011.

———. "Most Wars in American History Were Unnecessary and Undermined the Republic." *Mediterranean Quarterly* 23 (Summer 2012): 4–33.

———. "Warfare State to Welfare State: Conflict Causes Government to Expand at Home." *The Independent Review* 18, no. 2 (Fall 2013).

———. *Recarving Rushmore: Ranking the Presidents on Peace, Prosperity, and Liberty.* Oakland, CA: Independent Institute, 2014.

Elkins, Stanley, and Eric McKitrick. *The Age of Federalism: The Early American Republic, 1788-1800.* New York: Oxford University Press, 1993.

Elliot, Jonathan, ed., *The Debates in the Several State Conventions: On the Adoption of the Federal Constitution, as Recommended by the General Convention at Philadelphia, in 1787.* Philadelphia: J. B. Lippincott company, 1907.

Ely, John Hart. *On Constitutional Ground.* Princeton, NJ: Princeton University Press, 1996.

Farrand, Max, ed., *The Records of the Federal Convention of 1787.* New Haven: Yale University Press, 1911.

Fein, Bruce. "Comments at the Debate Between John Yoo and Bruce Fein on the War Power." Atlantic Council. February 8, 2018.

Fisher, Louis. *Presidential Spending Power.* Princeton, NJ: Princeton University Press, 1975.

Fleming, Thomas. *The Great Divide: The Conflict Between Washington and Jefferson That Defined America, Then and Now.* Boston, MA: Da Capo Press, 2015.

Folsom, Burton, and Anita Folsom. *FDR Goes to War: How Expanded Executive Power, Spiraling National Debt, and Restricted Civil Liberties Shaped Wartime America.* New York: Simon & Schuster, 2011.

George Washington, Farewell Address, September 17, 1796.

Gormley, Ken. "Introduction: An Unfinished Presidency." In *The Presidents and the Constitution: A Living History* edited by Ken Gormley. New York: New York University Press, 2016.

Gray, David, and Michael A. Genovese. "Introduction." In *The Presidency and the Law: The Clinton Legacy* edited by Adler and Genovese. Kansas: University of Kansas Press, 2002.

H.R. 2655, 106th Congress.

Healy, Gene. *The Cult of the Presidency: America's Dangerous Devotion to Executive Power.* Washington, DC: Cato Institute, 2008.

Heer, Jeet. "Don't Just Impeach Trump. End the Imperial Presidency." *New Republic*, August 12, 2017. https://newrepublic.com/article/144297/dont-just-impeach -trump-end-imperial-presidency.

Higgs, Robert. *Crisis and Leviathan: Critical Episodes in the Growth of American Government: 25th Anniversary Edition*. Oakland, CA: Independent Institute, 2012 [1987].

Hintze, Otto. "Military Organization and the Organization of the State." In *The Historical Essays of Otto Hintze*, edited by Felix Gilbert. Oxford: Oxford University Press, 1975.

Huntington, Tom. "Death and Taxes." *Civil War Times* 43 (February 2005).

James Madison, "Universal Peace," *National Gazette*, February 2, 1792. In Gaillard Hunt, ed., *The Writings of James Madison 1790–1802: Comprising His Public Papers and His Private Correspondence, Including His Numerous Letters and Documents Now for the First Time Printed*, vol. 6 (1906).

James Madison, *Federalist* No. 58.

James Madison, *Federalist* No. 39.

Jensen, Laura S. "The Early American Origins of Entitlements." *Studies in American Political Development* 10 (Fall 1996).

Jim Powell cites President Franklin D. Roosevelt's Executive Order Providing for the Stabilizing of the National Economy, October 3, 1942. http://www.ibiblio .org/pha/policy/1942/421003a.html.

Jones, C. C. "Class Tax to Mass Tax: The Role of Propaganda in the Expansion of the Income Tax During World War II." *Buffalo Law Review* 37, no. 3 (1989).

Kamarck, Elaine C. *Why Presidents Fail: And How They Can Succeed Again*. Washington, DC: Brookings Institution Press, 2016.

Kaplan, Fred. *Lincoln and the Abolitionists: John Quincy Adams, Slavery, and the Civil War*. New York: HarperCollins, 2017.

Kernell, Sam. *Going Public: New Strategies of Presidential Leadership*. Washington, DC: Congressional Quarterly Press, 1986.

Koh, Harold Hongju. *The National Security Constitution: Sharing Power After the Iran-Contra Affair*. New Haven and London: Yale University Press, 1990.

Letter from Abraham Lincoln to Albert G. Hodges, April 4, 1864. Reprinted in Christopher Pyle and Richard M. Pious, eds., *The President, Congress, and the Constitution: Power and Legitimacy in American Politics*. New York: Free Press, 1984.

Letter from James Madison to Thomas Jefferson, April 2, 1798. In *The Republic of Letters: The Correspondence Between Thomas Jefferson and James Madison 1776–1826, Vol. 2*. New York: W. W. Norton & Company, 1995.

Letter from James Madison to Thomas Jefferson, June 13, 1793. In *The Papers of James Madison, Vol. 15.* Edited by Robert Rutland et al. Charlottesville: University of Virginia Press, 1985.

Letter from Thomas Jefferson to James Madison, September 6, 1789. In James Morton Smith, ed., *The Republic of Letters: The Correspondence Between Thomas Jefferson and James Madison 1776–1826, Vol. 1.* New York: W. W. Norton & Company, 1995.

Letter from William H. Herndon to Wendell Phillips, February 1, 1861. In Fehrenbacher and Fehrenbacher, eds., *Recollected Words of Abraham Lincoln.* Stanford, CA: Stanford U. Press, 1996.

Lind, Michael. *Land of Promise: An Economic History of the United States.* New York: Harper-Collins, 2012.

Lofgren, Charles A. "War-Making Under the Constitution: The Original Understanding." *Yale Law Journal* 81 (1972).

Madison, *Federalist* No. 48 in Mason, *The Papers of James Madison.*

Madison, *Federalist* No. 51 in Mason, *The Papers of James Madison.*

Madison, James. "Helvidius Number 4." In *The Papers of James Madison, Vol. 15* edited by Robert Rutland et al. Charlottesville: University of Virginia Press, 1985.

Madison, James. *Letters and Other Writings of James Madison.* Philadelphia: Lippincott, 1865.

Mayer, Kenneth R. *With the Stroke of a Pen: Executive Orders and Presidential Power* Princeton, NJ: Princeton University Press, 2001.

McClanahan, Brion. *How Alexander Hamilton Screwed Up America.* Washington, DC: Regnery Publishing, 2017.

McClellan, James, and M. E. Bradford. *Elliot's Debates, Vol. III: Debates in the Federal Convention of 1787.* Richmond, VA: James River Press, 1989.

McClintock, Megan J. "Civil War Pensions and the Reconstruction of Union Families." *Journal of American History* 83 (September 1996): 456–80.

McClintock, Russell. *Lincoln and the Decision for War: Northern Response to Secession.* Chapel Hill: University of North Carolina Press, 2008.

Meyer, G. J. *The World Remade: America in World War I.* New York: Bantam Books, 2016.

Michener, James A. *Presidential Lottery: The Reckless Gamble in Our Electoral System.* New York: The Dial Press, 2016.

Morris, Seymour. *American History Revised: 200 Startling Facts That Never Made It into the Textbooks.* New York: Broadway Books, 2010.

National Taxpayers Union. "History of Federal Individual Income Bottom and Top Bracket Rates." Alexandria, VA: National Taxpayers Union, 2013. http://www.ntu.org/tax-basics/history-of-federal-individual-1.html.

Neustadt, Richard. *Presidential Power: The Politics of Leadership.* New York: Wiley, 1960.

Newman, Eric. *The Early Paper Money of America.* 3rd ed. Iola, WI: Krause, 1990.

Patterson, James T. "The Rise of Presidential Power Before World War I." *Law and Contemporary Issues* 40, no. 2 (Spring 1976).

Paul, Ron. "Congress Abdicates War Powers." *New American* (November 4, 2002).

Pleasonton, Alfred. Income Tax: Letter from the Commissioner of Internal Revenue. House Misc. Doc. 51 (January 23, 1871): 41–43.

Posner, Eric A., and Adrian Vermeule. *The Executive Unbound: After the Madisonian Republic.* Oxford: Oxford University Press, 2010.

Powell, H. Jefferson. "The Founders and the President's Authority Over Foreign Affairs." *William and Mary Law Review* 40, no. 5 (May 1999).

Powell, Jim. *FDR's Folly: How Roosevelt and His New Deal Prolonged the Great Depression.* New York: Three Rivers Press, 2003.

Prakash, Saikrishna B., and Michael D. Ramsey. "The Executive Power over Foreign Affairs." *Yale Law Journal* 3, no. 231 (2001).

Preble, Christopher. "The Founders, Executive Power, and Military Intervention." *Pace Law Review* 30, no. 2 (Winter 2010).

Roosevelt, Theodore. *An Autobiography.* New York: Da Capo Press, 1913), 372.

Rosenbaum, Sara, D. Richard Mauery, Peter Shin, and Julia Hidalgo. *National Security and U.S. Child Health Policy: The Origins and Continuing Role of Medicaid and EPSDT.* Policy brief. Washington, DC: School of Public Health and Health Services, George Washington University, 2005.

Ross, Tara. *Enlightened Democracy: The Case for the Electoral College.* Dallas, TX: Colonial Press, L.P., 2012.

Rothbard, Murray N. *A History of Money and Banking in the United States: The Colonial Era to World War II.* Auburn, AL: Ludwig von Mises Institute, 2002.

Rudalevige, Andrew. *The New Imperial Presidency: Renewing Presidential Power After Watergate.* Ann Arbor, Michigan: The University of Michigan Press, 2006.

Sautter, Udo. "Preparing the Welfare State: American Unemployment Reform in the Early Twentieth Century." *Journal of the Canadian Historical Association* 1, no. 1 (1990): 239–56.

Schaffer, Ronald. *America in the Great War: The Rise of the War Welfare State.* Oxford: Oxford University Press, 1991.

Schickler, Eric. *Disjointed Pluralism: Institutional Innovation and the Development of the US Congress*. Princeton and Oxford: Princeton University Press, 2001.

Schlesinger, Arthur M., Jr. *The Imperial Presidency*. New York: Houghton Mifflin, 1973.

Sinclair, Barbara. *Unorthodox Lawmaking: New Legislative Processes in the US Congress*. Thousand Oaks, CA: Sage Publications, Inc., 2017.

Skocpol, Theda. *States and Social Revolutions: A Comparative Analysis of France, Russia, and China*. Cambridge, UK: Cambridge University Press, 1979.

———. *Protecting Soldiers and Mothers: The Political Origins of Social Policy in the United States*. Cambridge, MA: Belknap Press of Harvard University Press, 1992.

———. "America's First Social Security System: The Expansion of Benefits for Civil War Veterans." *Political Science Quarterly* 108, no. 1 (1993): 85–116.

Stolzfus, Emilie. "Child Care: The Federal Role During World War II." Report for Congress. Washington, DC: Congressional Research Service, n.d. http://congressionalresearch.com/RS20615/document.php?study=child care the federal role during world war ii.

Suri, Jeremi. *The Impossible Presidency: The Rise and Fall of America's Highest Office*. New York: Basic Books, 2017.

Taft, William Howard. *Our Chief Magistrate and His Powers*. 1916. Quoted in Christopher H. Pyle and Richard M. Pious, eds., *The President, Congress, and the Constitution: Power and Legitimacy in American Politics*. New York: Free Press, 1984.

Talbot v. Seeman, 5 US (1 Cranch) 1, 28 (1801).

Tomasky, Michael. "Who Needs Congressional Districts?," *New York Times*, February 21, 2018, A23.

Transcript of Tonkin Gulf Resolution (1964). 88th Congress of the United State of America, 2nd Session. https://www.ourdocuments.gov.

Treanor, William Michael. "Fame, the Founding, and the Power to Declare War." *Cornell Law Review* 82 (1997).

Twight, Charlotte. "Evolution of Federal Income Tax Withholding: The Machinery of Institutional Change." *Cato Journal* 14, no. 3 (1995): 359–96.

US Constitution, Tenth Amendment.

US Constitution, Article 1, Section 9.

US Constitution, Article I, Section 8. In Linda R. Monk, *The Words We Live By: Your Annotated Guide to the Constitution*. New York: Hachette Books, 2015.

US Constitution, Article I, Section 8.

US Constitution, Article I, Section 9, and Louis Fisher, *Presidential Spending Power*. Princeton, NJ: Princeton University Press, 1975, 202-203, 205, 207.

US Constitution, Article I, Sections 8 & 9.

US Constitution, Article II, Section 1.

US Constitution, Article II, Sections 2 & 3.

US Constitution, Ninth Amendment.

US Constitution, Tenth Amendment.

Weston, Mark. *The Runner-Up Presidency: The Elections That Defied America's Popular Will and How Democracy Remains in Danger*. Guilford, CT: Lyons Press, 2016.

Wiener, Tim. *Legacy of Ashes: The History of the CIA*. New York: Doubleday, 2007.

Will, George F. "Foreword." In *Enlightened Democracy: The Case for the Electoral College* by Tara Ross. Dallas: Colonial Press, L. P., 2012.

Wilson, Woodrow. *Congressional Government: A Study in American Politics*. Boston: Houghton, Mifflin and Company, 1901.

Wolfensberger, Donald R. *A Brief History of Congressional Reform Efforts*. Bipartisan Policy Center, February 22, 2013.

Wood, John H. *A History of Macroeconomic Policy in the United States*. London: Routledge, 2009.

Woods, Thomas E. *Meltdown: A Free Market Look at Why the Stock Market Collapsed, the Economy Tanked, and Government Bailouts Will Make Things Worse*. Washington, DC: Regnery, 2009.

Wormuth, Francis D., and Edwin B. Firmage. *To Chain the Dog of War: The War Power of Congress in History and Law*. Dallas: Southern Methodist University Press, 1986.

Yoo, John. "Comments Made in the Debate Between John Yoo and Bruce Fein on the War Power." Debate at the Atlantic Council, Washington, DC, February 8, 2018.

Index

About the Author

IVAN ELAND is Senior Fellow at the Independent Institute and Director of Independent's Center on Peace and Liberty. Dr. Eland is a graduate of Iowa State University and received an MBA in applied economics and a PhD in public policy from George Washington University. He has been director of Defense Policy Studies at the Cato Institute, and he spent fifteen years working for Congress on national security issues, including stints as an investigator for the House Foreign Affairs Committee and principal defense analyst at the Congressional Budget Office. He also has served as evaluator-in-charge (national security and intelligence) for the US General Accounting Office (now the Government Accountability Office), and has testified on the military and financial aspects of NATO expansion before the Senate Foreign Relations Committee, on CIA oversight before the House Government Reform Committee, and on the creation of the Department of Homeland Security before the Senate Judiciary Committee. Dr. Eland is the author of *Eleven Presidents: Promises vs. Results in Achieving Limited Government*; *No War For Oil: U.S. Dependency and the Middle East*; *Partitioning for Peace: An Exit Strategy for Iraq*; *Recarving Rushmore: Ranking the Presidents on Peace, Prosperity, and Liberty*; *The Empire Has No Clothes: U.S. Foreign Policy Exposed*; and *Putting "Defense" Back into U.S. Defense Policy*; as well as *The Efficacy of Economic Sanctions as a Foreign Policy Tool*. He is a contributor to numerous volumes and the author of forty-five in-depth studies on national security issues.

His articles have appeared in *American Prospect, Arms Control Today, Bulletin of the Atomic Scientists, Emory Law Journal, The Independent Review, Issues in Science and Technology* (National Academy of Sciences), *Mediterranean Quarterly, Middle East and International Review, Middle East Policy, Nexus, Chronicle of Higher Education, American Conservative, International Journal of World Peace,* and *Northwestern Journal of International Affairs.* Dr. Eland's popular writings have appeared in such publications as the *Los Angeles Times, San Francisco Chronicle, USA Today, Houston Chronicle, Dallas Morning News, New York Times, Chicago Sun-Times, San Diego Union-Tribune, Miami Herald, St. Louis Post-Dispatch, Newsday, Sacramento Bee, Orange County Register, Washington Times, Providence Journal, The Hill,* and *Defense News.* He has appeared on ABC's World News Tonight, NPR's Talk of the Nation, PBS, Fox News Channel, CNBC, Bloomberg TV, CNN, CNN Crossfire, CNN-fn, C-SPAN, MSNBC, Canadian Broadcasting Corp. (CBC), Canadian TV (CTV), Radio Free Europe, Voice of America, BBC, and other local, national, and international TV and radio programs.

Independent Institute Studies in Political Economy

Independent Institute Studies in Political Economy

INDEPENDENT
I N S T I T U T E

100 SWAN WAY, OAKLAND, CA 94621-1428

For further information:
510-632-1366 • orders@independent.org • http://www.independent.org/publications/books/